Oxford Shakespeare

Shakespeare Criticism in the
Twentieth Century

17

OXFORD SHAKESPEARE TOPICS
Published and Forthcoming Titles Include:

Oxford Shakespeare Topics

GENERAL EDITORS: PETER HOLLAND AND STANLEY WELLS

Shakespeare Criticism in the Twentieth Century

MICHAEL TAYLOR

OXFORD
UNIVERSITY PRESS

Great Clarendon Street, Oxford OX2 6DP

Oxford University Press is a department of the University of Oxford.
It furthers the University's objective of excellence in research, scholarship,
and education by publishing worldwide in

Oxford New York

Athens Auckland Bangkok Bogotá Buenos Aires Calcutta
Cape Town Chennai Dar es Salaam Delhi Florence Hong Kong Istanbul
Karachi Kuala Lumpur Madrid Melbourne Mexico City Mumbai
Nairobi Paris São Paulo Shanghai Singapore Taipei Tokyo Toronto Warsaw
and associated companies in Berlin Ibadan

Oxford is a registered trade mark of Oxford University Press
in the UK and certain other countries

Published in the United States
by Oxford University Press Inc., New York

British Library Cataloguing in Publication Data
Data available

Library of Congress Cataloging in Publication Data

Taylor, Michael.
  Shakespeare criticism in the twentieth century / Michael Taylor.
    p. cm. – (Oxford Shakespeare topics)
  Includes bibliographical references (p.) and index.
  1. Shakespeare, William, 1564–1616–Criticism and interpretation–History–20th century. I. Title.
II. Series.

PR2970 .T39 2001   8223'3–dc21   00–045319

ISBN 0–19–871185–9
ISBN 0–19–871184–0 (pbk.)

1 3 5 7 9 10 8 6 4 2

Typeset by Kolam Information Services Pvt. Ltd, Pondicherry, India

Printed in Great Britain
on acid-free paper by
Biddles Ltd,
Guildford and King's Lynn

Preface

Shakespeare Criticism in the Twentieth Century surveys the major literary critical movements and critics of the twentieth century in their dealings with Shakespeare. Each chapter considers a particular aspect of Shakespeare criticism and its organization is roughly chronological. The twentieth century has of course seen an enormous proliferation of studies on Shakespeare so any survey of it must needs be highly selective, but I hope I have been able to give the reader a sense both of the continuity of Shakespeare criticism in this century, its ongoing conversation with itself, and of the important breakaways from traditional thinking that we believe to be peculiarly modern (and postmodern). In a work like this it is important for readers to know exactly where they are chronologically and to facilitate this I have adopted the sociological system of reference whereby the date of the work under consideration followed by the pages is given in parenthesis after each quotation. For the full reference, readers can then look up the work under the author's name in the List of Works Cited. Quotations from Shakespeare use the text of Wells *et al.*, eds., *William Shakespeare: The Complete Works* (Oxford, 1986; reissued in smaller format 1988).

Chapter 1 is an expansive introduction to the twentieth century showing how much of today's criticism relies upon yesterday's scholarship. The spadework of the Victorian Shakespeare industry, despite its sometimes blinkered commitment to an arid positivism, prepares the ground for the fancier cultivations of later critics. I try to show, however, that the Victorian and Edwardian obsession with the discovery of verifiable facts leads us in fact into a century of criticism characterized by doubt and scepticism. The more we know about Shakespeare and his texts, the more precarious sometimes seem to be the conclusions the hard-won information helps to generate. Precarious too is the critical act itself in its often self-conscious awareness of the weight of its predecessors' judgements. Self-consciousness produces the extraordinary efflorescence of critical positions that may well be the twentieth century's most distinguishing characteristic.

Chapter 2 deals primarily with the first decades of the twentieth century dominated by A. C. Bradley and his approach to Shakespeare's works through the intensive study of Shakespeare's characters. The chapter then traces the fluctuating fortunes of this critical approach through the rest of the century as opinion of it changes from sour disapproval to a qualified re-acceptance in the 1980s and 1990s. Chapter 3 investigates a criticism spawned by an adverse reaction to Bradleyism; namely, the study of the formal arrangements of Shakespeare's language divorced in most instances from a concern for the character of the speaker, the dramatic situation, or any of the play's extrinsic circumstances. In Chapter 4 I deal with a criticism that concerns what is arguably the least extrinsic of the plays' extrinsic circumstances, that is, their life in the theatre of (primarily) Shakespeare's time and that of the twentieth century. I then turn to a strain in the dramatic criticism of Shakespeare in the twentieth century that responds to his repeated use of theatrical metaphor and allusion in the structure and themes of his plays (and poems). Hence the importance of the final phrase in the chapter's title: 'Shakespeare in the Theatre and the Theatre in Shakespeare'.

Chapter 5 returns Shakespeare's works to the world. Focusing on Shakespeare's history plays, it outlines the various twentieth-century critical positions determined to see Shakespeare in terms of history—his own and later. A particularly important historical perspective for many critics in this (self-conscious) century is the one that finds in Shakespeare all kinds of Calpurnian anticipations and foreshadowings of situations and events in the twentieth century. But modern criticism is not only fascinated by the notion of Shakespeare as fortune-teller but as historian of his own past: hence a twentieth-century criticism that takes Shakespeare seriously as a historian of fifteenth-century England and first-century Rome. A final chapter deals with a number of different approaches to Shakespeare, unique to twentieth-century criticism, that diverge in their subject-matter and (often) in their intensity of commitment from mainstream criticism: feminist, ethnic, and religious criticism of Shakespeare. The book ends with the warning that what seems to be marginal and eccentric now may well be the orthodoxy of the future.

Acknowledgements

First and foremost I'd like to acknowledge the help and encouragement given me by the General Editors. Frances Whistler of OUP was unfailingly cheerful through the thousand shocks that book production is heir to. Carole Tattersall and Bozena Clarke, librarians at Carleton University Library in Ottawa, are models of their kind. Matthew Taylor provided me with information at a crucial moment. Marni Squire saved the day in the final stages. My thanks to all.

Contents

Illustrations

Introduction

Setting Endeavour in Continual Motion

The springboard for much twentieth-century Shakespeare criticism in all its sparkling variousness and speculative daring has to be the late nineteenth-century investment in scholarly apparatuses of various kinds: libraries, editions of Shakespeare, dictionaries, concordances, data banks, scholarly societies, bibliographies, checklists, and so on. This was the age of Grammar and Lexicography, the golden age of the philologist and the academic editor, described by M. C. Bradbrook as 'the Industrial Revolution of Shakespearian studies . . . the generation that constituted scholarship on a professional scale; the age of the "Variorum Shakespeare", a monument that time has to some extent surprised' (1954: 1). Equally monumental, and to a similar extent equally surprised by time, were the great dictionaries of the last three decades of the nineteenth century: among them, and centrally, *A New English Dictionary on Historical Principles* (1888–1928) from Oxford, Joseph Wright's *English Dialect Dictionary* (1890–1904), and Farmer and Henley's *Slang and Its Analogues Past and Present* (1890).

In 1869 E. A. Abbott, the headmaster of the City of London School, produced his *Shakespearian Grammar: An Attempt to Illustrate some of the Differences between Elizabethan and Modern English* which went into a second and third edition in the same year and is still necessarily consulted. Alexander Schmidt's *Shakespeare-Lexicon* appeared in 1874–75. Between 1875 and 1894 Edward Arber edited his five volumes of the *Transcript of the Registers of the Company of Stationers, 1554–1640*. In 1894 John Bartlett published his *New and Complete Concordance of the Dramatic Works and Poems of Shakespeare* to which generations of

Shakespeare's readers owed and continue to owe a profound debt. Carefully edited editions of Shakespeare by academics came on the market during this time. The nine-volume Cambridge Shakespeare (1863–66) 'differed from all previous editions in its emphasis upon the factual history of the evolution of the text' (Taylor 1990: 187). In 1864 it appeared in single format as the line-numbered Globe which for some ninety years was the standard edition of Shakespeare. The Clarendon Shakespeare, a series of editions of individual plays, appeared from Oxford between 1868 and 1906. This Industrial Revolution of Shakespearean studies also witnessed the extraordinarily intensive, if often wayward, scholarship of The Shakespeare Society (1840–53) founded by J. P. Collier (1789–1883) and the more important New Shakspere Society (1873–94) by Frederick James Furnivall (1825–1910) which concentrated on establishing the plays' chronology. 'Here is', says E. K. Chambers justly, 'a ripe harvest gathered into the barns' (1944*b*: 23).

All of these endeavours were buoyed by the Victorian belief in progress, science, and evolution, so that it then seemed that Shakespeare's development, in Gary Taylor's words, could 'be measured with scientific precision, an evolution that confirmed the Victorian belief in progress, a progress that culminated in an affirmation of paternal pastoral "home-life"' (1990: 167). The very title of R. G. Moulton's *Shakespeare as a Dramatic Artist: A Popular Illustration of the Principles of Scientific Criticism*, written in 1885 at the height of all these scholarly endeavours, advertises this dedication to the scientific method and the pedagogical desirability of making its results widely known. Taking fifteen 'representative' plays by Shakespeare, Moulton's book, in a prose redolent of its author's sense of the magnitude of his pronouncements, subjects them to an analysis and interpretation based on the 'scientific' inductive method. 'If there is', Moulton intones, 'an inductive science of politics, men's voluntary actions in the pursuit of public life, and an inductive science of economy, men's voluntary actions in pursuit of wealth, why should there not be an inductive science of art, men's voluntary actions in pursuit of the beautiful?' (1966: 36–7). An inductive science of men's voluntary actions in pursuit of the beautiful would depend for its scientifically magisterial judgements on the establishment of a world of facts: 'The inductive sciences occupy themselves directly with facts, that is, with phenomena translated by observation into the form of facts; and the soundness of inductive theory is measured by the closeness with which it will bear confronting with the facts' (22). So much of the Victorian sense of arduous public duty is conveyed in this mode of expression, its imagery taken from the practical worlds of commerce and industrialization: once 'confronted' the facts should then be 'put together with business-like exactitude'; there should be 'a weighing, balancing, and standing by the product' (25). Such a positivistic, disinterested, 'industrialized' mode of enquiry must eschew what Moulton calls 'adjudicating' criticism, a mode he sees as purely ephemeral, the product of the unscientific practice of reviewing whose proper place is 'on the creative side of literature, as a branch in which literature itself has come to be taken as a theme for literary writing; it thus belongs to the literature treated, not to the scientific treatment of it' (21–2). For better or worse 'scientific' became one of the shibboleths of twentieth-century literary criticism.

On the other hand, criticism that belongs to the literature treated—that is, literature rather than criticism—anticipates an important strain of writing on Shakespeare (and on everyone else) in the twentieth century, and, despite Moulton's scorn for it in 1885, is something that he himself might be said to practise.[1] For all his insistence on the scientific nature of his endeavours, and for all his distaste for a literary-sounding criticism—and despite the afflatus of his own style—what is curious about Moulton and many of his contemporaries, as we shall see, is his real indifference to the enormous amount of genuine, productive scholarship going on around him. In his 'scientific' inductive system, the literary work itself provides the only mechanism that needs to be studied: 'A play of Shakespeare may present a system of wheels within wheels, like a solar system in motion as a whole while the separate members of it have their own orbits to follow' (373). Ironically, it is the very laws of scientific induction—as he here astronomically imagines them—that enable him to ignore the more truly scientific bibliographical and lexicographical research. The cogs of those wheels within wheels that he describes don't require, it seems, oiling from any external sources; as the process of inductiveness implies, they obey the laws of their own being in the smooth inter-meshing—the symmetry, the balance—of 'the federations' of Shakespeare's plots in which 'we trace a common self-government made out of elements which have an independence of their own, and at the same time merge a part of their independence in common action' (359).

So on the one hand we have in Moulton in 1885 an enthusiastic proponent of a scientific criticism, and on the other we have in him an exponent of a critical writing that essentially ignores the factual scholarship that Moulton claims animates his vision of a scientific criticism of Shakespeare. No doubt Moulton's unconscious resistance to the scientific approach he claims to be the spokesman for is an inheritance of the Romantic insistence on the primacy of the imagination. Whatever its origins, the struggle between the two approaches surfaces in a variety of forms throughout twentieth-century criticism of Shakespeare. As Karl Kroeber remarks: 'Increasing imitativeness of the "scientific" has accompanied, interestingly, ever more strident proclamations of the "creativity" of criticism' (1984: 329). (A book could be written on this tension-ridden symbiosis.) In the late nineteenth century, however, the new 'scientific' nature of literary criticism was embraced with such religious fervour by its practitioners that it can be considered a symptom of Russell Jackson's diagnosis of the place of art in the late nineteenth century whereby '[a]n increasingly secular state looked to artists for a definition of the purposes that might complement if not replace those attributed to God' (1996*b*: 113). (Moulton himself contributed to this spiritualizing movement in 1903 with a ponderously entitled book *The Moral System of Shakespeare: A Popular Illustration of Fiction as the Experimental Side of Philosophy.*)

Moulton's better known contemporary, the admired precursor of A. C. Bradley, Edward Dowden, whose *Shakspere: A Critical Study of His Mind and Art* went through twelve British editions between 1875 and 1901 and is still in print, is another case in point. Gary Taylor suggests that Dowden's version of Shakespeare as the self-made entrepreneur 'satisfied the mercantile mentality, but he was harder to relate convincingly to the sublimely imaginative poet who had been worshipped for more than a century' (1990: 215). But there is an intense effort in *Shakspere: A Critical Study of His Mind and Art* to rescue Shakespeare from mere mercantile criticism, and Dowden does this in part by taking Moulton's scientific notion of 'fact', with its inevitable Gradgrindian overtones, and giving it a Bunyanesque infusion. Dowden talks admiringly of Shakespeare (and of Bacon and Hooker) as possessing '*a rich feeling for positive, concrete fact*' (emphasis in original, 1962: 23) which bows down before 'the one standing miracle . . . the world itself' (24). The 'logic of facts' (32) leads to the religious experience (the one standing miracle) and to a moral decisiveness because its pursuit enables us to be 'thoroughly free from lassitude, and from that lethargy of heart, which most of us have felt at one time or another' (29). Subscribing to the logic of facts enables Shakespeare not only 'to compass and comprehend the knowable' but to 'brood with a passionate intensity over that which cannot be known' (34); through its process 'we come anew into the presence of most stupendous mysteries, and, instead of our little piece of comfort, and support, and contentment, we receive the gift with solemn awe, and bow the head in reverential silence' (34). '[B]rought back once again to Shakspere's resolute fidelity to the fact' (46) we ourselves by some kind of sympathetic osmosis might be permitted 'the strength and courage to pursue our own path, through pain or through joy, with vigor and resolution' (41). In contrast, '[t]he protest against fact, against our subjection to law made by such men as Marlowe and Greene, was a vulgar and superficial protest' (47).

The Madness of Discourse

For Dowden, then, Shakespeare's resolute fidelity to the fact was a form of spirituality of a sternly Protestant kind and the spiritual in Dowden himself—as in Moulton and Bradley—might be said to flourish in his own resolute indifference to the facts of Shakespeare scholarship as they were then proliferating. The quasi-paradoxical relationship between fact and feeling, the frequent lack of connection between the critical writing and the scholarship on Shakespeare, anticipate in their own way the grand irony of all this scholarly activity on the threshold of the new century: it didn't produce the certainty its adherents fondly imagined it would.[2] It was the bell-wether, on the contrary, to a century of Shakespeare criticism characterized—gloriously some say, frustratingly others—by an awareness of increasingly intricate uncertainties. As Paul Gottschalk argues, piling interpretation upon interpretation doesn't necessarily produce anything definitive as each interpretation takes its restricted place in 'the procession of new techniques and disciplines brought to bear on the artifact' (1972: 1). A further anticipatory irony in a tale riddled with it lies in the fact that much of this Victorian scholarly endeavour was devoted to proving that Shakespeare did not write parts of the works attributed to him. The 'disintegrationist' argument, as it came to be known, stretches back at least to Johnson in the eighteenth century who expressed profound doubts as to the accuracy of the texts in the 1616 Folio and the quartos that preceded it. Parts of the plays were thought to be simply too inferior for the hand of a master craftsman like Shakespeare, and the Victorian scholars jumped at the chance to be able to expunge 'scientifically' those allegedly indecorous, feeble, and ill-mannered passages that only an inferior talent could have cobbled together. W. W. Greg calls this textual scepticism 'the quagmire of nineteenth-century despondency' (1955: p. v).

In this complicated history, the chief purifying disintegrator was F. G. Fleay (1831–1909), the industrious flea as he was known, a major activist in the New Shakspere Society for the cleansing of Shakespeare's texts. E. K. Chambers observed in 1924:

Fleay distributed and redistributed *Henry VI*, *Richard III*, and *Titus Andronicus* among Shakespeare, Marlowe, Greene, Peele, Lodge, and Kyd; found much of Lodge and a little of Drayton in *The Taming of the Shrew*, traces of Peele in *Romeo and Juliet*, traces of Kyd in *Hamlet*, debris of Dekker and Chettle in *Troilus and Cressida*. He also gave parts of *Julius Caesar* to Ben Jonson. (1944*a*: 4)

With a magisterial asperity Chambers passes judgement on the pernicious influence of the industrious flea's redistributing system: 'His self-confidence has hypnotized his successors, and many of his improvisations recur in the works of serious students, not to speak of those school-books, compiled at starvation wages for competitive publishers, which do so much in our day for the dissemination of critical and historical error' (5).

And yet, as Hugh Grady (1991*b*) points out, modern criticism of the canon owes its origins to Fleay, and it could be argued that his work— and the work of his colleagues—anticipates that of the poststructuralists who are equally disintegrationist in their critical tendencies, if not for the same saintly reasons as Fleay and co. For Grady disintegration 'seems like a strange, empiricist deconstruction *avant la lettre*' (1991*a*: 63). Even some of the most controversial re-attributions in the most important edition of Shakespeare in our time, the Oxford, owe Fleay a debt; and Fleay had his later twentieth-century devotees in those like J. M. Robertson who, in Chambers's words, were 'repelled' by what they (and perhaps Chambers himself) considered to be 'child-ish work' in Shakespeare, 'by imitative work, by repetitive work, by conventional work, by unclarified work, by clumsy construction, by baldness and bombast' (1944*a*: 8). Instead, as Chambers says, the disintegrators longed for a 'smoothly progressive curve' (10) in Shake-speare's development, unlike, of course, their odd bedfellows, the poststructuralists, who long for something in his development along much more jagged lines.

Fleay's well-meant depredations in Shakespeare's texts were repu-diated by the 'scientific bibliography'—claimed to be more 'scientific', that is, by the new bibliographers than the 'scientific' procedures of their Victorian predecessors—of Greg, McKerrow, and Pollard in the first two or three decades of the century, who between them authentic-ated the Folio text. What really scuttled the disintegrators was A. W. Pollard's division of the known quarto texts into 'good' and 'bad' ones in his ground-breaking study in 1909, *Shakespeare's Folios and Quartos: A Study in the Bibliography of Shakespeare's Plays, 1594–1685*. The 'new paradigm', established in the main by the work of these three biblio-graphers, proved to be—for a time—a vindication of the Folio editors. The importance of such a vindication can best be seen by pondering Chambers's worried observation in 1927 that all of the disintegrators

share a dominating conception of a standing stage text, preserved as a valuable possession in the tiring-room, transferred, it may be, from company to com-pany, remodelled and written up to date, in accordance with shifting standards of taste, by dramatist after dramatist, but preserving some kind of continuous life and bearing to the end some traces of its successive reincarnations. (1944*b*: 31–2)

This is something that Chambers finds difficult to swallow:

But it is certainly disturbing to the literary mind; for who can be said to be the author of such a play, and how is such a genesis reconcilable with the internal evidence which Shakespeare's plays at least seem to carry, for all their offhand-edness and inconsequences, of a ruling idea or sentiment in each, due to the unifying power of a shaping spirit of imagination? (32)

What is at stake here, in other words, is the continued validity of another shibboleth of the literary mind of the modernists in the twentieth century: the organic unity of Shakespeare's texts.

Weary of Solid Firmness

The industrious flea might well be considered prescient. The difference in Shakespeare criticism between the twentieth century and the centuries preceding it is paradigmatically signalled by an overwhelming awareness by critics in this century of the instability of Shakespeare's texts. What was once considered to be the bedrock for all hermeneutic activity has now cracked open to reveal a molten flow. We might consider, for instance, David Willbern's presentation of a representative textual crux in Shakespeare in these lines from *Troilus and Cressida*:

> For speculation turns not to itself
> Till it hath travelled and is mirrored there
> Where it may see itself.

> (3.3.104–6)

In both quarto and Folio the middle line reads 'Till it hath travail'd and is married there'. 'Travail'd' and 'married' have been traditionally rejected by editors for 'travell'd' and 'mirror'd' despite the fact that the former pair makes some sense and, in the case of the first term, 'travail'd', makes, arguably, richer sense. Which of these four alternatives is the *real* Shakespeare here, Willbern asks. How can we ever know is his answer: 'how can we establish an authoritative text when the words themselves won't stay still?' (1989: 243). For him it's more an occasion for enjoyment than anxiety: the words won't stay still because the processes of their production unhinge them from a determinate meaning. It's inevitable so we might as well enjoy the ride. But the words also won't stay still because of criticism's fashionable new awareness of the indeterminate nature of the reading process itself: the words fly up, their thoughts remain below.

An amusingly exasperated experience of this phenomenon—much less enjoyable it seems than Willbern's textual dizziness—occurs in Harry Berger Jr.'s ruefully unfettered, anxiety-inducing experience of reading lines from *King Lear*. His article begins with the phenomenon Willbern notices: 'Whenever I open my text of *King Lear* and look fixedly at certain phrases sitting on the page, they begin to move, change shape, dance, wriggle, turn inside out, sprout wings, and fly about flapping from one speech to the other until my wits begin to turn' (1987: 144). In Willbern's case, the dance of the words is to the music of the editorial process; in Berger's, the music is composed by the readers themselves, the score is in their heads.[3]

Twentieth-century Shakespeare criticism finds the indeterminate everywhere. The indeterminate nature of the editorial and reading processes finds a parallel source of discomfiture in the interventions of the Elizabethan printing-house personnel. Traditionally, the aim of a modern editor of a work by Shakespeare was, in Antony Hammond's words, 'to recover the author's text from the corruptions of the printing house, and thereby restore the author's linguistic and lexical intentions'. Now, on the contrary, Hammond suggests that 'one valid editorial role ... should be to collaborate with the original *printing house*, rather than to ignore its vital function in dressing for the public what the author entrusted it with' (1994: 235). Such a collaboration is made difficult, of course, by the complicated and often whimsical nature of the printing process itself. And this process is in turn made more complicated by the new realization that, as Alvin Kernan points out, the texts of the plays must now be treated not as 'successive corruptions of an unprinted ideal text but historical versions of a text continually changing in the give-and-take of theatrical production' (1987: 91). Which historical version should have authority though? After all, even in the twentieth century and since, when scholarly and commercial presses continue to add to a plethora of different editions of Shakespeare in English, usually only one version of a play is published at any one time.[4]

The 1986 Oxford edition of the *Complete Works of Shakespeare* can help us here as an indicator of the prevailing tendency to accord respectability to the notion of a restlessly indeterminate 'script', a performance text. The modern editor has a basic choice: either to aim for editions of the plays as Shakespeare originally wrote them, or as they were performed by his company and perhaps revised by him for performance. The Oxford editors plump for the playhouse versions of Shakespeare's plays as representing Shakespeare at his most professionally authentic: 'Performance is the end to which they were created, and in this edition we have devoted our efforts to recovering and presenting texts of Shakespeare's plays as they were acted in the London playhouses which stood at the centre of his professional life'

(1986: p. xxxix). In these heady times all these processes—the reading, editorial, printing, and theatrical—combine to make the task of dealing with Shakespeare an excitingly precarious one. There are no fixed landmarks in these journeys of discovery—scepticism rules, as is suggested, for example, by the title of an essay by Ernst Honigmann, 'On not trusting Shakespeare's stage-directions' (1989: 169). Leah Marcus sums up the volatility of it all:

What if, rather than flowing effortlessly and magically from Shakespeare's mind onto the unalterable fixity of paper, the plays were from the beginning provisional, amenable to alterations by the playwright or others, coming to exist over time in a number of versions, all related, but none of them an original in the pristine sense promised by Heminges and Condell? Nothing we know about conditions of production in the Renaissance Playhouse allows us to hope for single authoritative versions of the plays. (1988: 44)

Consequently, however conservative the editorial process, the fact of the matter is that all editions of Shakespeare at all times, as Gary Taylor argues, are necessarily invasive (some more so than others of course): 'All texts of Shakespeare are editions; all have been edited; all have been mediated by agents other than the author' (Wells and Taylor 1987: 1). And who—really—are these agents? They are 'the pimps of discourse' (7). Such invasive language on Taylor's part is not merely an attempt to enliven a traditionally strait-laced area of scholarship[5]— though it certainly does that—but to direct our attention to the momentousness of the twentieth-century discovery that all Shakespeare studies are built on the shifting sands of textual indeterminacy.

The critical language presses the case. In Anthony Dawson's variation on Taylor's excited rhetoric, Taylor's pimps become Dawson's rapists: 'Every production, every critical reading, is an act of violence, an attempt to wrest meaning from the recalcitrant text. And the text's revenge is to keep allowing meanings to proliferate, in the knowledge that there always is as much left in *as* was there before' (1991: 320). Pimps, rapists, and—perhaps most heinous of all—authors. Editors of Shakespeare, like their critical confrères (see p. 2 above), must take decisions whether they like it or not, that assume the creative mantle of authorship when there is no certain evidence one way or the other as to the correctness of variant readings.

To complicate matters further twentieth-century criticism has revived the earlier hypothesis that all authors may well be editors. In other words, we no longer take on face value—twentieth-century Shakespeare criticism tends to take nothing on face value—the traditional view of Shakespeare's unblotted papers. Ernst Honigmann vividly portrays 'Shakespeare at work: preparing, writing, rewriting' (1989: 188). Shakespeare, Honigmann maintains, was simply not as fluent as Heminges and Condell claimed; their praise 'like much else in their prefatory epistles in the First Folio, simply echoed the cliches of their time' (198). Instead, we should trust Edison's version of genius rather than Milton's: Shakespeare was more the perspiring reviser than the warbler of wild woodnotes. He was, in other words, his own first editor (though not presumably in the manner suggested by Taylor and Dawson).[6]

There is no doubt that the relationship between editions of Shakespeare and the criticism of Shakespeare is mutually reinforcing. Criticism spawns new editions based on new critical principles and editorial procedures, and these in turn inspire critics to rethink their critical positions. So it's arguable that the extraordinary number of (apparently) thriving new or renewed or reprinted editions of Shakespeare's works (single, collected, or partly collected) is an index of the extraordinary number of critical works. And of course the symbiotic relationship between edition and critical work is not confined to Shakespeare. Jerome McGann talks about the fruitful collaboration between editions and translations of Homer's *Iliad* and a variety of readerships:

To read, for example, a translation of Homer's *Iliad* in the Signet paperback, in the edition published by the University of Chicago Press, in the Norton Critical edition, or in the limited edition put out by the Florio Society (with illustrations), is to read Homer's *Iliad* four very different ways. Each of these texts is visually and materially coded for different audiences and different purposes. (1991: 115)

More than this, perhaps, the traditional divorce between editorial/ textual matters and ('real') criticism has been shown to be a self-serving chimera. Margreta de Grazia writes: 'It is our sense that it is a major triumph of this latest generation of critics to have effectively crossed the Great Divide, now concerning themselves with textual matters once relegated exclusively to the editor and bibliographer' (1997: 70). The notion to ponder is that authors do not write books—they write stuff that is then turned into books.

Base Authority from Others' Books

The notion that Shakespeare's critics and to a lesser extent his editors are in some significantly creative sense *authors* has taken a firm hold on the imaginations of some twentieth-century critics.[7] And in the shuffle Shakespeare himself tends to get lost. The most extreme statement I've come across of the case for a missing Shakespeare can be found in Scott Wilson's *Cultural Materialism: Theory and Practice*:

> He is as temporally remote as the sun in space, empirically unknowable, as dead as it is possible for an author to be, yet all the more radiant for that. If we cannot have access to Shakespeare, cannot have access to his mind, his person, the world in which he lived, if we cannot have access to the pre-Shakespear- ized world in which his work first irrupted and almost completely disappeared, then we cannot properly know the meaning of Shakespeare or his work: Shakespeare himself, as a totality, as a Work, is never properly present in discourse; there is certainly no access to the meaning of Shakespeare (Shak- spere) or the work through the dead letters that signify them. (1995: 88–9)

There is much to take issue with here, not least the hyperbolic manner in which the difficulty of reading Shakespeare/Shakspere in some- thing like his own terms is magnified. In Wilson's extremist vocabu- lary, Shakespeare's signifying letters, his works, are 'dead', and the dead cannot convey meaning, significance, or anything else. It's not enough of course to point to the huge amount of 'meaning' already excavated by critics from the tombs of these dead letters. As far as Wilson is concerned that meaning isn't Shakespeare's but the critics'.

Although his position may be extreme, Scott Wilson does touch a nerve. Richard Halpern notes that one of the unexpected results of the enormous amount of anthropological research in the twentieth cen- tury was to distance rather than to bring closer the societies under scrutiny. Perhaps the Elizabethan age 'was separated by an unbridge- able cultural and historical distance from our own, and that increased historical contextualization, far from enriching the imaginative consumption of older works, might actually alienate them from modern sensibilities' (1997: 32–3).

T. S. Eliot's remarks in his Introduction to Wilson Knight's *Wheel of Fire* in 1930 express the conservative Modernist's belief in the distant strangeness of Shakespeare's times: 'But with Shakespeare we seem to be moving in an air of Cimmerian darkness. The conditions of his life, the conditions under which dramatic art was then possible, seem even more remote from us than those of Dante' (p. xiv).

There is more than a suggestion of the self-willed in the writings of some influential twentieth-century Shakespeare critics on the air of Cimmerian darkness in which they stumble. Shakespeare in these instances seems not so much unknowable from an epistemological point of view—despite the asseverations of a critic like Scott Wilson— as unknowable in the sense of its not now being desirable to know him from a political point of view, or to know him any more comprehensively than we already do. Enough already. The times call for a different kind of involvement with Shakespeare; there are now more important things to do than interpret (read?) him; interpretation of his works should give way to, let's say, analyses of his presence—for better or for worse—in the culture of our and other times. What is/was his political significance? Where was/is he in ideology? In the face of these pressing questions—the kind that animate a work like Frank Lentricchia's *Criticism and Social Change*—we should now care less than ever to know how many children Lady Macbeth had. As W. B. Worthen says in a slightly different context: 'the intensity of the "text versus performance" skirmishing suggests that the stakes are mainly ideological, having less to do with Shakespearean drama than with how competing visions of culture are sustained by a "legitimate" vision of "Shakespeare"' (1996*a*: 211).

That the stakes are mainly ideological may be seen quite clearly in the position taken by Terence Hawkes in his books, *That Shakespeherian Rag* and *Meaning by Shakespeare*, in his considering 'how constitutive contexts are of meaning' (1986: 67). If contexts—the contexts, that is, of the reader's times—were completely constitutive of meaning then there would not be any necessity to summon up the effort of will that Hawkes thinks needed to refuse the text's blandishments; we must, he urges, 'refuse absolutely to encounter the text on its own terms, to refuse the text's own hierarchy of character and event, and to read and re-read it seeking out what it suppresses, marginalizes and silences as part of its own project' (1992: 39).[8] Scott Wilson doesn't think that the text has its own terms; Hawkes thinks it probably does but that they should be resolutely rejected.

There is no doubt that these and similar urgings by influential critics have fluttered the dovecotes of Shakespeare criticism. Exactly to what extent may be gleaned perhaps by a brief consideration of the tone and tenor of Michael Bristol's valuable study, *Big-Time Shakespeare* (1996). The blurb on its jacket tells us that 'Bristol attempts to bridge the gap between conservative demands for unreflective affirmation of the ideals and achievements of Western civilization and the equally unhelpful oppositional programs of compulsive resistance and critique'. So the book attempts a 'controversial and even inflammatory' (p. xii) argument for the possibility 'that Shakespeare is the common possession of Western modernity and a definitive expression of its experience' (p. xii). It's an indication of the current state of affairs that Bristol, nervously looking over his shoulder, should consider inflammatory what many critics might think is an unimpeachable ambition to interpret Shakespeare as 'the common possession of Western modernity'. We must now look, he says, with scepticism on 'fragmentary appropriations' (26); Shakespeare's works are not merely 'empty signifiers freely available for opportunistic appropriation' (26).

It may seem strange, outrageous even, that in 1996 we should need to be reminded that Shakespeare's works are not merely empty signifiers. Yet Bristol's prodigal-son return to the plenitude of the signified comes, as we have seen, at a time when symposia like the one worriedly entitled *Is Shakespeare Still Our Contemporary?* (1989) are very much in vogue.[9] Some kind of compromise between those who do and those who do not interpret Shakespeare as the common possession of Western modernity is obviously in order, whereby his work, we might say, can be experienced as both empty and full, as signifier and signified, and whereby both reader and work are granted some degree of participatory autonomy. Jean Howard argues in her discussion of the issue of the generically unstable text and the inevitability of interpretative changes—persuasively it seems to me—that the best interpretation of a Shakespeare text 'arises from the interaction between the strategies of the text and the strategies of the reader. Neither is a negligible force' (1986: 140).[10] After all, as Naomi Liebler writes:

If discrete cultural experience were so ghettoized as to prevent access by all but native inhabitants, then none of us would have useful access even to the culture that produced Shakespearean tragedy, separated from it as we are by four centuries of history and change. Blinkered relativism has no greater purchase on accuracy than does a reductive essentialism. The kinds of rigorous and diligent efforts that are now made by theoretical laborers in historicist, materialist, anthropological, and other fields of inquiry allow informed and 'sympathetically imaginative' access to cognitively analogous representations in tragic drama. (1995: 32)

Equivocation Will Undo Us

The scepticism we may feel about the author's very existence[II] is no doubt among other things a symptom of a more generally held scepticism in this century about the possibility of establishing any truths about anything. About language itself for instance. How can we establish the truth of anything when the very language we use, like the words in Shakespeare's texts, will not stand still. Ordinary language philosophy, a dominant strain in the twentieth century, is deeply suspicious of the ability of language to convey truth. By its very nature, such a philosophical position argues, language is a cracked and fissured thing, especially in its fictionalizations. In drama, for instance, the critic is dealing with the inherently slippery nature of exchanges between fictional characters moving around in a fictional space, the stage, where, inevitably, much of the dialogue may simply not be sufficiently contextualized, may be enigmatic, cryptic, inherently vulnerable to competing interpretations. Hence the different interpretations of Prospero's forgiveness of Antonio in *The Tempest*, the nature of Cleopatra's love for Anthony, of the Macbeths for each other, of Leontes for his wife in *The Winter's Tale*, and so on.

Not to labour the obvious, this difficulty with language is compounded when the language isn't ordinary, or at least not ordinary to the modern reader, but comes from distant times, carrying its own strange freight of ambiguity and multiple-choice meanings. What does it say about Hamlet's insurrectionary nature, for instance, when David Margolies (1988) tells us in his discussion of Hamlet's cryptic 'I am but mad north-north-west; when the wind is southerly, I know a hawk from a handsaw' (2.2.380–1), that the traditional interpretation of 'handsaw' by editors and commentators as the aristocratic 'heron-shaw' is no more valid than its meaning as a carpenter's saw with 'hawk' as a plasterer's hawk, the board on which plasterers carry their plaster? What the tendentiousness of Margolies's story of his sally into etymology does tell us points to what Cedric Watts believes to be the peculiar characteristic of twentieth-century scepticism, the way 'Shakespearean studies have become part of a study of social inscription—of the ways in which individual people are inscribed by society with roles, beliefs, identities and allegiances' (1986: 277). And this is because '[t]hese days the "meaning" of a work may be regarded not as a lightly buried treasure awaiting the treasure-seeking interpreter but rather as a multiplicity of possibilities in constant process of generation and regeneration' (277).

There has never been such a constant process of generation and regeneration as in the criticism of Shakespeare in the twentieth century. Industrious fleas are everywhere: in the academy, the theatre, commerce, diplomacy, politics, music, films and television, creative writing—the name of Shakespeare is invoked, abused, manipulated, and traduced. It would be tiresome to indulge more than a rapid excursion into the statistics of proliferation but everywhere we turn there are examples of 'an amazing monument of veneration' (25), there is a 'bewildering abundance' of 'new and even revolutionary positions' (p. v): 'in the number and variety of the minds at work, and especially in the extent and closeness of their scientific grip upon their subject-matter... here the last thirty years surpass any previous generation' (p. vi). This is C. H. Herford looking back over the thirty years before 1923. He would be hard put to it to find the appropriate vocabulary of astonishment were he to look back at the bewildering abundance of the criticism on Shakespeare over the thirty years before 2000.

Sixteen years later in 1939 Ivor Brown and George Fearon recoil fastidiously from the spectacle of 'the Headquarters of the Shakespeare Industry' (2), Stratford-upon-Avon, which has become 'both shrine and tripper-dump' (16). The Shakespeare Industry goes 'on and on and up and up' (5) exasperatingly: 'Really there's no escaping William Shakespeare now' (307). Their book's conclusion, however, is surprisingly upbeat: 'Ubiquitous now and unquenchable, outward, onward, upward go the story, the glory, and the commerce. The existence of a Shakespeare Industry is not only inevitable: it is desirable' (326). Ten years later in 1949 J. I. M. Stewart is much less sanguine: 'In Shakespeare criticism ... all is confusion' (3). In 1964 George Steiner remarks that 'it requires a fair-sized library to house what has been written and spoken about Shakespeare in 1964' (1970: 200). By the 1990s Gary Taylor can write: 'Even for hard-core Shakespearians, lifers, it is impossible to digest the hundreds of books and thousands of articles published on the subject in any year' (1990: 369).

All this frenzy spawns and has been spawned by a myriad competing theories: performance criticism, prophetic, metaphysical, creative, formalist criticism, reader-response criticism, phenomenological, semiotic, deconstructionist criticism, Lacanian, Foucauldian, Derridean criticism. There is a flourishing in this century of Polonian conjugations: Derridean-Marxist-feminist criticism, for instance (this example is taken from Mark Krupnick's book on Lionel Trilling). As Jonathan Culler remarks with some dismay: 'Never has so much been written about Shakespeare; he is studied from every angle conceivable, interpreted in feminist, Marxist, psychoanalytic, historicist, and deconstructive vocabularies' (1997: 48–9).

Indeed the specialist vocabularies are often arcane, forbiddingly so, as in Richard Wilson's chapter on Shakespeare's will ('Shakespeare's Dead Hand') in his fine book *Will Power: Essays on Shakespearean Authority* (1993) where we have to come to terms with usufruct, parcenary, alienation (in the strictly legal sense), mortmain, testation, devisable (in the strictly legal sense), partibility, and so on. Shakespeare criticism has in other words become an appropriative force sallying forth into adjacent and not so adjacent disciplines. Company mergers and marriages of modes mark this syncretizing tendency, leading Lisa Jardine to believe that '[w]hat we should be looking at ... is the converging practices of social historians, intellectual and cultural historians, text critics and social anthropologists, as they move together towards a more sensitive integration of past and present cultural products' (1996: 36). And Louis Montrose notes that recent developments in Shakespeare criticism point towards 'a potential synthesis of historicist and formalist, materialist and textualist or tropological, interests and analytical techniques' (1996: 5). Shakespeare criticism is 'a *jeu sans frontières*', as Ernst Honigmann says (1989: 2).

Issues of gender, race, and sexuality in Shakespeare are, according to Carol Neely, 'inseparable, unstable, disunified, and mutually constitutive' (1995: 303).

Mutually constitutive they may be, as may be many of the other issues taken up by Shakespeare criticism in the century, but it is noticeable that very frequently there is a driving agenda behind their reconstitution, so that when Valerie Traub, for instance, applies psychoanalysis to the plays of Shakespeare it is 'to provide a historical account which restores agency/participation to groups hitherto marginalised or left out of what counts as historical explanation—nonelite men and all women' (1995: 136).

So much activity, on so many fronts, not only produces a criticism of an often shameless partiality but one which is more than occasionally unhinged.[12] As Richard Halpern says: 'The sheer mass of Shakespearean scholarship, criticism and speculation provides an archive vast enough to "prove" virtually anything, and thus to manufacture Shakespeares to order, "as you like it"' (1997: 175). Not everybody likes it, as Haines reminds us in James Joyce's *Ulysses*: 'Shakespeare is the happy hunting ground of all minds that have lost their balance' (1966: 248). And even as early as the end of the nineteenth century Oscar Wilde could contemplate writing an essay called 'Are the Commentators on *Hamlet* Really Mad, Or Only Pretending to be?'.

Packs and Sects of Great Ones

Sensitive integrations, potential syntheses, happy marriages between consenting ideologies, then, are by no means the whole, or even the main, story of Shakespeare criticism in the twentieth century, though I would certainly argue that these alliances have produced major contributions to our understanding and greater enjoyment of Shakespeare. An analysis of the way things have gone, closer, perhaps, to the spirit of our times, occurs in Chris Baldick's justly admired book, *Criticism and Literary Theory 1890 to the Present* (1996), where he talks of the various critical movements in the twentieth century as comprising 'short-lived fashions and spectacular contests . . . generating a cutthroat intellectual bazaar of contending critical "schools" whose only point of agreement is that the critical methods of twenty years ago are too shop-soiled to be put on sale at all' (7).

A slightly more charitable way to view these spectacular contests is through the lens of Harold Bloom's theory of the relationship between writers and their predecessors, 'the anxiety of influence', a phenomenon by no means restricted to the twentieth century (or to poets). Many literary artists after Shakespeare especially (and particularly those writing for the theatre) have at times thought his genius a baleful influence, the 'bitter-sweet of this Shakespearean fruit' as Keats says, and an influence difficult to get out from under in their attempts to establish voices of their own. George Steiner responds to Shakespeare's painful majesty: 'We do him honour, also, if we recognize how heavy is the burden of his glory' (1970: 211). Scott Wilson, as we have seen, compares Shakespeare to the sun—Shakespeare is 'just as ambivalent as the sun in nature and in myth: he is both productive and destructive, illuminating and blinding, castrated and castrating' (1995: 88). ('Castrated', that is, because of his 'inability to communicate directly'.) And the ambivalent sun with its castrating rays has long been popular with critics as a metaphor for Shakespeare's benevolent tyranny. Sir Sidney Lee writes in 1906: 'But Shakespeare was the sun in the firmament: when his light shone, the fires of his contemporaries paled in the contemporary play-goer's eye' (30).

It's hard to imagine Shakespeare, the sun itself, prey to this anxious frame of mind. Yet the opening lines of Sonnet 59 suggest otherwise:

> If there be nothing new, but that which is
> Hath been before, how are our brains beguiled,
> Which, labouring for invention, bear amiss
> The second burden of a former child!

There is here, as Jonathan Bate points out, 'the melancholy implication that all writing is mere imitation of previous writing' (1993: 91). According to Linda Woodbridge, 'Shakespeare and his contemporaries felt they were contending against a world of overshadowing ancestors: they wrote in an age when those upstart youths the vernacular languages were doing battle against the ancient patriarchy of Latin and when modern writers were striving to come into their own against the almost deified shades of the Greek and Roman classics' (1994: 274).

Critics too—especially of the kind singled out by G. D. Atkins—
can feel their predecessors breathing down their necks, or as Paul Bove
more elegantly phrases it: 'modern intellectuals (perhaps all successors)
repeat the dynastic patterns that they hope to transcend in revisionist
acts meant to establish their own authority and priority' (1986: 4). And
while it is hard to imagine Coleridge feeling threatened by the critical
acumen of Johnson or A. C. Bradley by that of Coleridge, it's
undoubtedly the case that much of what they say is in reaction and
often in contradistinction to their great predecessors. As E. K. Chambers says: 'Heresy and the reaction against heresy and the search for a
reconciliation have always been the dialectical process by which
knowledge has advanced its frontiers and consolidated its territory'
(1944*b*: 25). Gary Taylor talks about a general anxiety for the professional critic: 'The contemporary scholar like the contemporary scien-
tist, must keep routinely producing new ideas at an accelerating rate,
while keeping up with everybody else's new ideas' (1990: 351). In our
own time, some of the most stimulating criticism of Shakespeare
has been stimulated by argument either with individual critics or
with critical movements then thought out of date, or even pernicious.
Edward Dowden's opening sentence of the Preface to the first edition
in 1875 of *Shakspere: A Critical Study of His Mind and Art* (1962)
attempts to distinguish it 'from the greater number of preceding
criticisms of Shakspere' by his observing the growth of Shakespeare's
'intellect and character from youth to full maturity' (p. xiii). Much of
the animus of William Empson's essays on Shakespeare, to take
another random example, is in response to what he finely describes
as John Dover Wilson's 'odd power of making a deep remark without
seeing its implications' (1987: 86). In *Making Trifles of Terrors: Redistributing Complicities in Shakespeare* (1997), Harry Berger Jr. redistri-
butes an initial complicity of his own by announcing that his work as a
Shakespeare critic is largely in reaction to the Shakespeare criticism of
the philosopher, Stanley Cavell, 'whose Shakespearean meditations
initially stimulated and still haunt the interpretation developed in the
following pages' (p. x).

Making trifles of terrors suggests, however inadvertently, the strain
that twentieth-century Shakespeare critics feel themselves under from
a variety of sources. Can twentieth-century criticism of Shakespeare as
a result fairly be characterized—at least in part—as being dog-in-the-

manger? Is there more of the adversarial in twentieth-century criticism of Shakespeare than in previous centuries? Heather Dubrow for one thinks so but claims that it is only after 1970 that celebration of Shakespeare comes to be thought 'a dangerous lionizing' (1997: 38). Shakespeare's time, she says, has now become known—ominously—as the early modern period as opposed to the Renaissance: it is 'the site of proto-capitalism, the source of twentieth-century conceptions of subjectivity and authorship, and the arena for modes of patriarchal suppression...' (39).

It might be appropriate, then, given this return to the future, to think of the twentieth century in the words of John Donne's famous description of the beginning of the seventeenth when 'new philosophy calls all in doubt'. For Hardin Craig, writing in 1949, and clearly influenced by the destruction of the Second World War, 'it is the presence of doubt that chiefly distinguishes our world from that of Shakespeare' (107). For Craig, Shakespeare and his world somehow escape Donne's censure; not so for Paola Pugliatti and many other more recent critics, who are much more Donnian than he. In her discussion of Shakespeare's history plays she argues that their 'instability of meaning, their perspectivism, their irresolution, their dialogism, and their heteroglossia constitute, I believe, a significant breach with the orthodox practice of contemporary historians' (1996: 345). What gets reinstated in them is the 'strict discipline of doubt' (346), the creative discipline of our time according to Robert Hughes's masterly book on the origins and triumph of modern art, *The Shock of the New* (1981). In literary criticism the 'hermeneutics of suspicion' replaces the 'hermeneutics of faith', and formalism's celebration of texts as well-wrought urns is abandoned for the pleasurable pursuit of what in them is ill-wrought and unintended: cracks, fissures, slippages, and—a favourite word—aporias.[13]

Study's God-Like Recompense

The reign of doubt in the twentieth-century criticism of Shakespeare is coextensive with the rise of the academy, where professional doubters were institutionalized and rewarded for replacing readings of works of literature as sacred cows by readings of them as, so to speak, brinded cats. At first the sacred cow aspect predominated as the latter half of the nineteenth century was concerned more with the education of children than of university students. As Brown and Fearon observe, in the latter half of the nineteenth century '[t]he Shakespeare industry's great discovery... was the value of the child' (1939: 252), but it was a value that required a fumigated Shakespeare: 'William the Outspoken' had to be replaced by 'St. William the National Hero and ornament of school curricula' (256). As an icon of everything noble and British—the terms were interchangeable—Shakespeare assumed the kind of status that would later be exploited for his role in Britain's tourist and manufacturing industries.

Many social commentators see his iconic status in the education system in the late nineteenth century—and after—as part of an Arnoldian conspiracy driven by evangelism and utilitarianism to unite the country in the face of social unrest. D. J. Palmer's *The Rise of English Studies* (1965) gives us fascinating glimpses into the huge importance of adult education in the late nineteenth century with its Foucauldian ambitions to police and humanize the lower classes. (A remarkable proportion of Victorian Shakespeare criticism, incidentally, originated in adult education lectures.) Hugh Grady observes that 'English literature and Shakespeare entered the education system in the nineteenth century as part of the effort to preserve a sense of cultural unity in the face of the fragmentation and differentiations brought on by mechanization' (1991a: 65); they became 'part of a liberal humane education, providing a cultural continuity that otherwise seemed in danger of extinction in the social upheavals of a new industrial democracy' (78). Investment in secondary education bred investment in post-secondary, and the late nineteenth and early twentieth centuries witnessed a large expansion in university education that was only to be surpassed by the spread of the new universities after the Second World War. In English studies at the university it was inevitable that Shakespeare would be granted his familiar sun-like authority, the study of him made intellectually respectable by an early emphasis on philology and historical criticism.

If anything the experience of European revolution and the 1914–18 war intensified the pressure on English literature and Shakespeare to be seen as beacons of civility shining in a naughty world. During the First World War, Chris Baldick tells us, literary education attempted 'the binding of class to class in common respect for the national heritage and all that was precious in it, against the threat of its destruction by the barbaric Hun' (1983: 82). In 1915 Henry Newbolt chaired the committee into the teaching of English literature which included as some of its members the prominent Shakespeareans, Caroline Spurgeon, Guy Boas, Sir Arthur Quiller-Couch, and John Dover Wilson. In 1921 he published its extremely popular report *The Teaching of English in England* which Baldick describes as a 'large-scale exercise in mental health' (1983: 141), responding to the universal fear of chaos, the dishonesty of wartime propaganda, and the need to buttress social order with poetry. It was also an attempt to correct the taste of the masses without offending commercial interests. Shakespeare was seen in it as Arnold saw him—superior in every way but especially in the possession of a superior normality, and many critics between the world wars responded positively to this version of Shakespeare as the great artist of super-normalcy. The Leavises launched *Scrutiny* in 1932 to celebrate the moral centrality of all great literature including Shakespeare's works, and critics like T. S. Eliot and I. A. Richards placed great importance on the therapeutic capacity of literature to make the individual mind whole. M. H. Abrams describes such approaches as 'treatments of literary works as symbolic modes for encompassing and coping with experience' (1997: 111). After the Second World War Shakespeare became part of the coverage of the Welfare State; according to Russell Jackson, the aim of the British government was to make theatre-going an affordable experience for everybody 'like state-funded provision of national insurance, health care, housing, education, and the other elements of the "Welfare State"' (1996a: 211).[14]

Shakespeare's enthronement in the seats of higher learning and his new pedagogic status as a guru in the art of discriminating living entailed, as Hugh Grady puts it, 'the de-legitimation of the competence of lay readers' (1991a: 70). Difficulty itself has been seen as part of a kind of class exclusiveness, as John Fiske argues: 'Artistic complexity is a class distinction: difficulty is a cultural turnstile—it admits only those with the right tickets and excludes the masses' (1989: 121). Such a new emphasis on instruction in the high-minded, however, sat well with a modernist literary culture. T. S. Eliot famously argued in 1932 that twentieth-century literature had no choice but to be difficult:

We can only say that it appears likely that poets in our civilization, as it exists at present, must be *difficult*. Our civilization comprehends great variety of complexity, and this variety of complexity, playing upon a refined sensibility, must produce various and complex results. The poet must become more and more comprehensive, more allusive, more indirect, in order to force, to dislocate if necessary, language into his meaning. (289)

This last sentence can be applied just as well to the refined sensibilities of twentieth-century literary critics as to twentieth-century poets. And the sentence also has equal authority for many twentieth-century critics as a description of Shakespeare's own refined sensibility, even though it operated in the sixteenth and seventeenth centuries rather than in the twentieth—illustrating yet again Shakespeare's wonderful capacity to live up to Jonson's famous description of him as not of an age but for all time. Gary Taylor writes: 'By midcentury Shakespeare looked as polyglot as Joyce and Eliot and Pound, his poetry, like theirs, the product of a cosmopolitan intellect' (1990: 252). A polyglot Shakespeare demands a polyglot critic, though he doesn't often get her.

Since the 1960s criticism has often been fiendishly difficult. Although I wouldn't have thought that an early play like *The Two Gentlemen of Verona* could be considered as representing Shakespeare at his most polyglot—especially in the vicinity of that other early play, the ultra-sophisticated *Love's Labour's Lost*—the following extract from an essay on the play by Jonathan Goldberg might suggest otherwise: 'The letter is "for" Valentine if he can read his name as "the secret, nameless friend". Only if, that is, auto-affection will allow him to find within himself the valentine that enfolds the letter from Valentine that another (himself as that other), writing for Silvia has written within' (1986: 73). This kind of writing—polymorphic if not polyglot—seems to be responding to Foucault's belief—as relayed through Karlis Racevskis—that '[t]he critic's major responsibility is to "problematize" the processes through which truth is produced' (1989: 237–8).

Academic Shakespeare critics these days take their problematizing function very seriously and search for unproblematized areas in which to practise their art. A symptomatic plea from Susan Bennett for 'an area in desperate need of some theorization as well as a much more complicated scholarship' asks the critical community to help problematize and theorize 'the cross-cultural, if not global, imperatives of . . . performances' (1996: 15). There is no doubt that this relatively new-found need to theorize has contributed heavily to the demands on the reader that Shakespeare criticism now makes. Theory is inter-disciplinary, analytical, and speculative; it critiques the unexamined assumptions of common sense (and a good thing too); it is reflexive, it demonstrates a thinking about thinking, addressing the problem of why we think the way we do, and at its finest presents us with a sophisticated and powerful set of procedures for understanding a text's place in the world as well as the text itself. It also appeals—once more—to the creatively inclined critic; in the hands of some theorists it can be, in G. D. Atkins's words, an 'intellectual poem' (1989: 12). We have moved from criticism as a kind of fiction in the hands of a story-telling critic like A. C. Bradley to the much denser often heavily metaphoric 'poetic' language of the poststructuralists and deconstruc-tionists.

At the same time, we should bear in mind that the difficulty of twentieth-century Shakespeare criticism—and not just the diffi-culty—sometimes has a factitious quality. Graham Bradshaw's polem-ical Epilogue 'The New Historicist as Iago' in his book assaulting the materialists reminds us that '[o]nly the very naive or saintly could fail to see how contemporary theoretical and ideological disputes have an institutional setting, where they are practically and inevitably asso-ciated with other kinds of "contestation"—personal or group advance-ment, promotions, and patronage', but he hastens to add—and in the nick of time perhaps—'on the other hand only the very cynical would think it sufficient to explain such disputes in that insultingly reductive fashion' (1993: 229). None the less the moral of his book is to 'be suspicious of the hermeneutics of suspicion' (231). I might also hasten to add here perhaps also in the nick of time that we should of course be even more suspicious of the hermeneutics of credulity.

Moulded of Things Past

And yet. And yet. Despite the proliferation of new-fangled ways of doing things with Shakespeare, much twentieth-century Shakespeare criticism (a great deal in fact, perhaps most) does what it does regard-less of fashion and change. Heather Dubrow writes: 'An essay referring to "dramatic form," for instance, might have been written in 1910 or

1950 as well as in 1990 . . .' (1997: 27). (Though I don't think it could have been written in 1840 or 1880.) When we consider the rise of English studies in D. J. Palmer's *The Rise of English Studies* (1965) we can see it as a constant process of the reconstitution of traditional elements. If, as Jonathan Dollimore observes, 'the new defines itself against the established', it is also the case, as he goes on to say, that with time 'sharp differences may dissolve into obscure similarities' (1990: 405).

Frequently the similarities are not all that obscure, and not too much time needs to pass for us to be able to notice them, and much of this book is concerned to bring the reader's attention to the *plus ça change* aspect of the history of Shakespeare criticism in the twentieth century in response to the notion, here formulated by Robert Hughes, that '[h]istories do not break off clean, like a glass rod; they fray, stretch, and come undone, like rope' (1981: 375). And despite the fact that an anxiety of influence may well prevail in elite critical circles in the twentieth century it is also true that many critics see their work in terms of a tradition of Shakespeare criticism with which they are more than happy to be associated.[15] In his Prefatory Note to the 1949 edition of *The Wheel of Fire*, first published in 1930, G. Wilson Knight thinks of his own criticism—nostalgically and probably erroneously—as part of the great tradition of Shakespeare criticism which includes A. C. Bradley, but his way of putting it suggests that his own assessment is not the same as other people's: 'It was, and is, my hope that my own labours will be eventually regarded as a natural development within the classic tradition of Shakespearian study' (pp. v–vi). James Calderwood sees himself as one of those partaking of the great feast of criticism: 'Criticism, one likes to feel, perhaps nostalgically, is a corporate venture, or at least a potluck meal to which each of us brings something, without, we all hope, too much duplication of dishes' (1983: 18). Graham Bradshaw puts a somewhat more negative spin on this classic tradition by drawing our attention to critics who mirror each other's bad habits: in *Radical Tragedy*, he argues, Jonathan Dollimore 'carries on the old bad Tillyardian habit of giving particular characters and speakers a supradramatic significance, which is then identified with what the play or the dramatist "really" thinks, and usually coincides with what the critic thinks' (1993: 9). What you find in Shakespeare, he declares, depends on what you're looking for.

It's arguable that the later twentieth-century's re-emphasis on the historical context(s) of a literary work renews in a different kind of way the later nineteenth-century emphasis on the historical, political, and philosophical value of philology as opposed to the eighteenth-century indulgence in what *The Rise of English Studies* describes as 'verbal criticism and mere elegant scholarship' (1965: 42) (whatever they might be). Or we might consider how the present sense of a crisis in the humanities in the conduct and ideology of literary criticism(s) continues—if in shriller, more apocalyptic vein—a traditional view that we are always, already, living in desperate times. Gerald Graff's *Professing Literature* (1987) and—especially—Jonathan Culler's *Framing the Sign* (1988) valuably pursue these continuities. In 1997 M. H. Abrams ventured a concluding prophecy to his article: looking back fifty years hence, the literary critic 'will conclude that literary studies, having undergone some such changes as I have sketched, are (in a favorite expression of my favorite literary theorist, S. T. Coleridge) *alter et idem*. The Latin may be translated freely as "transformed yet recognizable"' (1997: 129). And in the same year Richard Halpern aligns recent twentieth-century critical movements: 'Our "postmodern condition"', he writes, 'represents a mutation, rather than a cessation, of the modernist paradigm' (1997: 2).

Mutations can be looked at inversely. We may look back at this stage to the book that began this chapter, R. G. Moulton's *Shakespeare as a Dramatic Artist: A Popular Illustration of the Principles of Scientific Criticism*, published in 1885. As far as Eric Bentley is concerned in his introduction to the 1966 reissue it remains 'the only notable book on Shakespeare's handling of plot' (p. vii). And he adds: 'May I refer the man of tomorrow to a critic of yesterday?' (p. viii). We may see in the next chapter the extent to which that invitation is taken up by the men of tomorrow (and the women too of course), referring in particular to a great critic of yesterday, A. C. Bradley.

'Anxiety of influence' has its sunnier counterpart—at times anyway—in the communality of the theatre. J. L. Styan begins his chapter on the advent of stage-centred criticism in the twentieth century with a remark by Tyrone Guthrie: 'We all learn, borrow, steal, if you like, from one another' (1977: 64). The bonhomie of this remark suggests that the influence of previous directors is less anxiety-causing than that of writers in the literary or critical worlds. And the same might be said of the acting tradition: actors learn from actors in extraordinarily fruitful ways.

Of course this tradition can also be seen in the by now more familiarly obverse, perhaps more twentieth-century, view as it is unrestrainedly presented in Martin Buzacott's alarmist book, *The Death of the Actor* (1991), where, for instance, a self-effacing, Stanislavskian actor, Alec Guinness, is shamelessly upstaged by a boorish, tyrannical, Brechtian actor, Ralph Richardson. Buzacott claims that it is Richardson, not Guinness, who is in the great tradition of Shakespeare (over)acting, a tradition that has been a pernicious influence in the British theatre. A particularly reverberating ego, according to Buzacott, belonged to Donald Wolfit whose 'greatness as a Shakespearean actor lay in his . . . ability to play characters badly and confidently' (24). Although Buzacott prefers the term 'intertextuality' to Bloom's 'influence', his description of its inhibiting operation on both directors and actors takes us into a nightmare world of self-destructive passions conveyed in the metaphors of deviant sexuality. The result of this heavy burden of theatrical intertextuality, especially in the case of Shakespearean acting, is that 'the actor's impotence is particularly abject, indeed deathly, because of the sheer weight of intertexts which constitute the cultural icon' (132).

On the other hand, to ignore the heavy burden of theatrical intertextuality entirely is to invite trouble as when critics ignore the work of *their* predecessors. Peter Holland draws a more general lesson from a typically disastrous production of the 1990s:

The staging of some plays suggests that directors are only too willing to ignore the lessons of history while leaving behind them a trace that their successors will perhaps not heed either. No one could respond to the experience of such catastrophes with any belief in the inevitability of progress. Theatre historians cannot be Whiggish. (1997a: 216)

The choice between succumbing to the tyrannical traditions of the past and heedlessly ignoring its line of admonishing failures is no real choice at all. All directors in the twentieth century are anxious to overthrow tired interpretations. In one of his productions of *Hamlet* Jonathan Miller describes how necessary it is to get out from under performances like Olivier's. His counter-interpretation of Hamlet's character would not receive universal approbation: 'I have always been interested in the idea of Hamlet as a rather unattractive character, a tiresome, clever, destructive boy who is very intelligent but volatile, dirty-minded and immature' (1986: 111). Entirely playful (mis)appropriations of Shakespeare, unsullied by anxieties of any kind, are possible of course as Stephen Bretzius reminds us in his chapter on the Beatles and Shakespeare where he notes that '*Abbey Road* refashions *A Midsummer Night's Dream* in much the way that *Sgt. Pepper* recalls *Julius Caesar* and *Magical Mystery Tour* replays *King Lear*' (1997: 130).

One of the most traditional of the *plus ça change* critical positions in this and any other time is simply to shut one's ears to the siren songs of current debate. In their ongoing attempts to make him new, many twentieth-century critics continue to take to heart Heminges and Condell's simple injunction to the 1623 Folio's 'Great Variety of Readers' to read Shakespeare 'againe, and againe'. We can understand Heminges and Condell's emphatically iterative 'and againe' as a pre-emptive (and anachronistic) admonition to us to read 'him' as opposed to reading around him, through him, or ourselves via him—all such readings indulged to excess in the twentieth century. That 'him', as far as Heminges and Condell are concerned, then, is his works—reading them is reading him.

This salutary admonition seems to be being newly heeded these days, against the grain of much modern criticism. A book like Howard Mills's *Working With Shakespeare* (1993), for example, takes Dr Johnson's advice to heart: 'Read every play from the first scene to the last, with utter negligence of all his commentators'. All very well, we might say, for someone like Johnson writing in the eighteenth century when commentators were few and far between, and many of those few only too deserving of our utter negligence. This is not the case today surely when it would be criminally unprofessional to ignore the mass of sophisticated criticism from commentators deserving our utter consideration. Yet Mills's project is just one of a number that attempt to bring fresh eyes to bear on (over)familiar material—the works and 'him' in them, at the expense of the critical controversies swirling around them. To advert to Dr Johnson again, we should read Shakespeare, we should read anyone, 'uncorrupted with literary prejudices'. To heed this injunction is to write criticism in the manner of, say, William Empson who asks us to taste Shakespeare's plays with as clean a palate as we can. Richard Strier writes: 'Empson is a model for me by virtue of his verbal and philosophical alertness, his non-programmatic curiosity and bafflement, and his complete lack of theoretically imposed inhibitions in approaching texts' (1995: 7).

A clean palate in point perhaps is Tony Tanner's series of Introductions to the eight-volume Everyman edition of Shakespeare's works (1992). In an interestingly conflicted review of it in the *Times Literary Supplement* (7 Nov. 1997), Peter Holland praises Tanner's acumen as a critic highly—each page worthy of repeated readings, Holland writes, in Heminges and Condell vein—but he goes on to warn us that because Tanner is not a professional Shakespearean he seems to be writing in a time warp. Does this mean that if Tanner were writing in some more up-to-the-minute way his pages would be worth—how many more re-redings? Re-readings of re-readings? The fact of the matter is that Tanner's sophistication as a critic is everywhere apparent in the Everyman Introductions, his pages *are* worth the re-readings Holland urges on us, despite—maybe because of even—Tanner's lack of concern for what the 'professional' Shakespeareans out there are now doing, and I don't think we should ask much more of any critic, whether or not he is a professional Shakespearean, than that his work should be sufficiently cogent and pleasurable that his pages demand to be read again and again. What Tanner is demonstrating, it seems to me, is the validity of John Dewey's notion of the 'artful innocence' of our thinking about experience (though of course Tanner is no literary innocent—far from it). In this respect, he is in the tradition of critics like Bradley, Dowden, and G. Wilson Knight in their cavalier disregard for the scholarship of the early twentieth century. Which does not mean to say, of course, that 'professional Shakespeareans' aren't equally capable of a kind of 'artful innocence' or at least the self-confidence required to travel over well-trodden ground and reach different, sometimes more desirable, destinations, nor does it mean to say that artful innocence is superior to artful professionalism. (That is, the profession of Shakespeare critic.) There is a plenitude of unignorable examples in twentieth-century Shakespeare criticism of Shakespeare having been read again and again in both artfully innocent and artfully professional ways, each worthy of many re-readings.

The Cup of Alteration

Whether artful and innocent, or artful and professional, these readings could only have been produced in the twentieth century. Because of the new concerns with Shakespeare, new ways of looking at the plays from differently angled coigns of vantage, under new rubrics, with different expectations, critics from the twentieth century have tended to group the works in untraditional ways. Peter Holland explains: 'Critics often complain about the taxonomic systems used for Shakespeare. Dissatisfied with the Folio's "comedies, histories, tragedies", bored with divisions like "the major tragedies", "the problem plays" or "the romances", we try to find new and invigorating subdivisions of the canon, new juxtapositions to illuminate the plays' relationships' (1997*a*: 75).

There are still, of course, the traditional groupings; books by the score continue to appear on Shakespeare's tragedies or on his comedies, on his histories or on his romances, as self-sufficient units for investigation, but there are also hundreds of investigations that track elements across traditional genres.[16] As far as these critics are concerned, what is at work here is a quite intricate intertextuality, an intramural intertextuality as it were, linking Shakespeare's plays and poems in a *mélange* of cross-echoings in which one work complicates, ironizes, or maybe interrogates the assumptions and modes of being of another or others.

Writing for undergraduates, Northrop Frye painlessly practises this Shakespearean intertextuality: 'If Hamlet had been in Othello's situation, there'd have been no tragedy, because Hamlet would have seen through Iago at a glance; if Othello had been in Hamlet's situation, there'd have been no tragedy, because Othello would have skewered Claudius before we were out of Act One' (1986: 4). A model for these kinds of readings of the plays is the one demanded by the Sonnets whose interdependence is of course unignorable (and has never been ignored).

But we might consider here the recent criticism of a romantic comedy, *Much Ado About Nothing*. While not denying that the play is a romantic comedy, the three major twentieth-century editions of *Much Ado*—A. R. Humphreys's Arden (1981), F. H. Mares's New

Cambridge (1988), and Sheldon Zitner's Oxford (1993)—all deal with the play in terms of its affinities with the problem plays and romances rather than with its traditional bedfellows, the other major romantic comedies, *As You Like It* and *Twelfth Night*. Similarly, Carol Neely (1985) interrogates the broken nuptials in *Much Ado* in the light of the collapsed relationships in *All's Well*, *Antony and Cleopatra*, *Othello*, and *The Winter's Tale*.[7] And when Gary Taylor (1985) analyses some Shakespeare titbits he does so in a variety of ways with some arbitrarily chosen moments of pleasure: Act 3, scene 1 from *Julius Caesar*, the character Viola from *Twelfth Night*, the Royal Shakespeare Company's 1975 production of *Henry V*, and a single scene from *King Lear*.

Reading Shakespeare anew in the twentieth century often involves what Carol Neely felicitously calls 'over-reading'. In her case, a feminist over-reading of Shakespeare's plays is necessary in the face of what she believes to be the built-in patriarchal slant to the criticism of the New Historicists and cultural materialists. A feminist critique, she urges, 'needs to over-read, to read to excess, the possibility of human (especially female) gendered subjectivity, identity, and agency, the possibility of women's resistance or even subversion' (1988: 15). Feminists need to read 'men's canonical texts with women's uncanonical ones' (17).

We could extrapolate the term 'over-reading' and apply it to a variety of twentieth-century Shakespeare readings which 'over-read' Shakespeare in the face of a traditionally myopic critical approach. Of course there's over-reading and over-reading. The dangers of over-reading, or of partial reading, of reading adversarially against the grain of the text (and of tradition), are, as we have seen, apparent everywhere in twentieth-century Shakespeare criticism. Certain cruxes seem to breed fanciful over-readings. One such is the—allegedly—infamously under-motivated jealousy that Leontes conceives for Polixenes in *The Winter's Tale*. For Michael Bristol, Leontes's jealousy is a 'type of spatio-temporal derangement of the ethos of gift, hospitality, and expenditure, mandated by the observances of the Winter Festival or Christmas-tide' (1996: 158). It's 'motivated by a barely conscious fantasy or wish in which he gives his wife to Polixenes for his sexual enjoyment in order to intensify the social bond between the two men' (159). All this 'despite their protestations of love and friendship, then, and despite the imagery of the "twinned lambs"' (160). Despite, that is, specific (if not precise), indirect (if not crystal-clear) textual admonitions as to the exchange's psychic history.

We need to put this emphasis on 'over-reading' in a larger cultural context, the pedagogical one especially. Some critics talk, for instance, about the desirability for a conservative agenda of Great Books courses as opposed to those that take in other, often marginalized, cultures. But 'over-reading' tends—fortunately I think—to find otherness in the great books themselves. It's hard to imagine, say, a course on the Greek classics constrained by definition merely to re-issue civilized pieties of a conservative nature. Any given course may do so—so may any given course on Shakespeare—but the potential for the unconstrained reading to excess is always inherent in the hospitable greatness of the work itself.

An illuminating example of this tendency (more unfortunate perhaps than not) can be found in the (relatively) unlikely milieu of the reference book. (Relatively unlikely because we have come to expect such books to be more objective and dispassionate, more sincerely factual than any others.) Only in the twentieth century could a reference work as farcically indiscriminate as Frankie Rubinstein's *A Dictionary of Shakespeare's Sexual Puns and their Significance* (1984) run into a second edition in 1989. On the other hand, only in the twentieth century could there be such a frank acceptance and appreciation of Shakespeare in the Sonnets as a homosexual activist. (See Chapter 2 for further discussion.) In an updated application of Dowden's version of Shakespeare's earthy spirituality, Bruce Smith notes that although there is sexual desire in Sidney, Spenser, Daniel, and others, it is only in Shakespeare's sonnets that 'sexual desire remains uncontained by spiritual metaphor' (1991: 229). The sonnets are 'discourses of homosexual desire' (269).[18]

The coigns of vantage in Shakespeare criticism in the twentieth century become more and more oblique. Shakespeare's reception in the four corners of the world, the lives of Shakespeare critics, all kinds of anthropological and materialist practices that impinge on Shakespeare, the advanced technologies of the modern theatre, Shakespeare in the movies, Shakespeare in all aspects of economic life, the make-up of Shakespeare's audiences in his and other centuries, the make-up of the make-up used in Shakespeare's time[19]—even the photographs in theatre foyers[20]—all now clamour for the attention of the

century Shakespeare critic as legitimate areas for discussion
h. A ripe harvest gathered in the barns, indeed. But even
:rease in subject areas there is perhaps a hint of panic in the
ranks of Shakespeare critics seeking new worlds to conquer. Hence the
interest in increasing the number of Shakespeare's works. Giorgio
Melchiori (1994) puts the case for Shakespeare's authorship of *Edward
III* and has the support of Wells and Taylor (1987) and Meredith Skura
who writes: 'The text is so enmeshed in reciprocal relations to Shakespeare's other works that it seems rather to issue from the same mind
than to have come from outside and impressed Shakespeare so totally'
(1993: 296). Gary Taylor controversially finds a 'new' poem by Shakespeare. Quartos of Shakespeare's plays long dismissed as corrupt and
inferior compete now with their more respectable brethren—sometimes shouldering them aside—as versions that should stand on their
own—and so the 1997 Norton Complete Shakespeare gives us three
*King Lear*s, and a case can be made for additional *Richard II*s, *Troilus
and Cressida*s, and *Othello*s, and maybe three (or even four) *Hamlet*s.

In performance, there is a tendency today to re-shuffle and add to
whatever Shakespeare has written. M. C. Bradbrook observes: 'The
pluralist interpretation of the plays in performance now extends to rewriting the text, improvising upon it, blending it with other texts'
(1976: 129). Some of these productions attain memorable notoriety as
in the case of Michael Bogdanov's *The Taming of the Shrew* for the
Royal Shakespeare Company at Stratford-upon-Avon in 1979. (See
Chapter 4 for further discussion of this and other creative invasions of
Shakespeare's plays by the hypertrophic imaginations of today's directors.)

When we think about reshuffling and pluralism in the twentieth
century, Heather Dubrow reminds us, we need to take into account
the propensity for critics to change their minds, especially given our
century's greatest gift to those of us who live in the West, an increased
life-span. And, for that matter, we need to take into account the shifts
in focus and alterations of emphasis in critical movements. A collection of essays on myth and ritual criticism in 1992 differs materially
from the concerns of myth and ritual criticism thirty years earlier. In
the former we find the proud disclaimer: 'Our essayists make no
mention of archetypes, for example, or of Jung, and invoke the ideas
of Northrop Frye, if at all, only to supplant them' (1). The collection

celebrates what its editors believe are now presumably the true rites; Jung's and Frye's the maimed. Another, edited by Deborah Barker and Ivo Kamps (1995), charts the maturing of the feminist response to Shakespeare over the previous twenty years. As for individuals, R. W. Babcock's essay (1952) takes amused note of E. E. Stoll's Polonius-like shifts in critical position over the years from the sceptical-historical to the historical-aesthetic to the aesthetic-historical. Chronological changes in a critic's position can be matched by the number of straddling positions that a critic might hold at any one time. A critic doesn't have to be an intellectual gadfly like Empson to pursue legitimate, interpenetrating interests in a number of different critical camps. T. S. Eliot, whose importance as a founding critic would be acknowledged by formalists, mythicists, and historicists alike, is a case in point. It is primarily because Eliot employs anthropological methods and themes that he is so important for twentieth-century Shakespeare criticism: from him, such major Shakespeare critics as C. L. Barber, Northrop Frye, René Girard, and Robert Weimann spring.

Degree, Priority, and Place

It's hardly surprising in the circumstances that the twentieth century should revalue Shakespeare's canon and be drawn to those plays that seem to anticipate the obsessions of our own time. The abrasive intellectuality of Shakespeare's 'problem plays', for example, their cynicism in the face of moot points of morality, especially, have many admirers in this doubting century. *Measure for Measure* in particular casts an intellectual spell. Although there were rumblings of approval for it in the late nineteenth century, it wasn't until the 1920s, so Rosalind Miles (1976) tells us, that *Measure for Measure* came to be universally highly regarded. By 1989 T. F. Wharton can argue that the play is now Shakespeare's most popular. The most aggressive defence of it, as high-toned and scornful as Isabella and Angelo themselves, continues to be F. R. Leavis's (1942). In less pugnacious terms, D. L. Stevenson argues, in a scene by scene analysis, that this Jonsonian play is a 'brilliantly intellectual tour de force on moral obtuseness' (1966: 11). Harriett Hawkins's Harvester Introduction to the play (1987) strikes a chord with us in its promotion of the play as a maelstrom of conflicting interpretations and positions each of which is powerfully supported in the play itself which pits character against character and sometimes the same character against his/her previous or later self. What is a sin for Isabella is laudable for Mariana. John Dover Wilson insists that

> *Measure for Measure* is written in much the same key as *Point Counter Point* and others of Mr. Aldous Huxley's novels. The hatred of sentimentalism and romance, the savage determination to tear aside all veils, to expose reality in its crudity and hideousness, the self-laceration, weariness, discord, cynicism and disgust of our modern 'literature of negation' all belonged to Shakespeare about 1603. (1932: 117)

Similar arguments have been made in this century for the overwhelming relevance for our times of *Measure for Measure*'s companion plays *All's Well that Ends Well* and *Troilus and Cressida*.[21]

The play of all Shakespeare's plays that seems to speak most powerfully to our time—especially since 1960—is *King Lear*. R. A. Foakes (1993) writes a book in which he traces the declining value of *Hamlet* as the cultural icon of our civilization in the face of the bullish rise to cultural predominance of *King Lear* as the play that best mirrors our experience of this century's desolations. The nineteenth-century identification with the dilemma of the individual conscience that makes cowards of us all has given way to the twentieth-century identification with the grimmer possibility that none does offend in a world where all do.

The rise in popularity of *King Lear* in this century is matched by that of the Roman plays which are valued especially for their usefulness as proleptic political commentary on the political conundrums of our own times. '[I]t is there, and there alone, that something like an urban, public space emerges', so Richard Halpern argues (1997: 52). In these plays we get charismatic, dictatorial leaders and turbulent plebeians which anticipate developments in early twentieth-century politics. Of *Antony and Cleopatra* and the Roman plays generally, Northrop Frye writes, 'It's amazing how vividly Shakespeare has imagined a world so much more like ours than like his' (1986: 122). (His nomination for the Shakespeare play of the twenty-first century, interestingly, is *Antony and Cleopatra*.)

The twentieth century has also seen an upsurge of interest in the Sonnets, the Histories, and all of Shakespeare's comedies not just those with problems. Indeed, Samuel Crowl considers that '[o]ne of the great achievements of modern Shakespearean criticism is the way in which it has liberated the comedies from secondary consideration within the canon' (1992: 64). We have to thank critics like C. L. Barber (1959) for the beginnings of this liberation in his ground-breaking study of the connections between the comedies and Elizabethan society's festive traditions which give them universality and depth. By now we have become used to reading claims like the one Richard Wilson makes for *As You Like It*: 'No Shakespearean text transmits more urgently the imminence of the social breakdown threatened by the conjuncture of famine and enclosure' (1993: 65). In plays like *As You Like It*, indeed, in 'these seemingly benevolent texts we can detect the discursive formation of a new sensibility that would transform the operation of discipline and punishment in Europe' (125). We need to read *As You Like It* not just in the company of the problem comedies but under the stern tutelage of Hobbes's *Leviathan*.

Imperious in Another's Throne

The twentieth century has consolidated and expanded the already bustling Shakespeare export market. If the nineteenth century saw the triumph of Shakespeare in Europe and of course in English-speaking countries, the twentieth century has witnessed world-wide dominion. (For facts and figures Gary Taylor (1990) is a convenient and readable guide.) Productions of Shakespeare's plays in languages other than English are now legion and are often considered threatening by repressive governments: the militaristic government of Japan in 1938 felt threatened by a production of *Hamlet*, and Stalin also banned this always controversial play. Dennis Kennedy writes: 'If new plays and films critical of a repressive regime are regularly censored, producers are sometimes tempted to make the classics into coded messages about the present: Shakespeare thus became a secret agent under deep cover' (1996: 135). Obviously, productions of Shakespeare in a foreign language will lose something; but Kennedy argues that they will not lose everything, and they may gain some things. They may in fact have 'a more direct access to the power of the plays' (136). (Peter Brook's most radical productions of Shakespeare have been done in French.) It's probably true to say then that the twentieth century had a greater tendency to see Shakespeare in terms of world literature than did other centuries. The Danish critic, Georg Brandes begins his best-known book on Shakespeare (1905) by talking about him in the company of Michelangelo and Cervantes. In the 1990s it is very fashionable to see Shakespeare in a European context. If the world is now a global village then Shakespeare is arguably its headman. But before exploring this vast terrain we need to return to a criticism that has its roots closer to home: the criticism of Shakespeare's characters.

The Age of Bradley

What a Piece of Work Is a Man

And a woman too of course. Despite what Heather Dubrow says about the study of character in Shakespeare's plays—'character has virtually become a dirty word, quite as taboo in many circles as frank glosses on Shakespeare's sexual wordplay were to an earlier generation of editors' (1987: 17)—the fictional hearts and minds of Shakespeare's characters (and the even more fictive heart and mind of Shakespeare himself) continue to exert a fascination on theatre-goers, readers, and sophisticated critics alike. 'The age of Bradley', then—manifested most triumphantly in the first two or three decades of the twentieth century—in its insistence on the special value of character criticism as a means of understanding Shakespeare's plays, constitutes in all probability one of those eternal moments in criticism that will survive the predations of its competitors. At all events, there is a critical consensus in this century on the contribution that Shakespeare made to the thickening of dramatic characterization whether we read his characters 'as rhetorical constructs confined to the text or as mimetic representations of imagined persons' (Dubrow 1997: 30).

For Barbara Everett, indeed, Shakespeare is a proto-modernist, finding a way out of the sixteenth and into the seventeenth century by making his characters centres of consciousness as well as of action. Each play after 1600, she says, 'is also a poem to the degree that it is, at its deepest, a reasoned dream: an experience of the individual mind embodied as never before' (1998: 229). And despite the obvious danger in periodization, critics seem to agree that the transition from the sixteenth to the seventeenth century coincided with a change in

Shakespeare's techniques of characterization. After 1600, so George Wright argues, we hear a voice from the major characters in the plays 'in some ways like the voice that speaks the sonnets—a ruminative, private voice that deepens our sense of the dramatic character's inner self' (1998: 324): we are privy to a 'language of inner thought and feeling' (329). There's been nothing like this before, according to Alvin Kernan (1995), except perhaps in the psychological self-presentations of the great religious writers, Augustine, Luther, and Calvin. Lawrence Danson illuminatingly contrasts Marlowe and Shakespeare: 'Shakespeare's characters may undergo radical shifts in apparent identity, psychic slippages that unsettle a spectator's expectation for the unity of person; while Marlowe's heroes amaze or dismay us by the sheer tenacity of their will to be always themselves' (1986: 217). Somehow or other Shakespeare's characters, unlike Marlowe's, aren't always themselves; they seem to be unconfined by the texts they inhabit; they're autonomous, slippery, spontaneous, exhibiting, in Karen Newman's words, 'a residue beyond their function as agents' (1985: 2). And it's this tendency to burst out of their textual seams that persuades A. D. Nuttall in 1984 to pronounce Maurice Morgann's treatment of Shakespeare's characters in 1777 more credible than L. C. Knights's in 1933: '[Morgann] is aware in Shakespeare of a special dimension of inferable identity, an independent integrity *over and above* the usual dramatic allowance' (1963a: 27). The best-known exploiter in our century of inferable identities from Shakespeare's characters over and above dramatic allowance is of course A. C. Bradley (1851–1935).

What Majesty Should Be

A. C. Bradley is the Shakespeare of modern literary critics. What is the basis of his egregious popularity? For one thing, while Bradley is assuredly an academic critic he is one of the most accessible of them, and offers his readers what at first sight seems to be a sure-footed guide through the antres vast of Shakespeare's thought and language—his thought anyway, as Bradley rarely deals with the intricacies of Shakespeare's language despite his claim to analytic rigour.[1] As Katherine Cooke (1972) points out, Bradley was always more interested in the why rather than the how of dramatic characterization, in synthesis rather than analysis. Indeed the difference between him and later critics is often characterized, as it is by the philosopher Stanley Cavell (1987), as the difference between a character-based criticism and a—later—word-based one. The vast majority of Bradley's quotations from Shakespeare are illustrative; he very rarely attempts to investigate the way they work despite his being one of those souls unbewildered by analysis, as he jocularly claims at the beginning of *Shakespearean Tragedy*. Shakespeare's passages tend just to sit there on Bradley's pages as exemplary instances of seventeenth-century poetry round which Bradley weaves the sentences of his exemplary Victorian prose. At times, in fact, Bradley writes about a Shakespeare play like a novelist or a dramatist. (See especially 'The Rejection of Falstaff' in his *Oxford Lectures on Poetry* (1965).) In Bradley's hands, Gary Taylor observes, 'Shakespearian criticism became a philosophical novel' (1990: 230).

So it's pleasant to read literary criticism that sounds like a story. Bradley's tendency to write his essays in the form of narrative, often of an overheated kind, combines with other friendly characteristics of style and rhetoric. Cumulatively, they amount to what we might call a discourse of good breeding: his essays are peppered with polite phrases of the 'if the phrase may be pardoned' (1904: 85) variety and others that suggest—often disingenuously—hesitancy, second thoughts, and being unequal to the task.[2] Arthur Eastman talks of Bradley's 'aggregational style' (1968: 189) and observes that it is 'calm as Coleridge's is nervous, personal as Pater's, yet far more public' (189). Calm, magisterial, confident, reasonable, and orderly—and yet passionate also—it's the voice of the authoritative pedagogue, one who can say such things as 'if we prefer to speak (as we might quite well do if we know what we are about) ...' (1904: 17), a parenthesis that could only have been written by a man who clearly believed that he knew what he was about. To this avuncular style and assured tone and passionate commitment generations of readers have responded appreciatively. There is something peculiarly comforting about the way Bradley writes and, more importantly, in what it is he wishes to convey. The message as well as the medium is one of reassurance, a gospel of good news. Despite Bradley's conviction in the first lecture in *Shakespearean Tragedy*, 'The Substance of Tragedy', that the spirit of Shakespeare's tragedy moves in mysterious ways, his essential belief, expressed throughout the rest of *Shakespearean Tragedy* and the *Oxford Lectures*, is in the explicability of Shakespeare's work.

Thus, despite Bradley's own demonstration of the worthlessness in *Othello* of the motives Iago 'fingers' in his soliloquies, he rejects Coleridge's famous assessment of Iago's 'motiveless malignity' for one that—like so many others—relies upon an intelligible psychology. Iago, he believes, plumes up his will in double knavery out of a thwarted sense of creative superiority. Bradley quotes approvingly Swinburne's notion that Iago is an inarticulate poet (1904: 231) and 'infatuated and delivered over to certain destruction' (232), leavened with a glimmering of moral feeling as in Iago's remark about Cassio that 'He has a daily beauty in his life / That makes me ugly' (*Othello*, 5.1.19–20). Here, as quite often, Bradley's Nietzschian view of Iago strikes an authentically twentieth-century note, struck again more provocatively in an extension of it by W. H. Auden in his essay, 'The Joker in the Pack', in which Iago's diabolic exercises in creativity are seen as those of 'a practical joker of a peculiarly appalling kind' (1968: 253). Auden goes on to argue that Iago's practical joker's contempt for others stems from his own sense of insufficiency, 'of a self lacking in authentic feelings and desires of its own' (256). He is for us if not for the Elizabethans 'a parabolic figure for the autonomous pursuit of scientific knowledge through experiment' (270). Whether he realizes it or not, Auden is extemporizing on Swinburne's and Bradley's Faustian notion of a misbegotten artistic/scientific creativity. At moments like these, in linkages like this one, the accusation of fustiness against Bradley's Victorianism seems misconceived.

Just as there is no mystery for Bradley in the evil of Iago so there is none for him in the tragedies' manifestations of the good. Of the good characters in *King Lear* he writes: 'We do not ask in bewilderment, Is there any cause in nature that makes these kind hearts?' (1904: 305). (As opposed, that is, to Lear's bewildered question about the mystery in nature of the existence of hard hearts.) And this is because we—and Shakespeare—are 'hardened optimists' (305). 'Hardened' is an interesting choice of adjective in the light of Bradley's judgement on the death of the best of the good characters in *King Lear*, Cordelia. There's something in her death, he maintains, 'in some way which we do not seek to define' (324), that mitigates the harshness (the tragedy?) of it. It's this notion that brings out the rhapsodic in Bradley—never far from the surface—this idea of the triumphant martyrdom of the tragic victims, especially Cordelia: 'And here adversity, to the blessed in spirit, is blessed. It wins fragrance from the crushed flower. It melts in aged hearts sympathies which prosperity had frozen. It purges the soul's sight by blinding that of the eyes' (1904: 326–7). What could be more comforting for the reader to be told, and to be told in this winsome way, that the one death in Shakespeare that even critics as tough-minded as Dr Johnson can hardly endure exudes a life-enhancing fragrance?

There is a good deal to be said, however, for Bradley's full-hearted commitment to Shakespeare's tragic characters. The suffering men in particular awake in him an eloquent sympathy. They too for him are crushed flowers. The case for Lear, late in the play, as one more sinned against than sinning, can hardly be put more justly: 'His sufferings ... have been so cruel, and our indignation against those who inflicted them has been so intense, that recollection of the wrong he did to Cordelia, to Kent, and to his realm, has been well-nigh effaced' (1904: 280). We respond equally sympathetically to Bradley's contempt for those vulgarizers of *Macbeth* who see the play's protagonists in Malcolm's terms: 'The way to be untrue to Shakespeare here, as always, is to relax the tension of imagination, to conventionalise, to conceive Macbeth, for example, as a half-hearted cowardly criminal, and Lady Macbeth as a cold-hearted fiend' (349–50).

Bradley's tension of imagination doesn't relax in his reading of the History plays, either, especially in his defence of Falstaff, 'The Rejection of Falstaff', in the *Oxford Lectures*. Here, in an interesting improvisation on his remarks about Iago's creative urges, Bradley emphasizes the degree to which Falstaff's responses to friend and foe alike are conditioned by his sense of himself as audacious performer. Thus the often vexed question of morality and Falstaff is convincingly set aside as an irrelevance.

At moments like these, especially in the ones that anticipate the concerns of later readers—Iago as frustrated creator, Falstaff as amoral entertainer—we may feel that Bradley is justified in thinking of himself—as he clearly does—as speaking for the consensus of readers, the 'we' in those sweeping introductions he indulges, of the 'we should all say' (1904: 71) kind. We may know who we are, but who does *he* think 'we all' are? It turns out—flatteringly enough I suppose—that

'we all' are members of an exclusive club, entrance to which is determined by taste rather than gentility (although that taste was no doubt
determined by a genteel upbringing), a club consisting of those 'readers of taste who are unbewildered by analysis' (208), 'who really enjoy
the Falstaff scenes (as many readers do not)' (1965: 251), who know that
Shakespeare as a person was not like Shelley or Wordsworth or Milton
but like Fielding or Scott (see 'Shakespeare's *Antony and Cleopatra*' in
the *Oxford Lectures*).[3] The club is not exclusively exclusive, more
popularly exclusive, one might say, but nevertheless, like most clubs,
it is more welcoming to gentlemen than to ladies, and behind its
veneer of polite informality stands a carefully considered constitution
rigorously enforced by an authoritarian committee. Bradley's style and
attitude, in other words, while comforting, are in fact vehicles of a
quite tyrannical set of beliefs, an almost adversarial certainty. 'We' part
company with him, for instance, when he speaks with such dogmatic
conviction about the unspoken feelings of Shakespeare's characters—
or, for that matter, their spoken ones. Or when he speaks—just as
dogmatically—about 'our' feelings: 'a fact it certainly is' (1904: 83), he
says, of 'our' distaste for aspects of *Othello*, for the repulsiveness of its
presentation of sexual jealousy (and for the vileness of sexual jealousy
generally). An equally certain fact for him (and therefore for 'us', as far
as he is concerned) is Gertrude's 'adulterous' affair with Claudius in
Hamlet.[4]

Bradley can be as tyrannical with Shakespeare as he is with us. He is
at his most confidently high-handed when he quotes then contradicts
evidence from the text; when, for instance, he argues that '[i]t is
nothing to the purpose that Macduff himself says "sinful Macduff"
etc.' (1904: 393) because it is nothing to Bradley's purpose that Macduff
should say so, though it may be to Shakespeare's (and to Macduff's of
course). Just as he knows when Shakespeare or his character isn't
speaking what either of them means, so he knows when Shakespeare
is speaking particularly for himself, when he is being Shakespeare as
much as if not more than the character who is speaking. Hence his
remark about Isabella's attack on man's glassy essence in *Measure for
Measure*: 'Shakespeare himself is speaking' (1965: 348), or when he says
on the same page, '[w]e can hardly err in hearing his [Shakespeare's]
own voice. . . . when we read Hamlet's or Lear's attacks on the insol-
ence of office. It's hardly surprising that Bradley should believe that he

can discriminate in this way among utterances, picking and choosing whose is their real voice, as his critical desideratum is the same as that of his great predecessor, Edward Dowden, in *Shakspere: a Critical Study of his Mind and Art* (1962), first published in 1875, which is to come as much as possible into the presence of Shakespeare's living mind, a desire that Katharine Cooke suggests owes something to the Victorian cult of the hero (1972: 51).[5]

At times, however, Bradley nudges us further into the twentieth century when he implicitly acknowledges the relativism of such perceptions: 'To everyone, I suppose, certain speeches sound peculiarly personal' (1965: 351). And he sees very acutely how Coleridge's theory of chronic procrastination in Hamlet is really more of a description of Coleridge himself; it's not so much a matter of there being a little of Hamlet in everyone, including Coleridge (as Coleridge famously claimed), as of there being a great deal of Coleridge in Hamlet. Bradley argues that it is the specific circumstances in which Hamlet finds himself that paralyse him, that induce 'a state of profound melancholy' (1904: 108), not an habitual excess of reflectiveness (as Coleridge believed). And very early on in *Shakespearean Tragedy* Bradley openly acknowledges the immense power of our own insertions of ourselves into what we read: 'our reflecting mind, full of everyday ideas, is always tending to transform it [the driving tragic force] by the application of these ideas' (24). (For many post-Bradley critics this is of course a transformation devoutly to be wished.) Or again he talks about the mistakes we make 'for substitution of our present intellectual atmosphere for the Elizabethan' (1904: 139).[6]

Yet, as we have seen, there may well be as much Bradley in Hamlet (and in Shakespeare) as Coleridge. Hence, for instance, the lyrical manner in which Bradley discusses Hamlet's first soliloquy in which he castigates his 'wretched mother' (Bradley's words, 1904: 147) for the speed with which she remarried. It never occurs to Bradley that Hamlet's reaction may be excessive, pruriently puritan even. He is in complete sympathy with Hamlet's judgement over what Bradley himself calls Gertrude's 'astounding shallowness of feeling... an eruption of coarse sensuality' (1904: 188). Is this an expression of Shakespeare's living mind here or Bradley's?

Bradley's moral certainty, his easy loquacity, his living mind, were vastly congenial to generations of readers and students of Shakespeare,

and still are. But just as there are many reasons to explain the phenomenon of Shakespeare in the drama of the sixteenth and seventeenth
centuries—reasons that have to do with the converging on a particular
moment in history of the conditions that enabled Shakespeare's genius
to flourish—so, in this overdetermined manner, were there forces at
work to help to explain the predominance of Bradley as the Shakespeare critic of our time—or at least, let's say, our time up to the late
1930s (with something of a revival in the 1960s). One of the reasons for
Bradley's dominance has to do with the gigantic shift in the kind of
attention paid to Shakespeare in the early part of our century. We can
see with critics like Bradley and Dowden the beginnings of what
Randall Jarrell called the age of criticism, although he was referring
only to the 1950s. Bradley was one of the first of our critics to make his
living as a university lecturer in English and his concern with Shakespeare, while by no means academically esoteric, was predominantly
that of the reader rather than the theatre-goer.[7] In *The Rise of English
Studies* (1965) D. J. Palmer considers the extent to which English
Literature with Shakespeare as its flagship began its dominance of
secondary education as 'part of a liberal humane education, providing a
cultural continuity that otherwise seemed in danger of extinction in
the social upheavals of a new industrial democracy' (78). For the
students of Shakespeare at these new institutes of learning, Bradley's
avuncularly pedagogic manner and profound self-confidence made
him an irresistible guide to the meaning and significance of Shakespeare, especially at examination time:

> I dreamt last night that Shakespeare's Ghost
> Sat for a civil service post.
> The English paper for that year
> Had several questions on *King Lear*,
> Which Shakespeare answered very badly
> Because he hadn't read his Bradley.[8]

As the century wore on, education in English literature, Shakespeare,
and Bradley became mutually sustaining, an alliance for what Chris
Baldick describes as 'the binding of class to class in common respect for
the national heritage and all that was precious in it' (1983: 82) with
Bradley providing 'the responsible correction of taste by knowledge'
(1996: 31).

Yet, as we have already seen, Bradley was more subversively twentieth century than he's been given credit for, and Katharine Cooke (1972) is one of a number of critics determined to rescue him for our time.[9] She argues that there has always been a crucial distinction between the reality of Bradley's texts and the critical commentaries on them (just as there is for those critics who still believe in such realities between the 'reality' of Shakespeare's texts and the commentaries written on them). Critics, in other words, often seem to get Bradley wrong, and they do so for rather complicated ideological reasons. At the same time, as Cooke also makes clear, Bradley's influence most often takes the ironic form of repeated denials by critics that he has or should have any influence on them. Of course, this massive campaign on their part to deny his influence is a back-handed compliment to the force of his presence as a critic of Shakespeare in the twentieth century. The fact that they do (or do not) get him wrong is immaterial really in the face of his relentless popularity, which has scarcely waned in Shakespeare studies since the publication of *Shakespearean Tragedy* in 1904, at least for the 'ordinary reader' and the general student of Shakespeare.

But even sophisticated critics seem to be returning to him, or to his example, at the close of the century. Sometimes they seem to be doing so as prodigal sons and daughters coming home, critics coming in from the cold rigours of modern academic criticism, finding warmth and sanctuary in what they nostalgically conceive as a more sane way of proceeding. Hence, for instance, William Kerrigan's protest against what he calls the 'shocking decadence' (1994: 3) of the *Hamlet* criticism of the 1980s; he suggests that we should return basically to the Romantic Hamlet, or, better still, the Bradleyan one. And a subtly argued book, Bert States's *'Hamlet' and the Concept of Character* (1992), takes up again the subject that dominated Bradley's discourse and which many critics thought had long since been exhausted. Derek Cohen in *Shakespearean Motives* (1988) analyses language, ritual, and narrative in order to study character more carefully. Edward Pechter's defence of character analysis is unapologetically Bradleyan:

This is Bradley-talk. Whatever was misdirected in Bradley, treating characters as isolated monads abstracted from the action, an intense affective engagement underwrote his criticism and the traditions culminating in his work. In this sense, my modest proposal for the critical new world order at the end of the millennium is: back to the nineteenth century. (1998: 372)

Back to the future, then, despite the obloquy, according to Karen Newman, that critics who do so may face: 'To show an interest in a complex character reveals a failure of critical nerve, an irresistible and sentimental urge to give in to the seductive power of mimesis' (1985: 2).[10] In similarly defensive mode, Cooke (1972) talks of Bradley's inveterate play-going—he's not just an armchair critic. Kenneth Muir says flatly: 'Bradley did not read *Hamlet* as though it were *Middlemarch*' (1981: 2).[11]

This Is [and Is Not] Cressid

Bradley may not have read *Hamlet* as though it were *Middlemarch* but he certainly read it as though its characters had lives of their own. Interior lives, that is. One of the great debates in twentieth-century Shakespeare criticism revolves around the nature of this interiority— if, indeed, it exists at all. For many critics still, Shakespeare's characterization suggests the unplumbable depths that terrorized Gerard Manley Hopkins: 'O the mind, mind has mountains; cliffs of fall / Frightful, sheer, no-man-fathomed'.

J. I. M. Stewart's book, *Character and Motive in Shakespeare* (1949), argues that the minds of Shakespeare's characters were indeed unfathomable, no-man-fathomed, until the advent of Freud whose fathoming psychoanalytic procedures were, as Freud himself claimed, transhistorical and equally applicable to fictional seventeenth-century dramatic characters as to his real-life nineteenth-century patients from the Viennese bourgeoisie. Freud's description of *delusional* jealousy, for instance, captures for Stewart the essence of *The Winter's Tale*'s triangle of Leontes, Hermione, and Polixenes where Leontes's position 'represents an acidulated homosexuality which takes the form of: "Indeed *I* do not love him, *she* loves him!"'[12] As far as Stewart is concerned, we need to *deepen* the psychologizing in reading Shakespeare's characters not to abandon it, for it encompasses the 'stability of truth' that lies out of sight somewhere beneath the words and off the page, although the directions it takes off the page might well have surprised Bradley who probably hadn't read his Freud.

Someone like Macbeth, Stewart writes—in defence of the underlying coherence of the incoherence attacked by the 'realist' school of Shakespeare criticism—may be 'inexplicable after the fashion in which his sort of person is often inexplicable' (89); in Macbeth's case, and in that of many others, there's a 'confluence of motives' (94) at work. Macbeth behaves much as 'real' criminals behave; he acts from archaic strata of the mind. We may need to abandon naturalism, Stewart concludes, but we must not abandon psychological truth. In other words, Shakespeare 'is penetrating to nature, and once more giving his fable something of the demonic quality of myth or folk-story, which is commonly nearer to the radical workings of the human mind than are later and rationalised versions of the same material' (36).

If Bradley might well have been surprised by the Freudian and anthropological turn of things in Stewart's book in 1949 he would have been nonplussed, one suspects, at the Lacanian turn fifty or so years later. This is deepening the psychologizing of Shakespeare's characters with a vengeance (interiors within specular interiors). A brief contrast between two psychoanalytic works that deal mainly with *Hamlet*, a play that many feel insists on its status as analysand, may be taken as indicative of the extraordinary demands that psychoanalytic Shakespeare criticism makes on the reader these days—and much other postmodern criticism of Shakespeare, for that matter. In the same year as Stewart, Ernest Jones published *Hamlet and Oedipus* (1949), a heavily Freudian work that has proven almost as popular with readers of Shakespeare criticism as Bradley's *Shakespearean Tragedy*. In 1993 Julia Lupton and Kenneth Reinhard, building deconstructively on Jones's analysis, published their *After Oedipus: Shakespeare in Psychoanalysis*, a work that is highly imaginative and ambitious but gives no quarter to readers not soaked in Freud and Lacan. The difference between Jones's short book and *After Oedipus* rests in the almost Bradleyan way in which Jones considerably negotiates for the unfamiliar reader the difficult terrain of Freudian discourse; *After Oedipus*, on the other hand, is brutally technical, its last pages replete with curvaceous Lacanian graphs and diagrams of subtle, elusive sets of binary oppositions. It is very difficult to read *After Oedipus*, itself full of frightful, sheer cliffs of fall, without a thorough grounding in the major works of Freud and Lacan; reading Jones, on the other hand, is like reading a plainer-writing yet more specialized

Bradley. What *Hamlet and Oedipus* and *After Oedipus* have in common, though, is their total commitment to the psychoanalytic inferability of fictional characters and, from them, as in Bradley's *Shakespearean Tragedy*, the inferability of Shakespeare's living mind. For Jones, writing *Hamlet* was Shakespeare's response to intolerable personal circumstances: 'In so doing he assuaged his own suffering and saved his sanity of mind....' (1949: 136); for Lupton and Reinhard, more cryptically (of course), '*Hamlet* is the death mask worn by Shakespeare as son and father, a mask he bequeaths to Freud and ourselves' (1993: 19).

I began this section with a quotation from *Troilus and Cressida* 'This is and is not Cressid' (5.2.149) and bracketed 'and is not' to indicate the emphasis I'm placing here on the possibility of knowing who Cressida is; we can infer her mind's condition, so say the critics I am dealing with at the moment, as we can that of any other character in Shakespeare's plays. And yet the psychoanalytic inferability discussed in the immediately preceding paragraphs, in its tortuous, paradoxical, metaphoric, and metonymic mode of investigation, suggests that what is *not* Cressid is what she *really* is. What we see on the surface, that is, in the text's words, are not a sufficient disclosure of the interiors of the characters—they have that within that passes show in regions that only psychoanalysis can penetrate. And the psychoanalytic investigation of Shakespeare's fictional characters in the twentieth century is often quite breathtakingly confident in expressing its practitioners' belief that it alone is the answer to the Shakespeare critic's prayer for definitive interpretation. For Ernest Jones Shakespeare trawls the psychic depths: 'I would suggest that ... Shakespeare's extraordinary powers of observation and penetration granted him a degree of insight that it has taken the world three subsequent centuries to reach' (1949: 76). The world has reached it at last because of the work of Sigmund Freud. Norman Holland's 'Introduction' to *Shakespeare's Personality*, a collection of recently gathered psychoanalytic studies of Shakespeare's characters, proudly proclaims that '[t]he psychoanalyst studies an individual in the Renaissance as psychoanalysis defines an individual, not as the Renaissance defines it' (1989: 5), and the essays in this collection are the kind that you might expect to encounter on the coffee-table in the consulting room of a twentieth-century practising psychiatrist.

Psychoanalytic investigation of Shakespeare's characters is predicated on the putative difficulty we have in coming to any judgements at all about them.[13] And this is particularly true of the characters in the tragedies because of Shakespeare's dramatic use, in Ernst Honigmann's words, 'of blurred impressions: different kinds of mixed response, the zigzagging of response, the interweaving of contrary impressions, the strategy of confusing the audience, compelling it to suspend its judgement' (1976: 192).[14] But a case can be and has been made in the twentieth century for the inner lives of the characters in Shakespeare's comedies both before and after 1600. Indeed, Leo Salingar in his important study *Shakespeare and the Traditions of Comedy* (1974) argues that Shakespeare's comic characters differ from those of classical and Italian comedy precisely in their possession of the quality of an inner life. And they possess this quality not just in spite of the drama's enabling conventions but in co-operation with them—the dramatic and theatrical conventions and psychoanalysis are thought to be in this view mutually sustaining. As Karen Newman argues: 'Shakespeare's plays . . . demonstrate how he used inherited comic conventions, not in opposition to realistic characterization, but as a strategy for accomplishing it' (1985: 5). And she goes on to say that '[p]aradoxically, we discover, a character often becomes more real by doing what are patently unrealistic things—speaking soliloquies, thinking aloud, and the like' (6). None the less, both the paradoxical nature of the investigative process and a concomitant worry about the possible waywardness of psychological procedures continue to vex critics of character criticism, and they often demonstrate Honigmann's zigzagging of response in their own sometimes desperate attempts to avoid the accusation of Bradleyism. Here, for example, is Alan Sinfield, bobbing and weaving, in a dexterous justification of an updated application of Bradley to Shakespeare's characters:

None of the opponents of character criticism I have been invoking disputes altogether that the dramatis personae in Shakespearean plays are written, at least some of the time, in ways that suggest that they have subjectivities. The objection is to jumping from that point to a Bradleyan all essentialist-humanist conception of character. My contention is that some Shakespearean dramatis personae are written so as to suggest, not just an intermittent, gestural, and problematic subjectivity, but a continuous or developing interiority or consciousness; and that we should seek a way of talking about this that does not slide back into character criticism or essentialist humanism. This way of talking would not suppose that performances attempted an unbroken illusionistic frame; or that this continuous interiority is self-constituted and independent of the discursive practices of the culture; or that it manifests an essential unity. The key features in this redefined conception of character are two: an impression of subjectivity, interiority, or consciousness, and the sense that these maintain a sufficient continuity or development through the scenes of the play. (1992: 62)

I'm not sure that talking about 'an impression of subjectivity, interiority, or consciousness' does not constitute a slide into 'character criticism'. At all events criticism of Shakespeare's characters these days is much concerned with Sinfield's 'continuous or developing interiority or consciousness' as Bert States indicates, for instance, in his persuasive argument that the open-endedness of a character like Hamlet has limits to it: 'Hamlet could no more forsake the company of Horatio for that of Osric than Mrs. Micawber could leave Mr. Micawber' (1992: 10) for 'character expresses itself in accordance with its own probability' (13). Hence, Ophelia is 'a character [who] always goes crazy in character' (15).

I have been speaking here about a particular kind of interiority, the twentieth-century psychoanalytic one. Equally twentieth-century in its obsession with history—countering its equally powerful obsession with an atemporal formalism—is an interiority necessarily predicated on and explained by Elizabethan psychology. Twentieth-century psychoanalysis, that is, takes a back seat at times in the twentieth century to Renaissance faculty psychology. From Lily B. Campbell's *Shakespeare's Tragic Heroes* (1930) to the present, various attempts have been made to explain Shakespeare's characters in terms of what Louis Montrose describes as 'the historical specificity of psychological processes, the politics of the unconscious' (1983: 63), though Montrose is much more concerned with the larger social context, the political one particularly, than merely with how the Elizabethans in their day perceived the workings of the mind. In recent years the most formidable attempt to repossess the Elizabethan mind in its Renaissance configuration is J. Leeds Barroll's *Artificial Persons: The Formation of Character in the Tragedies of Shakespeare* but even he concedes an ultimate frustration: 'It would seem that if we adhere to the ways offered through formal Renaissance theories of physiology, rhetoric, or faculty psychology, we cannot ultimately ask what we take to be the relevant questions about "character" in Shakespearean drama' (1974: 34–5). In the end 'everything' is subsumed and controlled by the 'artistic process' (101). Elizabethan faculty psychology, then, is simply too mechanistic and monochromatic for the tastes of most twentieth-century Shakespeare critics who would in all probability endorse Robert Hellenga's conclusions:

Did Shakespeare imitate life or did he imitate Elizabethan theories about life? Presumably he imitated the life itself, in which case we should expect modern psychology to provide a more adequate interpretative framework for *Othello* than the Elizabethan faculty psychology; and we should expect Freud's *Interpretation of Dreams* to throw more light on Hamlet than Timothy Bright's *Treatise of Melancholy* (1981: 29).[15]

[This Is] and Is Not Cressid

On the one hand, twentieth-century Shakespeare criticism bestows a dazzlingly complex interiority on Shakespeare's major characters, responding to what Graham Bradshaw describes as 'Shakespeare's compulsive habit of creative interiorization' (1993: 132); on the other, it has wondered at different times in the century if it makes sense to talk about such an interiority at all. The circularity of this process is entertainingly probed by Gary Taylor: 'Modernist critics had said good-bye to character analysis and biographical narrative; postmodernist critics say hello again to both—an aggressive, knowing hello' (1990: 334). In the 1920s and 1930s angry voices were raised as to the legitimacy of psychological interpretation, partly, to do them justice, in response to the 'disintegrationist' arguments that attempted to find alternative writers for 'corrupt' parts of Shakespeare's plays. One of the most scornful of them comprised the works of E. E. Stoll (1874–1959) who attacked what he called 'the psychological formula offered, with its claptrap and legerdemain' (1933: 21). His greatest contribution to Shakespeare studies, spurred on by his distaste for what he considered to be the excesses of Bradley and his followers, was a renewed emphasis on the theatricality of Shakespeare's plays, stoked by an awareness of the powerful forces of theatrical convention that had become second nature to writers and theatre-goers alike in the sixteenth and seventeenth centuries.

There's a lot to be said for Stoll's exuberant advocacy of the importance of an understanding of the historical dimensions of Shakespeare's
dramaturgy[16] and much subsequent good work owes a debt to his
pioneering scepticism.[17] Yet Stoll and many of his supporters strike
us now as vulgar and reductive interpreters of Shakespeare's plays,
especially in the kind of pedagogic anti-intellectualism they indulge;
as Stoll says in this vein, 'A play is not a study or a puzzle—really
nowadays it is not' (1933: 12).[18] The gentle exasperation conveyed in
this sentence produces startling judgements, turning Iago, for
instance, into a mechanical device rather than a complex character:
'It is a mechanical device, to be sure, this intrusion of the villain; but
there is something of the mechanical in most art, once we get to the
bottom of it' (20). Stoll has a similarly reductive view of the delay in
Hamlet: it is merely '[a] mechanical matter again, which . . . should not
surprise in a crude old play rewritten. The effort to postpone the
catastrophe is apparent in some of the greatest tragedies, like the
Oedipus, apart from those which deal with revenge' (101). We should
not therefore criticize Hamlet's conduct: as Stoll goes on to say, 'To
interpret Hamlet's conduct against him to the point of taking his delay
or his aversion for a psychical defect, is somewhat like taking Othello's
trustfulness for mental paralysis or stupidity' (106). We can find half-
truths like these everywhere we turn in Stoll's considerable body of
work on Shakespeare.

The same can be said for Stoll's important contemporary Levin
Schücking who, like Stoll, regards Shakespeare's characters as functions rather than characterizations, and who, also like Stoll, attempts
to be more scientific in his approach to reading Shakespeare. 'The
question arises', he writes in 1922, 'whether it is not possible to stem, to
a certain extent, this subjective current in the contemplation of Shakespeare' (7–8). We need to stem it because 'the interpretation of Shakespeare has strayed into hopelessly wrong paths' (8), and returning to
the straight and narrow involves acknowledging the primitive methods of Elizabethan dramatists, whereby, for instance, the intervention
of topical comic remarks in *Macbeth* is the equivalent of interrupting
the performance in 1922 'by reading the latest edition of the evening
papers to the audience' (24). We must not make the mistake, Schücking lectures, of reading Shakespeare as though he were Ibsen; we must
recognize that such a populist writer is often at the mercy of his

primitive plots, taking over their 'inherent faults into the bargain without examining them too closely' (169): 'It is most characteristic of him that he does not rebel against his historic model to which he owes so much, but unhesitatingly submits to it even where it reports events that are quite impossible from a psychological point of view' (144). As far as Schücking is concerned, Shakespeare uncritically gave his audiences what they wanted, which is why he was successful in his use of traditional, direct, primitive, and almost childish devices. The notion of unity was simply not the same for Shakespeare or for Chaucer as it is for us today; consequently, as Schücking points out, 'dramas of that time might actually be nothing but *bundles of scenes*' (113); there is 'a tendency to episodic intensification' (114); there is a 'rhetorical necessity of increasing the momentary effect' (116). A psychological consistency in characterization, given these other more important considerations, is simply not an issue.

Refurbished, more sophisticated, versions of this earlier position regarding the instrumentality of Shakespeare's characterizations continue to find proponents. A. R. Braunmuller, for instance, believes that 'Elizabethan playwrights will sacrifice virtually any inferred fictional character in order to get things said that need saying' (1983: 130). Like Schücking he asks us to consider the dominance of the scene as a structural unit, arguing, in 1990, that the English Renaissance dramatists composed in scenic units, 'in short stretches of sequential actions and speech' (68) with little thought beyond the effect of the immediate sequence.[19] Howard Mills suggests that we should abandon the term 'character' altogether and replace it with 'part', a term that would not have the onerous implications of psychological consistency and would therefore be far more appropriate for a character like York (and many others) in *Richard II*: 'Like the chameleon poet in Keats's and Coleridge's idea, he has no character; or at best it's made up as Shakespeare goes along—and remade quite without scruple to fit the dramatic needs of the moment' (1993: 40).

The most fruitful kind of character criticism these days is that which attempts to fit together individual psychology and the dramatic needs of the moment as Bert States does in his remarks about Polonius's expressions of long-windedness in *Hamlet*: 'In Polonius's catalogs we have a comic extension of the play's cancerous preoccupations metastatized to the seat of thought' (1992: 116). Even more impressive in late twentieth-century Shakespeare criticism is the marriage of post-modern character - psychoanalysis with Renaissance mythologies in a version, I suppose, of an historicized Freud. An exemplary instance of this productive co-operation can be found in T. G. Bishop's book *Shakespeare and the Theatre of Wonder* (1996). Talking of Shakespeare's Romances, Bishop writes:

> By this late stage in his career, Shakespeare's dramatic language has become an instrument subtle and searching enough to register not only the surface gestures of a character, but also the secret affections or intentions that inform those gestures. The imagination has become a layered thing, often obscure to itself, inventing its purposes moment by moment at several levels. Characters at times hardly hear what they say, so deeply can they become self-enchanted. In order to read such a language, it is sometimes necessary to extrapolate or extend an obscure inkling into an entire line of thought. (149)

Hence, he suggests, the necessity of using a psychoanalytic approach, but one constrained by and interpreted through the various subtending mythologies of Shakespeare's time: in *Pericles* and *The Winter's Tale*, for example, the Ovidian myths, especially that of Niobe and Narcissus for the former, and that of Perdita/Proserpina for the latter.

The twentieth-century inclination at times to counter its tendency to grant Shakespeare's characters a hugely significant inner life by granting them no inner life at all has to be read in the more general context of a relatively new concern for the possibility of subjectivity for anyone at any time. This concern has been given both a modernist and post-modernist inflection. For the former, we might consider S. Viswanathan: 'Related to the changed, modern attitude to character in Shakespearian drama is the twentieth-century anti-Renaissance, anti-Romantic and anti-humanist rejection of the claim of personality—an askesis and attempt to quell the ego, or efface the personality' (1980: 60). For the latter, Louis Montrose gets to the heart of an enormously complicated subject for an understanding of the postmodern retreat from interiority: 'Although it continues to thrive in the mass media, in the rhetoric of politicians, and in the hearts and minds of the general population, the freely self-creating and world-creating Individual of so-called bourgeois humanism has, for quite sometime, been defunct in the texts of academic theory' (1996: 15).

In a sense there is no such thing as an inner self, so this argument runs, the self is purely exterior; as Lisa Jardine writes, 'selfhood is read off the outside of the body, and is inseparable from that body' (1996: 37). Or, as she later says, this time about us as readers, 'the confused responses to woman which psychoanalysis internalises to the individual subject (and thus effectively prevents women from challenging) may also be produced as culturally constructed and historically specific' (177). In this context, we should consider—as Bishop does—interpretations of individual Shakespeare characters in terms of constructs larger than their individual psychological selves. For example, Naomi Liebler, in her study of character as pharmakos, argues that in Shakespeare's tragedies of state the real subject for examination is the institution of monarchy rather than the monarch himself. This new emphasis on the context of the hero's dilemma makes us think in new ways about the notion of the tragic flaw or *hamartia*: 'The "failure," if any, that tragic heroes "commit" is the one committed by their society. Their *hamartia* is their community's *hamartia*' (1995: 21). And so rather than its being an issue of individual characterization, 'Tragedy is a meditation on social and political order, on hierarchy, the differential structure that embeds conflict, tension, or anxiety in its very existence' (22).

Another larger, more embracing construct is the linguistic medium itself: the claim here is that Shakespeare's strategy in the rhetorical construction of his characters is a better way of analysis than that of Bradley, let us say, or recent subtle psychological investigation. As Giorgio Melchiori writes about *Othello*, 'each character has been endowed with a personal linguistic code and ... with different rhetorical habits in the construction on their respective speeches' (1981: 68). None of these larger positions, looking before and after, obviates the continuing critical concern with what we might call character as such, and perhaps the last word here should go to Linda Woodbridge's fine book *The Scythe of Saturn: Magical Thinking in Shakespeare* when she writes:

My position is ... that Shakespeare lived on the cusp with regard to subject unity—he could still create 'splits' and project parts of a personality onto other characters. ... But he was also starting to create complex characters who contain internal inconsistencies and act multiple and shifting roles, quite in the manner of subjects we meet in the extraliterary world. (1994: 195–6)

What's Aught but as 'Tis Valued?

Twentieth-century criticism of Shakespeare's characters ranges much more widely than formerly. There is now an exuberant engagement with characters in the plays who were heretofore thought too minor to be worthy of notice. Such a new concern is not restricted to major minor characters like Rosencrantz and Guildenstern in *Hamlet*, Emilia and Bianca in *Othello*,[20] or Duncan in *Macbeth*. It extends to the fleeting presences of, say, the Clowns in *Othello* and *Antony and Cleopatra*, the First Servant in *King Lear*, Grumio and Curtis in *The Taming of the Shrew*, Philharmonus in *Cymbeline*.[21] Sometimes a minor character thrusts himself or herself into the main action and onto our attention by a major act, breaking the decorum of their subaltern anonymity. Perhaps the most famous instance of this is the First Servant in *King Lear* whose courageous intervention in the blinding of Gloucester has done so much for some critics in the twentieth century in their attempt to offset Jan Kott's sentimentalized reading (1964) of an exclusively brutal *King Lear*, itself an extraordinarily influential interpretation of the play for our time. When a peasant stands up thus he makes an important contribution to the democratizing readings of Shakespeare in the twentieth century.

There has been a tendency for twentieth-century critics of Shakespeare's plays to give minor characters an interesting role in a narrative that sometimes seems to have been written by the critic rather than the dramatist. On the basis of slim or no evidence, minor characters are awarded interesting, complex, and provocative personalities, and we might see in this tendency a reworking of the kind of concern that Bradley demonstrates in his infamous endnotes to *Shakespearean Tragedy* on the anterior lives of Shakespeare's characters. Bradley's speculations about the facts of the characters' pasts have been replaced by speculations about their hidden motives and complex desires. John Gillies (1994), for instance, argues that the Duke in *Othello* is shifty and equivocal in his rejection of Brabantio's case against his son-in-law's role in his elopement with Desdemona; an equally convincing case could be made—and has been made (much more frequently)—for the Duke's statesmanlike judiciousness. T. G. Bishop spins a wonderfully circumstantial tale for the centrality of Mamillius to the meaning of *The Winter's Tale* whereby his father, Leontes, is 'this dark cartoon of himself [Mamillius] grown up' (1996: 130) who conveys 'male terror at the nature and implications of sexual desire' (144).[22]

The *locus classicus* in our time of a concern with the lives of the most minor of minor characters in Shakespeare is M. M. Mahood's book *Bit Parts in Shakespeare* which deals with those

> numerous First, Second, and Third Messengers, Citizens, and Soldiers; a host of gardeners and gaolers, knights and heralds, ladies-in-waiting, murderers and mariners; the odd day-woman, haberdasher, poet, vintner, hangman, scrivener, king, cardinal and goddess; John Bates, Tom Snout, George Seacole, Simon Catling, Peter Thump, Neighbour Mugs; and four men who are all called Balthasar. (1993: 1)

The interpretative screw is almost comically turned in this critical approach when these minor characters' silences are enthusiastically interpreted by Mahood, as when she explores, for instance, the silent presence of Francisca the nun during Isabella's conversation with Lucio in Act 1, Scene 4 of *Measure for Measure*, which could have its effect on the conduct of the interlocutors; or when she considers the silent Justice in the scene involving Froth and Pompey. But of all the minor characters' silences in *Measure for Measure* that of 'Barnadine's silent participation in this last scene is one of the most striking uses Shakespeare makes of any peripheral character' (154) in that the Duke's decision to let him live caps, for Mahood, the meaning of the play.[23]

A compensatory babble of talk from twentieth-century critics fills in the silences of Shakespeare's major characters. How they don't say what they don't say is of course an important concern for any director of Shakespeare's plays, and the twentieth century has seen an immensely fruitful collaboration between theatrical and literary interpretation. This century has seen more productions of Shakespeare in more parts of the world at more levels of cultural signification than at any time previously. Major characters (and minor ones too) often do intensely interesting and unexpected things on stage—often unexpectedly apropos—depending on the nature of the director's (and actors') ideological commitments, and on the history of the play in the theatre, now often recorded for posterity on video and film—about which more later.

The problem of a character's challenging silence was explored by Leslie Fiedler in his remarks on Antonio in *Twelfth Night* who, as Fiedler points out, doesn't speak a word in the last scene through nearly 200 lines of recognitions and reversals, though he is awkwardly parked on stage throughout. Fiedler takes up the actor's cause:

> And God knows what the actor does who is playing his equivocal part—simply melt into the scene like one more bystander, or try somehow by stance and gesture (but how?) to indicate what becomes clear at this point to the reader: that Antonio is not what he may have seemed at the first, another actor in the dream play, but rather its 'shamanized' dreamer. (1973: 92)

That 'but how?' has been addressed by numerous productions since 1973, not many of them cleaving to Fiedler's line about the shamanization of Antonio's character that he finds so compelling.

A more interesting silence, perhaps, from the same play, one not explored by Fiedler, is Viola's, who is excluded from the last 125 lines of the play's dialogue. This is one of the silences in Shakespeare pondered by Jonathan Bate in his exemplary book exploring the relation between Shakespeare and Ovid: 'It remains for the judicious spectator to choose between a reading in which Viola empties Illyria of narcissism (Malvolio apart) and is rewarded with love—a Lucentio and Bianca reading, if you will—and a darker interpretation—a Petruchio and Kate one—in which woman is reduced to the status of man's echo' (1993: 151). One might add here the obvious point that the judicious (or injudicious) director invariably nudges the judicious spectator in the direction of one or other (or a combination) of these interpretations.

Bate's other pregnant silence emanates from another Antonio, the Antonio of *The Tempest* 'when the elder brother offers him [i.e. Antonio] grudging forgiveness' (240). Much can be and has been made of the lack of response from this second Antonio by directors and critics. An equally famous pregnant silence is Isabella's at the end of *Measure for Measure* when Vincentio tells her that he has a motion that much imports her good (marriage with him, that is): does she or does she not incline the willing ear he demands? Only the director knows.[24] And only he or she knows the significance of the silence of that 'most silent of Shakespeare's female figures' (1989: 146), as Shirley Garner describes her, Hero in *Much Ado About Nothing*, another woman pregnantly silent again while the men around her are arranging her marriage for her.

If much can now be made of characters who are hardly in the plays, even in—or especially in—their silences, almost as much can be made of characters who aren't in the plays at all, as we may enjoy in Stephen Orgel's witty and provocative disquisition on Prospero's wife who isn't in *The Tempest* but whose absence in it is for Orgel a symptom of the 'absent, the unspoken . . . the most powerful and problematic presence in *The Tempest*' (1986: 50). Such a reverberating silence in the play about Prospero's wife's absence, Orgel suggests, intimates that the relations that marriage 'postulates between men and women are ignorant at best, characteristically tense, and potentially tragic' (56). Orgel believes that the function of Prospero's wife's absence is to cast a shadow on the married future of Ferdinand and Miranda, but this pessimistic conclusion—a strikingly twentieth-century one—is, it seems to me, a misleading exaggeration of the suggestions of fragility in their relationship, as is perhaps the whole emphasis in this essay on the brooding presence of the wife's absence in the play.

Carol T. Neely similarly finds an ominous function for the potent non-presences of female characters, this time in *Othello*. But here the play itself isn't exactly silent about these women's lives, as is *The Tempest* about Miranda's mother; *Othello* summons up its own remembrances of its characters' pasts. Othello's mother is recalled as 'the powerful sybil, the Egyptian charmer' in contrast with Desdemona's childhood maid, Barbary, 'who is killed by her love and sexuality rather than controlling them; [and] is dislocated and disempowered sexually and socially, as Desdemona discovers herself to be' (1995: 309). Prospero's wife, Othello's mother, Desdemona's maid, these critics suggest, all participate in a drama of a threatening augury of the later dramatic life of the plays' central characters.

Casting the net for characters *in absentia* ever wider, twentieth-century critics refuse to restrict themselves to those legitimated by the play's *fabula*. Louis Montrose, for instance, constructs an elaborately haunting argument for the powerful non-presence of Queen Elizabeth in the subtexts of *A Midsummer Night's Dream*: 'My point is not that the structure and ethos of *A Midsummer Night's Dream* are indifferent to the cultural resonance of the Queen but rather that the play's own cultural resonance may be said to depend precisely upon the dramaturgical exclusion of the queen, upon her *conspicuous* absence' (1996: 176). The Whole books can be written on conspicuous Shakespearean absences as Ernst Honigmann's *Shakespeare: The Lost Years* (1985) demonstrates, while George Wright argues for the huge importance of the absence of their subject for the Sonnets: they are, he argues, 'more about the absence ... of their radiant center than about the enjoyment of its presence, though there is enough testimony about its presence to make its absence seem all the more poignant' (1998: 315).

Pursuing this line of enquiry into radiant absences, almost as much can now be made in Shakespeare criticism of Shakespeare's *disinclination* to pursue the lesser fates of his minor and absent characters as of his *inclination* to give them a dense local habitation and a name. Stephen Greenblatt's fascinating essay 'The Eating of the Soul' begins with a paragraph or two on Shakespeare's counter-willingness to sketch 'often in baroque detail' (1994: 105) the existence of minor characters who never appear on stage: Lamord in *Hamlet*, Marcus Luccicos in *Othello*, the perfumed Lord who offends Hotspur in *Henry IV, Part 1*. The absent in these cases make their presences felt in the language of the other characters in the plays. Shakespeare's willingness to materialize these absent characters linguistically if not corporeally makes the absence of any such verbal presentation, so writes Greenblatt, all the more significant, especially in Shakespeare's obtrusive silence about all those absent wives and mothers in his plays, the mothers in particular: the mothers, that is—who significantly aren't there and who aren't recalled by the other characters—of Hotspur, Bolingbroke, Hal, Lavinia, Katherine of Padua and her sister Bianca, Jessica, Rosalind, Celia, Hermia, Lucentio, Cressida, Hero, Edgar—the list goes on and on. And the missing mothers that Greenblatt deals with are the wives of husbands who, unlike their wives, are importantly present in their plays, so this list does not take into account the absent mothers of Viola and Sebastian in *Twelfth Night*, Portia in *The Merchant of Venice*, and Helena in *All's Well that Ends Well* 'whose husbands are also absent but are by contrast conspicuously and insistently invoked' (105). Yet Greenblatt goes on to claim that it all seems somehow perfectly natural in these plays that the women should not be mentioned, not even in passing references, for instance, to their passing. Why is this, he asks. Shakespeare, he then argues, 'can make the unexplained absence of certain characters, mothers in particular, seem to signify a non-theatrical, perhaps implicitly anti-theatrical extinction. For over against death as a natural feature of the ordinary, everyday world—a feature that does not need to be accounted for, that is the condition of existence itself—are set the deaths to which his art is repeatedly drawn' (106). So, if nothing else, the absence of significant female members of the family has the negative force of making the mostly male deaths in the tragedies more powerful and significant.

One impetus for this new interest in minor figures in twentieth-century Shakespeare criticism (apart, that is, from the professional need to make new tracks in the snow) could loosely be described as adversarially democratic. There is a self-conscious, perhaps republican, urge in the twentieth century in particular not only to de-glamorize all those kings and queens, but to replace them with a concern for ordinary folk and sometimes a glamorization or justification of them. Leonard Tennenhouse, for instance, argues that, although the romantic comedies are primarily a 'vehicle for disseminating court ideology' (1986: 39), there is in them also a mockery of aristocratic culture 'which sharply distinguished Elizabethan romantic comedy both from preceding comic forms and from the Jacobean city comedy' (37), and he points to the importance of Mikhail Bakhtin's concept of the 'grotesque body' for a better understanding of this subversive thrust in modern criticism.[25]

Such a thrust, however, can be found in Shakespeare not only by Shakespeare himself but by the critics of Shakespeare at Shakespeare's expense. Among many examples of this particular brand of adversarial left-wing revisionism, I think with pleasure of Richard Wilson's discussion of Jack Cade, the rebel, in *Henry VI, Part 2* in his fascinating book, *Will Power: Essays on Shakespearean Authority* (1993). Here, Wilson notices and deplores Shakespeare's reworking of the portrait of Cade that he found in Hall's *Chronicles*. Whereas Hall was more or less even-handed in his presentation of Cade, granting him a due seriousness and civility, Shakespeare chooses to turn Cade into a madly stupid, if sometimes amusing, monster. Wilson calls this transmogrification a 'brazen manipulation of documentary records practised to buttress the regime' (27), and goes on to explain it further in terms of 'a self-interested aggravation by the Rose managers of an opportune crisis, designed to play off the "national interest" against the City council' (43).

However, Paola Pugliatti reminds us that this brazen manipulation of the documentary records parallels the presentation, unbrazenly manipulated, of the aristocracy Jack Cade is fighting. In other words, '[t]he deformity of the rebels . . . holds a mirror up to the deformity of the party in power. The political lesson is there for those who want to see it' (1996: 173). For her, this emphasis by Shakespeare on the rebels and other minor characters in the history plays—those choric and pedagogical messengers in particular and of course the similarly inclined ordinary soldiers, John Bates, Alexander Court, and Michael Williams in *Henry V*—constitutes 'a scandal of historiography' (188).

Most of the time twentieth-century literary critics have been eager to see Pugliatti's political lesson, to promote Shakespeare in scandalous fashion as a proto-democrat slyly cocking a snook at his aristocratic patrons. Hence the great interest, for example, in his fleeting individualizations of some of the ordinary Roman citizens in *Julius Caesar* and *Coriolanus*. Exactly what is their social status? Theodore Leinwand (1993) argues that they and others like them (e.g. those rude mechanicals, as Puck calls them, Snout, Snug, and Bottom in *A Midsummer Night's Dream* and Horner in *Henry VI, Part 2*) are not members of the rural and urban poor but, somewhat like Shakespeare himself in Leinwand's elastic definition, of the 'middling sort'. And Rosencrantz and Guildenstern in *Hamlet*, though not exactly ordinary citizens in the same way as the Roman cobblers and carpenters, have come in for a kind of Stoppardian attention from criticism in their roles as victimized minor functionaries in Claudius's court, as the winds of critical opinion have shifted to the north in perceiving Hamlet as the princely abuser rather than the traditionally abused prince.[26] We have come some way—though by no means all the way, as we shall see—from Walt Whitman's contention that Shakespeare and his ilk 'are poisonous to the idea of the pride and dignity of the common people' (cited in Taylor 1990: 225).

Indeed, at the beginning of the century it was possible to think of Shakespeare as someone who, through the use of his princely language, was able not only to gentrify his own family but to bestow a kind of instant linguistic aristocracy on the basest of his minor characters. Wyndham Lewis, for instance, celebrates the democratizing function of blank verse. 'It transforms everyone that uses it', he writes, 'into a member of a race of heroes. A serving-man speaking blank verse is of a different race to us, who speak prose' (1966: 162). C. L. Barber's classic account of social customs and Shakespeare's festive comedy brings into view the generally benign treatment on Shakespeare's part of the inarticulate members of the peasantry and lumpen proletariat whose representatives 'might be merely butts [but] win our sympathy by taking part, each after his fashion, in "eruptions, and sudden breaking-out of mirth" (*Love's Labour's Lost* 5.1.108–09)' (1959: 110). Barber's comment on Bottom in *A Midsummer Night's Dream* perfectly captures Shakespeare's rendering of the irreducible individualism of his leading representative of the play's hempen homespuns: 'His imperviousness, indeed, is what is most delightful about him with Titania and he remains so completely himself, even in her arms, and despite the outward change of his head and ears; his confident, self-satisfied tone is a triumph of consistency, persistence, existence' (157).

This century's inexhaustible desire to narrativize Shakespeare characters who barely exist in their plays has even colonized discussions of the various personnel involved in the complicated reconstruction of Shakespeare's Works as they lurched through the processes of the Elizabethan printing house. Here, in particular, the anonymous compositors of the 1623 Folio have assumed an alphabetical identity (A, B, C, and so on) and a kind of status of folk-hero (or villain). And in line with this concern for marginal characters both in and out of Shakespeare is a new emphasis on restoring meaning and significance to previously discounted knots of linguistic perplexity that sometimes both major and minor characters speak, especially in the incoherent language of madness. So, for example, the jumble of words that froth in Othello's mouth during the seizure brought on by Iago's fiendish lies about Cassio and Desdemona has been re-examined for its pattern of application to theme and situation. And the only-apparent nonsense of Ophelia's fractured language of madness in the fourth act of *Hamlet* has been analysed mightily by critics intent on justifying Horatio's insistence to Gertrude that the unshaped use of Ophelia's speech 'doth move / The hearers to collection' (4.5.8–9).

It's arguable that a perverse form of the adversarially democratic in our time not only rearranges our interest in the plays' social hierarchies but attempts to disturb our equanimity regarding the plays' 'good' characters. Richard Levin calls this rearrangement a kind of character assassination.[27] An interestingly outrageous example—compellingly so perhaps—can be found in Jonathan Dollimore's view of the lovers in *Antony and Cleopatra*. According to him, *Antony and Cleopatra* dramatizes the fact 'that sexual desire is not that which transcends politics and power, but is the vehicle of politics and power' (1989–90: 486). The play is neither decadent nor transcendental but camp, so that the famous speech beginning 'Eternity was in our lips and eyes' is 'not the voice of transcendent love, but the inflated rhetoric of camp: an extravagance which parades and delights in its own hollowness, and which satisfies our desire for the sentimental by reveling in rather than disavowing its shallowness' (489). In this view, perhaps, the play would best be served by Mick Jagger in drag playing Cleopatra.

Corresponding to this tendency in recent criticism to diminish the stature of the plays' protagonists is the twentieth century's counter-partiality towards Shakespeare's villains. It's as though in our hearts we are commending them for flouting the Great Chain of Being. They are—uneasily to be sure—co-conspirators with us in our latter-day endeavours to slash the canvas of Tillyard's Elizabethan world picture. We commend Shakespeare's ability 'to adjust the scenic perspective in an immoralist's favour' (1976: 22), so writes Ernst Honigmann, as though Shakespeare were the embodiment of Keats's poetical character that has no character: 'It enjoys light and shade; it lives in gusto, be it foul or fair, high or low, rich or poor, mean or elevated. It has as much delight in conceiving an Iago as an Imogen'. Many twentieth-century critics would argue that Shakespeare would probably have taken more delight in conceiving an Iago than an Innogen (or even an Othello). This is the critical counterpart of what Mark Krupnick calls 'the glamor of evil in modernist literature' (1986: 98).

What Braggardism Is This?

What is typically twentieth century about its approach to the question of character in Shakespeare's plays is its own theoretical thickening of the art of Shakespeare's characterization, unpacking the latent complexities in the use of the term and its cognates. Just how complex this process can be may be sampled by following the network of *character*'s cross-references and offshoots threading their way through Patrice

Pavis's *Dictionary of the Theatre: Terms, Concepts, and Analysis* (1998). Yet his dictionary amply—only too amply—illustrates that it is not a question of complicating something that isn't inherently complicated, but a question of bringing out a hitherto unrecognized, insufficiently theorized, history of ambiguity and imprecision in the use of the term that has been richly brewing for centuries.

Joseph Porter argues that the volatility of the term *character* in our time outmatches its volatility in Shakespeare's time and is now at its most fractured: 'Shakespearean characterology at the present time stands in the most richly unstable moment of its history, and ideology figures in it everywhere' (1991: 141). And Peter Holland considers some of the more recalcitrant chronic theoretical problems facing character criticism: the character who is individualized for only a brief part of the play; the occasional divergence of language from speaker; Shakespeare's changing conception of characterization over the length of his career; the relationship of actor to character, character to audience, and character to 'narrative'—for all of these relationships we need, he says, using a favourite word in Pavis, an 'actantial analysis' (1989: 122).[28] The moral Holland draws is a rueful one: 'the infinite variety of Shakespearian characterization' (123) eludes us.

One of the most interesting areas of the thickening process of Shakespeare criticism in this century lies in the first of these relationships, the productive inconclusiveness of the connection between character and actor. A particular concern for what has become known as *performance criticism* is its attempt to come to terms with a basic question: to what extent is the actor the character, or the character the actor? Characters are obviously at some level produced by actors, and it may be the case these days that the actor dwarfs the character.

Certainly this is what Martin Buzacott believes in his stridently entertaining attack on the excessive authority granted to modern actors by critics in discussions of the interiority of Shakespeare's characters. According to Buzacott, the new-found influence of actors is so great that in much 'actor-centric' criticism they may well have replaced the authority of the text with their own authority—the slave has become master. Buzacott describes this as a huge release of vanity in twentieth-century actors, and accuses them of offering us a 'mutilated Shakespeare' (1991: 24).

His book's second chapter draws an outlandish analogy between terrorism and Shakespearean acting in which the first victim is a text terrorized by the actor: 'Shakespearean texts become the virtuous Justines upon whom every degradation and every climactic shiver is perpetrated by an ecstatic butcher performing his atrocities for an audience deriding the abnormality of purity' (32). The terrorism of the actor is usually, he argues, in the service of a conservative agenda; Laurence Olivier, for instance, 'becomes the theatrical (and more successful) General Alexander Haig, enthusiastically proclaiming "Right now, I'm in charge here"' (110). Buzacott goes on to say: 'With no author to "close" the interpretation of texts, and no flesh to imbue the printed roles with physical attributes, a Shakespearean performance becomes a battleground where jealous and ambitious men and women struggle and rage to fill the vacuum of the sublime with the activity of their own bowels and egos' (117). Such scorn on Buzacott's part for the strutting egos of the contemporary actor has its counterpart in an equally dismissive scorn for the passive acceptance of these egos by modern-day 'fickle and perverted' (134) audiences who are 'rendered physically incapacitated by the architecture and tech- niques of theatrical production, . . . reverting to a position of hostage to the actor's authority' (114–15). The result of all this, Buzacott says, is that the actor is nothing more than 'the criminal lackey pretending to be dead on the street while her mistress picks the pockets of the assembled voyeurs and ghouls' (132).

A theatre filled with criminal lackeys, voyeurs, and ghouls hardly corresponds, it seems to me, to the pietistic crowd one usually finds at, let's say, a typical Shakespeare production at any of the world's Strat- fords. But there is something to be said for the new awareness in criticism of the new authority of the actor and its disturbing implica- tions for an understanding of Shakespeare's characters. Many twen- tieth-century Shakespeare critics have attempted to grapple with the intricate, intimate connection between the character of a character and the character as presented by the actor. As Michael Goldman says, '[p]erformance is inseparable from dramatic character' (1981: 77), what we see on the stage is not an object but a process, a character is something an actor does. How he or she does it encompasses many delightful variables, each expressive of what W. B. Worthen describes as 'the integrated, self-present, internalized, psychologically motivated "character" of the dominant mode of modern theatrical representation, stage realism' (1996*a*: 212). After all, as Worthen says in another piece in the same year, 'Characterization represents fictive individuals through a variety of shared codes—movement, language, behavior, dress, acting style, mise-en-scene, disposition of the audience—that render performance an act of ideological production' (1996*b*: 23). We must ask ourselves, he writes in an earlier article, 'how acting in a particular historical mode—the American Method, for instance—textualizes "character" as performance' (1989: 454).

A kind of complementary exercise in characterology to the textualization of the actor's performance, his or her 'character', is that of the critic's performance, his or her 'character'. In one of the many self-reflexive turns taken by twentieth-century Shakespeare criticism the life of the (Shakespeare) critic becomes an examinable enterprise. Our understanding of Bradley's living mind, that is, can be enhanced by asking similar questions about Bradley that Bradley asked about Shakespeare's characters in those notorious questions that form the appendices to *Shakespearean Tragedy* (and this is of course true about any critic had we world enough and time—and the inclination—to investigate their life-stories). To some extent in the twentieth century *The Lives of the Critics* has replaced *The Lives of the Poets* as a cultural pursuit: the character of the critic has become as important as the character of the playwright.

G. K. Hunter, for instance, pursues Bradley's biography to help us to understand Bradley's criticism: he tells us about Bradley's father, the Reverend Charles Bradley, who looked 'like a caricature of all that we suppose Victorian clergymen to have been—forceful, long-lived, dogmatic, a domestic tyrant, whose first wife "succumbed before the advent of her fourteenth baby" and whose second wife raised the total of his children to some 22' (1968: 101–2). This intriguing variation on the question of how many children had Lady Macbeth (a question Bradley never actually asked but has since come to epitomize the waywardness of his approach)—that is, how many children had the Mrs Bradleys—helps us to see in the chaotic circumstances of Bradley's childhood, in the spiritual crisis he underwent between school and Oxford primarily in reaction to his dominant evangelical father, in the influence of T. H. Green at Balliol who was 'a living testimony to the ethical power possible outside supernatural sanctions' (1968: 103),

Bradley's assumption of 'a metaphysics of morality' (103) which he followed for rest of his life and which suffuses his work on Shakespeare. More generally, as Arthur Eastman notes, Shakespeare critics like Harbage, Spencer, and Tillyard are not so much critics as 'illuminators of criticism' (1968: 305).[29]

The Observed of All Observers

The twentieth century has been just as avid as previous centuries—more so in fact given our obsession with celebrity—in its pursuit of Shakespeare the man. Biographies of him continue to spill from the presses at an alarming rate.[30] Attempting to pluck out the heart of Shakespeare's mystery has become a way of life for some critics. The most fertile ground for intimate speculation about the life of the private man continues to be the Sonnets whose coy cryptography—sugared sonnets among private friends—incites a criticism of excited prurience. 'With this key', Wordsworth maintained, 'Shakespeare unlocked his heart'. But it is clear from the immense amount of conflicting testimony that twentieth-century criticism has extracted from the Sonnets that while the key may have been turned, the door to 'truth' has remained closed, though that truth is by and large thought to be variations on Sonnet 29's despairing introversion 'With what I most enjoy contented least'.

One emphasis in twentieth-century Sonnet criticism—a rewarding one—is to see the speaker of the Sonnets, his antagonists, the fair young man, and the dark lady, as extensions, variations in lyric poetry, of the characters of the plays. Another is to see them as verbal artefacts, a perspective that leads Heather Dubrow, for instance, to argue that there's 'a strong case that Shakespeare's speaker [in the Sonnets] is not using rhetorical devices but instead being used by them' (1987: 200); he is therefore 'captive and victor, and he is both at once' (202). The notion that the speaker of the Sonnets, 'Shakespeare', is, as it were, the captive of a poetic tradition probably owes something to the more established tradition in this century of seeing him as the captive of larger social forces. For C. L. Barber the Sonnets are a response to life's humiliations: 'Shakespeare turns injury into poetry' (1959–60: 668). For other more politically minded critics Shakespeare's poems dramatize the humiliating manoeuvres of the writer-client—and by extension the dramatists' companies—in the semi-feudal obligations of the patronage system. For John Barrell, for example, the pathos of Sonnet 29, 'When, in disgrace with fortune and men's eyes', is that 'the narrator can find no words to assert the transcendent power of true love, which cannot be interpreted as making a request for a couple of quid' (1988: 42).

Twentieth-century biographers of Shakespeare, like their predecessors, have drawn many of their speculations about Shakespeare's character from the characters of his plays, or, more tangentially and even more speculatively, from the perception of some kind of overarching autobiographical narrative purpose stretching from *The Comedy of Errors* to *The Tempest* where the 'errors' in that preliminary play are either finally laid to rest in the last one or—depending on the interpreter's point of view—are shown to have been always fruitfully intransigent. Stanley Wells reminds us why biographers have had to move so indirectly and speculatively: there are 'no accounts of his [Shakespeare's] childhood or of his relationship with members of his family or with colleagues, no love-letters . . . no diaries, no working notebooks, no manuscripts—except for his "hand" in the manuscript of *Sir Thomas More*' (1994: 4). Wells goes on to argue that 'literary interpretation should not be based on biographical speculation' (12)—although of course it still often is—but the more far-reaching question perhaps is whether biographical speculation should be based on literary interpretation. The short answer is that biographers of Shakespeare have little choice other than to glean what they can of the man from a 'biographical' reading of his works.

This overarching biographical narrative of Shakespeare's life inspired by the plays takes many forms, ranging from the plausible to the outlandish. Somewhere interestingly between the two lies David Sundelson's version (1983) of Shakespeare's basic psychology which pivots on Lady Macduff's line about the plight of her son after Macduff's retreat into England: 'Fathered he is, and yet he's fatherless' (*Macbeth*, 4.2.27). Sundelson suggests that we not only think of other characters in Shakespeare's plays with Lady Macduff's words as guide—Hamlet, Juliet, Cordelia, and Edgar, for example—but see all the plays in terms of the death of the father and the hope of his restoration. The tragedies kill him off; the comedies, histories, and romances try to bring him back: they wake Duncan with their knocking, and, according to Sundelson, Shakespeare's own psychology throughout his life follows this pattern.

In his essay 'Shakespeare the Man' in the *Oxford Lectures* (1965), A.C. Bradley is convinced that we can infer in a more or less straightforwardly unproblematic manner something of Shakespeare the man from Shakespeare's plays—a not surprising belief, I suppose, from someone so certain that he can infer the characters of Shakespeare's characters from what they say and do. Bradley argues in fact that Shakespeare and his tragic heroes are similar (as they are similarly inferable): like them at their best Shakespeare was gentle, civil, upright, honourable, witty, free, and open. He was also, according to Bradley, good company, a free spender; he had been wild in his youth, of course, but he had also been modest and unassuming and he continued to be so after he had abandoned the wildness. From these inferences as to Shakespeare's character Bradley can infer others— inferences from inferences in a pattern that threatens infinite regress. Free and open natures, for instance, so Bradley infers, run the risk of being deceived, and they therefore may be tempted—as Shakespeare may have been (Bradley's 'may' introduces a weaker, more hypothetical inferential process at this stage)—to 'melancholy, embitterment, anger, possibly even misanthropy' (325). To imagine a Shakespeare at the mercy of such a set of debilitating mental conditions helps to explain, says Bradley—and others—, his production of satirical and tragic plays from 1602 to 1606 which must be in response to a difficult period in Shakespeare's life, aggravated, Bradley circularly believes, by Shakespeare's susceptibility to melancholy, embitterment, anger, and so on.

A. C. Bradley's work on Shakespeare, like that of many of his contemporaries, reveals a mind whose natural bent leads him, in the words of one of those distinguished contemporaries, the Danish critic, Georg Brandes, 'to delight in searching out the human spirit concealed and revealed in a great artist's work' (1905: 1). Dowden, Bradley, Raleigh (1907), Lee (1898), and Brandes all attempt, in Brandes's words, 'to declare and prove that Shakespeare is not thirty-six plays and a few poems jumbled together and read pele-mele, but a man who felt and thought, rejoiced and suffered, brooded, dreamed, and created' (1905: 689).

The commitment by these earlier critics to Shakespeare the brooder, dreamer, and sufferer, sometimes takes on an erotic intensity as though they were vying with the Shakespeare of the Sonnets in their adoration of the absent radiant centre of their ministrations. Here, for instance, is Walter Raleigh, working the metaphor of tumescent creativeness: 'But to know him [Shakespeare] as the greatest of artisans, when he collects his might and stands dilated, his imagination aflame, the thick-coming thoughts and fancies shaping themselves, under the stress of the central will, into a thing of life—this is to know him better, not worse' (1907: 7). Like Bradley, these critics believe in the relatively unproblematic nature of the ascertainability of Shakespeare through his works. And to know him thus is to know him as comforter, friend, sweetheart, redeemer; in the desolation of the end of some of the tragedies, Raleigh writes, sliding from the erotic to the churchly, there is 'the comfort of the sure knowledge that Shakespeare is with us' (13), a Shakespeare whose 'geniality clings to his name like a faded perfume' (14).

Although Sir Sidney Lee admits to the difficulty of knowing for sure when Shakespeare is speaking as Shakespeare, none the less 'one may tentatively infer that Shakespeare gave voice through his created personages to sentiments which were his own' (1906: 151), and these sentiments constitute a political and moral philosophy which 'for clear-eyed sanity is without rival' (151), demonstrating 'a robust common-sense' (161) in the establishment of high standards of public virtue and public duty. Lee has a very clear view of the man he is dealing with: 'I picture Shakespeare as the soul of modesty and gentleness in the social relations of life, avoiding unbecoming self-advertisement, and rating at its just value empty flattery, the mere adulation of the lips' (26). The fact of the matter, says Lee, is that 'Shakespeare's message is Carlyle's message or Ruskin's message anticipated by nearly three centuries, and more potently and wisely phrased' (161).

And it's important to record the fact about our more jaded century that some watered-down version of this view of Shakespeare is still—just about—the preponderant one. Even Bernard Shaw thought Shakespeare endearing; E. E. Stoll thinks that behind the mask Shakespeare was 'virtuous and kindly, not religious yet not irreverent, not cynical yet not fond of the rabble, and scornful of affectation, painted cheeks, and false hair' (1927: 17–18); and Alfred Harbage in his valuable book, *Conceptions of Shakespeare* (1966), describes him as essentially benign and speaks in Bradleyan terms about Shakespeare's ideal man being scholarly, courageous, and honest, and his ideal woman gentle, chaste, and fair.

So Shakespeare critics by and large at the end of the nineteenth century and at the beginning of the twentieth tended to read his works in the great puritan tradition of biblical exegesis through which God and right conduct were made known to believers. And for many of them what Shakespeare's readers will come to know is comfortingly Carlylian; if Shakespeare is an oracle to be consulted he is an honorary nineteenth-century one. In the twentieth century confidence in this critical process at first remains high but the readings themselves lose their Victorian *gravitas*. Yet it might be argued that these secular exegetes continue to resemble their religious counterparts in the controversial nature of their new conclusions: the medium remains the same, the message changes. What may be distinctively twentieth century, then, in some critics' responses to the story of Shakespeare's life is their recourse to Bradley's hesitant suggestion that Shakespeare may have suffered from bouts of misanthropy. Often more stridently than he, they offer us a Shakespeare harder-headed, more shrewd, less kind (loutish even) than the traditional picture of him.[31]

One of the earliest and most notorious, perhaps, of these debunkers was the sardonic, world-weary denizen of Bloomsbury, Lytton Strachey, whose famously infamous biographies of eminent Victorians did so much to dispel the aura of sanctification that his subjects had assiduously cultivated for themselves.[32] Strachey's most notorious essay 'Shakespeare's Final Period' (1948) judges Shakespeare in his last productive years to be suffering from a *fin-de-siècle* ennui, signs of which can be seen in *Coriolanus*, 'certainly a remarkable, and perhaps an intolerable play: remarkable, because it shows the sudden first appearance of the Shakespeare of the final period; intolerable, because it is impossible to forget how much better it might have been' (4).

This ominous judgement presages the more familiar one on the final plays: 'It is difficult to resist the conclusion that he was getting bored himself. Bored with people, bored with real life, bored with drama, bored, in fact, with everything except poetry and poetical dreams' (12). (As though poetry and its dreams had nothing to do with real life or drama.) Shakespeare is lost in a world of rhetoric,

Strachey argues, his plots 'hardly more than a peg for fine writing' (13). (As though fine writing had nothing to do with real life or drama.) Interestingly enough, Strachey's morose view of these last plays finds latter-day supporters among our own *fin-de-siècle* critics, as Paul Delany's article illustrates: 'His art may indeed still embody a "life-affirming humanism", as the Soviet critic Anisimov claims; but, in the later plays, at least, it is neither an optimistic nor a progressive human-ism—rather one whose essence is nostalgia, whose glory is that of the setting sun' (1995: 36).

If Shakespeare is to be identified with his characters maybe it should be with his less admirable ones. The iconoclastic Wyndham Lewis wants to set the record straight by redistributing the emphasis in this way: 'It will be my business here to relate the spasms of these scowling and despairing monsters to a particularly concrete figure, or to a mind experiencing things according to identifiable personal laws' (1966: 14). When characters are suffering misfortune 'they automatically become Shakespeare' (163). It's important to recuperate even a scowling and despairing Shakespeare, Lewis believes in a rare moment of procedural justification, as 'anyone who defines in the body of Shakespeare's work a personality and traces of passion and opinion is rescuing him for us from the abstract in which he might eventually disappear where less important men would survive' (20). What this approach clearly demonstrates is a belief that at the very least Shakespeare's thought can be gleaned from the depiction of his characters: 'In Achilles, Ajax, Hotspur, Coriolanus and the rest you get what Shakespeare thought of the chivalry of the physical hero. Falstaff is his Don Quixote, not Sancho Panza' (15).

However, the more vexatious and incidentally amusing critical pur-suit rests in the attempts by some twentieth-century critics to see this or that character as Shakespeare's *doppelgänger*. Hamlet and Richard III and, of course, Prospero are favourite candidates. So too, perhaps oddly, is Bottom in *A Midsummer Night's Dream*. Meredith Skura is convinced that all the Wills in Shakespeare's plays and Sonnets are 'ironically self-deprecating' (1993: 139) Hitchcockian cameo appear-ances by Shakespeare, and she enjoys making odorous comparisons between Shakespeare's relatives, the characters in his plays, and the modern actors' situations in life. 'As nearly all the psychoanalytic and feminist critics agree, the plays reveal pervasive assumptions about women's encompassing and dangerous maternal powers, and, to Shakespeare, Mary [Shakespeare's mother] may have seemed formidable in other ways as well' (77).

Skura revels in provocative fantasies of biographical speculation: in 1579 John Shakespeare and Mary Arden lost their seven and a half year old daughter Anne who died only two weeks before Shakespeare's fifteenth birthday. This death and John Shakespeare's decline may have prompted Shakespeare, mightn't they, to choose an acting career. And wasn't Shakespeare himself a replacement child for his two dead sisters? And what about the arrival of Gilbert, Shakespeare's brother? Wasn't Shakespeare as it were 'by a brother's hand/Of life, of crown, of queen at once dispatched' (*Hamlet*, 1.5.74–5)? Skura sums up her creed more soberly perhaps than her speculations suggest: 'No biographical event, whether the death of the patron or the death of a son, determines a text or simply reproduces itself in a text. But all events become part of the conditions for creating texts' (128).[33]

Even a critic as resolutely new historical as Louis Montrose can—somewhat more circumspectly—join in the fun: 'Thus, resonating through the dramatic persona of Nick Bottom, the weaver, are not only a generalized common voice but also the particular socio-economic and cultural origins of Master William Shakespeare, the professional player-playwright—and, too, the collective social cultural origins of his craft' (1996: 181–2).

Recent criticism continues to draw jaundiced conclusions about Shakespeare from the manner in which he presents his characters. Gary Taylor, for instance, asks us to consider—approvingly I think—Stephen Booth on *Julius Caesar* who argues that Shakespeare's characters in this play are unpleasant and Shakespeare himself unpleasantly manipulating: 'Booth's *Julius Caesar* is not a nice play; Booth's Shakespeare is not a nice guy' (1990: 330). Going a stage further in the chronology of Shakespeare's works than Lytton Strachey, Taylor points out—as have other critics—that Shakespeare's final piece of writing is not *The Tempest* (nor parts of *All Is True*) but his will, one 'full of complicated and cunning financial provisions' (330), unfair and selfish.

In Herbert Howarth's elegant cadenza on Ben Jonson's famous description of Shakespeare as 'gentle' in the First Folio's 'To the Reader', he pursues the notion of Shakespeare's pursuit of the 'gent' in gentle, and builds an elaborate biography around this ambition. The plays of the tragic period, Howarth argues, are in disgusted reaction to this pursuit of 'gentleness'—to Shakespeare's own honesty having been transformed into a bawd. In all of this, and even in his last plays where 'he even forgave himself for writing plays' (1961: 96), there's that 'inexpungable [*sic*] nucleus of that Proustian snobbery with which he started his work' (96).

Proustian snobbery is one thing, the gouging business man another. Yet Peter Thomson's *Shakespeare's Professional Career* (1992), despite a preliminary assertion as to its anti-biographical thrust—'This is not a book about Shakespeare but about Shakespeare's job' (p. xv)—casts a cold eye on Shakespeare as a hard-hearted entrepreneur, hoarding, for instance, 80 bushels of malt in 1598 at a time of great malnutrition in Stratford.

Casting a cold eye also distinguishes Ernst Honigmann's book, *Shakespeare's Impact on His Contemporaries* (1982), which sets out on a rather grim, someone-has-to-do-this mission to explore the negative side of Shakespeare's impact on his contemporaries offering us a re-reading of the records to throw 'new light on his personality, his development as a writer, his influence on other writers, and his response to criticism' (p. ix). Honigmann admits that his book may be no 'rounded biography' but it does offer in compensation 'a new "Shakespeare", and a new understanding of his achievement' (p. ix) which proffers a Shakespeare who is not as likeable as 'the old senti-mental model', but one who is, according to Honigmann, a 'more credible human being' (p. x).

Michael Bristol (1996) equally hard-headedly argues for a Shake-speare complicit with the groundlings and with patriarchy, 'morally unprincipled and opportunistic' (50), shrewdly strategical and market-driven. So Shakespeare doesn't have the peaceful retirement in Stratford in his posthumous years that he no doubt anticipated and probably enjoyed while he was alive. Richard Wilson, however, thinks it quite likely that Shakespeare 'died harried by a sexual scandal that may have hastened his end' (1993: 184).

Even when critics are dealing with Shakespeare at his most wor-shipful—namely in the last plays—there's a need to continue to anatomize his commercial instincts. Richard Halpern rather stuffily points out that 'Shakespearean romance, despite its redemptive and quasi-religious aspirations, still profits from the commercial world whose corruption and debasement it decries' (1991: 156). In the case of *Pericles*, he notes, the play doesn't really retreat into the romance world, 'it ransacks that world for a hodgepodge of numinous effects' and finally seems to be in the business of 'marketing of aura' (157). It's surely overstating the case to seize upon Shakespeare's unwillingness to invent any of his plots as an indication of a kleptomaniac tendency, but even this absurdity has been touted.

Critics of this ilk seem to be responding to Nietzsche who once remarked that 'dramatists are in general rather wicked men' (1909–11: 176). An entertaining, pugnacious, but curiously *de trop* climax to this saga of personal disenchantment with Shakespeare—as a person and as a writer—can be found in Gary Taylor's *Reinventing Shakespeare: A Cultural History from the Restoration to the Present* (1990) whose last chapter, 'Singularity', constitutes an attack on the notion that Shakespeare has any. For instance, Taylor argues that, as an all-round theatre man, Shakespeare was easily equalled by Sophocles, Aeschylus, Euripides, and Aristophanes; Molière was the greater performer. As for the longevity of Shakespeare's reputation, his hierophants are 'curiously blind' (377) to its relative recentness (a mere 400 years!). In any case, there is much to complain about: Shakespeare is now force-fed to the young in their 'captive classrooms' (384); there is an overrepresentation of men in his works, and his women are either pretty young or ugly old. And where are the mothers in his plays? Where are the lower classes? (Where are *Measure for Measure*'s prostitutes?) For Taylor's tastes, Shakespeare is simply not outraged enough about life's injustices and he is not surprised that someone as discriminating in his judgements as Wittgenstein distrusted him. Shakespeare lacks Plautus's 'hardness, toughness, exuberant and fantastic amorality. And what I dislike about Shakespeare's comedies—and tragedies—is their softness, their central mushiness, their inevitable "love interest," their wholesomeness' (400).

All this mayhem at the expense of Shakespeare's character in particular takes on a characteristically twentieth-century colouring in rapt discussions of his allegedly wavering sexual proclivities and his 'sex nausea'. The twentieth century is distinguished (if that's the right word) by its obsession with the sex life of its celebrities, alive or dead, perhaps simply because such an obsession is now allowable in print and all other media. No one writing about sex in Shakespeare could have done so with such freedom before the twentieth century. Preoccupied—but not exclusively so—with the Sonnets, critics attempt to assess the nature of Shakespeare's sexuality.

Wyndham Lewis, unsurprisingly, plumps for Shakespeare as a homosexual, referring to what he calls Shakespeare's 'sex organization, and to the fact that there is great reason to suppose that, like many of his contemporaries, his sentimentality was directed towards other men and not towards women' (1966: 153). As far as Lewis is concerned, Shakespeare in *Antony and Cleopatra* was clearly in love with Antony, and so the conclusion that Lewis reaches is 'to consider Shakespeare's attitude to the world somewhat as that of a woman— rather more that of a woman than of a man' (158).

Martin Green draws much darker conclusions from his study of the language of Shakespeare's Sonnets: the key Sonnet as far as Green is concerned is 99 'which tells of the friend's beauty, of his sexual relations with both the poet and the poet's mistress, and of the venereal disease which thereafter consumed him' (1974: 41). The Sonnets that are addressed to the rival poet make it clear that 'Shakespeare, whatever his endowment, was impotent' (52), and that there was 'the urgent necessity for the sodomite to conceal himself' (99).

William Kerrigan offers as his third clue to Shakespeare's personality 'an uneasy vulnerability to a peculiarly sexual or genital form of misogyny' (1989: 185); a sex nausea; 'a dark and terrible rage against woman's sexuality' (184). According to Kerrigan, it's not until *Antony and Cleopatra* that Shakespeare is able to undo the 'knot of sexual disgust' (186) (the undoing of which does not require Shakespeare to be in love with Antony).

The whirligig of time, however, continues to bring in its revenges. The sceptical reassessment of Shakespeare's personality is in the process (and will probably always be in the process) of reassessment. The Shakespeare of Shaw, Stoll, and Harbage will probably never be entirely effaced, and perhaps we should bear in mind at the close of the twentieth century Peter Erickson's impassioned protest against the de-elevation of Shakespeare's character: 'In a cankered, envious, smug, shameless response to authorial greatness, the reader will inevitably try to elevate himself or herself through a mean-spirited effort to diminish Shakespeare, to cut him down to the reader's size' (1985: 247). And Alvin Kernan repolishes a traditional, unfashionable proposition: 'In

odernist skepticism, we conceive, in our still romantic
of any worth as being the privileged expression of the
eative imagination of the individual artist' (1995: 169).
ied genius-worship continues to flourish. George Steiner,
owledging that 'the modern tone is more astringent. It
ı⸺ ere rapture' (1970: 199), declares that 'our essential stance is
heir to that of Coleridge' (200), that '[w]e seek Shakespeare's measure
and come short of breath' (198). Steiner believes that '[t]hose who
would challenge Shakespeare's stature do so with a betraying nervous-
ness' (200). (Perhaps a betraying extremism might be closer to the style
of more recent debunkings.)

From the moral point of view, Shakespeare's temperament is once
more reaffirmed as 'richly sociable, centered in kinship' (1989: 22) by
C. L. Barber, and Richard Wheeler, and a similar moral reaffirmation
of some of Shakespeare's characters continues to surface, as in Richard
Strier's strikingly persuasive essay 'Faithful Servants: Shakespeare's
Praise of Disobedience' (1988) which notes that for Shakespeare 'a
dog's obeyed in office only when its followers are also dogs' (123). In the
romances, Strier believes, with the partial exception of *The Tempest*,
'the distinction between the good servant who disobeys immoral
commands and the wicked who will do anything becomes a funda-
mental axiom' (123–4), and this theme is 'almost obsessive' (125) in
Cymbeline. Derek Cohen notes in his Introduction that '[t]he Shakespeare of today, in keeping with the dominant political value of
western society, is racially tolerant, a feminist, against war. That is,
we, his readers, have made him over in our image' (1988: 10).

The themes and characters of Shakespeare's plays, the argument
runs, reveal something essential about Shakespeare's own character.
And so too does the language he uses. Twentieth-century language
criticism takes its cue from Caroline Spurgeon's famous works on
Shakespeare's imagery, 'Shakespeare's Iterative Imagery' (1931) and
Shakespeare's Imagery and What it Tells Us (1935). What it tells Caroline
Spurgeon—among other things—is that Shakespeare was 'an intensely alive, incredibly sensitive, and amazingly observant man. And a
countryman through and through.' (1964: 199). It also tells her just
who is writing the works she's reading; Shakespeare's use of iterative
imagery is 'as an absolute beacon in the skies with regard to the vexed
question of authorship' (173), for what Shakespeare does is to give

himself away in his images, especially when they occur in clusters, 'that is, certain groups of things and ideas—apparently entirely unrelated— which are linked together in Shakespeare's subconscious mind, and some of which are undoubtedly the outcome of an experience, a sight or emotion which has profoundly affected him' (180). Subsequent investigations of Shakespeare's use of imagery and other verbal tics—Edward Armstrong's study (1946), for instance, which psycho-analyses Spurgeon's image-clusters—are often undertaken in order to probe Shakespeare's psychology and bring us closer to his living mind.

The King Hath Many Marching in His Coats

If we are to talk about the twentieth century's contribution to biographical speculation about Shakespeare we have to take into account those critics who talk about him as though he had never really lived.[34] One way to make him disappear as a flesh-and-blood-and-mind writer is to merge him with his partners in the theatre; it isn't Shakespeare we're dealing with really but a consortium of theatrical entrepreneurs who all had a hand in the production of his plays (maybe even in the writing of them)—if not of his non-dramatic verse. Sir Sidney Lee paved the way for this approach: 'The more closely Shakespeare's career is studied the plainer it becomes that his experiences and fortunes were identical with those of all who followed in his day his profession of dramatist, and that his conscious aims and ambitions and practices were those of every contemporary man of letters' (1906: 57).

This rich vein of reductive interpretative speculation continues to be tapped. The last chapter, and epilogue, of Louis Montrose's justly admired *The Purpose of Playing: Shakespeare and the Cultural Politics of the Elizabethan Theatre* (1996) expands upon Lee's suggestions that Shakespeare's genius needs to be considered in its causal context. It 'has historical conditions of possibility, which we should endeavor to specify before we genuflect to the ineffable' (206). So, according to Montrose, Shakespeare was allowed to be possible by the circum-stances of the theatre of his time in which he was one of only eight professional players who accumulated property in his lifetime, who was a sharer in a public company, and who stayed with one company throughout his career using a playhouse that he partly owned. 'Thus, he was able to enjoy both material and ideological conditions for artistic production that far surpassed those of most Elizabethan lit-erary professionals and patronage poets, as well as those of his notori-ously insecure fellow dramatists' (207–8).

Genuflecting to the ineffable may be something to avoid, but it now seems impossible not to avoid the substitution of those material and ideological conditions discreetly conjured up by Montrose for the reality of Shakespeare, the individual writer. For postmodern critics Shakespeare has become 'Shakespeare' (now almost more familiar to us than Shakespeare), 'Shakespeare' the ghost writer, the Keynesian confluence or conjuncture of intersecting cultural phenomena. Shake-speare is dead; long live 'Shakespeare'. 'Shakespeare' has now become, in Barbara Freedman's words, a 'privileged site of intersecting codes that reflect and effect discourse production and consumption' (1989: 245): 'site' and its cognates frequently replaces person, man, or char-acter as Lynda Boose casually illustrates in her description of him as 'this all important, powerfully political site called William Shake-speare' (1987: 710). Susan Bennett thinks of him as '[t]hat global industry of remarkable energy and profit' (1996: 1), as does Graham Holderness who describes Shakespeare as 'a set of social practices' (1984: 26).[35] In the popular consciousness, Holderness points out, pursuing his commercial definition of 'Shakespeare', he is alive and thriving in a glutinous mass of pop reference. Shakespeare has become a ubiquitous cultural phenomenon; 'a component of popular culture' (26). His name is now learned through 'advertisements, television comedies, the names of pubs and beers . . . a universal symbol of high art, of "culture", of education, of the English spirit' (26).

In the chapter on Shakespeare in his glorious history of American culture, *Highbrow/Lowbrow: the Emergence of Cultural Hierarchy in America* (1988), Lawrence Levine describes just how pervasively in the United States Shakespeare's name in the twentieth century has become the universal symbol of high art, of 'culture', of education, even though it is still useful to sell products and remains—thank-fully—available for parody. (In *Hamlet and Eggs* (1937), for instance, in a production of *Romeo and Juliet* Juliet awakes in her tomb and sings 'O Bury Me Not on the Lone Prairie' (55).) But by and large the twentieth-century American version of Shakespeare, Levine argues, is reverent and educational. In 1986 an advertisement on the Metro in

Washington pleads Shakespeareanly to the passengers to 'Help our colleges cope with inflation. The money you give may decide whether I'm to be or not to be' (73).

One impetus towards the abandonment of Shakespeare the self-generating writer lay in the notion modernist writers and their critical allies had about the essential nature of the artist. In contrast to the Romantic conception of the artist as the suffering (and insufferable) ego, modernist critics and writers espoused impersonality as the *sine qua non* of the artist's make-up. Richard Wilson writes that James and Arnold among many writers of the time thought that the author Shakespeare did not exist, but was in fact 'the prototypical modernist artist, who possesses genius in proportion to the dissolution of his personality, and who shrinks, like Jesus or the Cheshire Cat, from the sordid interrogation of historicism' (1993: 5). Or as Henry James puts it: 'the man himself, in the Plays, we directly touch, to my consciousness, positively nowhere: we are dealing too perpetually with the artist, the monster and magician of a thousand masks' (1964: 297). The downside of this remarkable example of Keats's 'negative capability', according to some critics, is the way the absence of Shakespeare's ego (of Shakespeare himself) has been eagerly replaced by the egos of his modern-day appropriators, whether they be editors (see G. Taylor 1988),[36] critics (e.g. Lewis 1966), actors (see Buzacott 1991), directors (see Marowitz 1991), biographers (Frank Harris (1969), say) or, late and soon, fanatics of every stripe, ranging from those who claim Shakespeare for their religions and ideologies to those who see him as a stand-in for their favourite nobleman (such as the Earl of Oxford) or intellectual (Francis Bacon is a popular choice).

It then became *de rigueur* for the New Critics (and others), whose formalist principles owed so much to the influence of modernism, to think of Shakespeare or 'Shakespeare' as consubstantial with his works, and there is a connection to be made here between the abolition of Shakespeare and the installation of 'Shakespeare' and the rise to legislative authority of the Intentional Fallacy in the 'New' criticism of poetry. If it is logically fallacious to argue that the interpretation of poetry depends upon or is revealing of the intentions of the poet, it is but a short step from this position to dispense with the writer altogether. Here is Peter Erickson wriggling free from any imputation that by Shakespeare he may mean a flesh-and-blood writer: 'I do not mean an entity prior or exterior to the specific play at hand; I do not mean the actual person, the biographical Shakespeare. Rather, I refer to the figure of the author as it emerges from the work itself' (1985: 245–6).

This position is commonplace for all formalist critics of Shakespeare, I would argue, but it is usually held less defensively, tending to go without saying. Yet as late as 1997 we can find an extraordinarily confidently written book arguing (as many twentieth-century books on Shakespeare have argued) for its author's having broken through to reveal the real thing, the holy grail, Shakespeare's Shakespeare. John Meagher believes that the real Shakespeare can be discovered through a careful study of his dramaturgy: 'The approach of this book is an investigation of Shakespeare's dramaturgy—i.e., his stagecraft, his repertoire of playwriting techniques, the strategies and schemes and tactics with which he put plays together' (1997: 14). He argues that his book is an attempt to 'to put Shakespeare in charge of the reading of his plays, and to assist readers to grasp, more intimately and accurately than seems to be the normal standard of even directors and scholars, what he was doing as a designer of drama and how he did it' (26). And the optimistic subtitle for his second chapter is 'How we lost, and may recover, Shakespeare's own dramaturgy'.

His contention is that the reading, editing, and understanding of Shakespeare has never recovered from the break in continuity between 1642 and 1660, and he goes on to argue that interpretation has dominated over the sometimes tedious labour of understanding 'how it is in fact designed to work' (33). There is discipline to be encountered in reading Shakespeare's plays as he wrote them; it's not a question of being pleasantly inventive. He ends this chapter by saying, 'This book is dedicated to the proposition that we can no longer easily read Shakespeare in his own terms; and that we can, and should, learn how to do so; and that his earliest texts can teach us how; and that this is the only way we can get close enough to conserving, in relatively primeval and unpolluted form, one of our greatest natural resources' (37). What is astonishing about these claims is not the claims themselves but that they can be put forward at such a late date with such conviction—as though twentieth-century close reading of Shakespeare began in 1997. Needless to say, Shakespeare's Shakespeare continues to elude criticism and will probably always do so—though the claims for pollution-free interpretation will no doubt continue to proliferate.

Formalist Criticism of Shakespeare

Such Apt and Gracious Words

If close readings of Shakespeare's works certainly did not begin in 1997 a case can be made for pushing back their time of origin to a date well before the twentieth century. A glance at the Variorum edition of any of Shakespeare's plays reveals the extent to which editors from the eighteenth century onwards have grappled with the meanings of words. How words work, how they mean, is a syntagmatic (and paradigmatic) process and dealing with them in their contexts is the basic act of formalist criticism. Immediacy is of course variable, and it may well be the case that the broadening and multiplying of Shakespeare's contexts while remaining ostensibly within the parameters of the works themselves is one of the twentieth century's main contributions to the formalist criticism of Shakespeare. Now it is commonplace for critics to deal with all kinds of structural combinations of Shakespeare's words, from those that make up images, couplets, asides, rhetorical patterns (such as isocolon and anaphora),[1] soliloquies, and sequences, to those forming larger structural units, the scene, the act, the entire play, or all of the plays thought of as one capacious, all-inclusive work. And then, spilling over the confining parameters of the works themselves, formalist criticism has to deal somehow with the formal groupings that make up the plays' genres.

Spilling over is perhaps a usefully tendentious phrase in discussing how words work; it is virtually impossible to restrict oneself to the words themselves as we can see when we follow Paul Jorgensen's pursuit of significant ones in some of Shakespeare's plays: *honesty* in *Othello*; *nothing* in *Much Ado About Nothing*; *honour* in *Henry IV, Part 1*; *time* in the *Henry IV*s; *noble* in *Coriolanus*. For *honesty*, Jorgensen explains, he had to study the morality play and the Diogenes literature; for *nothing* he had to read widely in ephemeral mock encomia and theological treatises on doctrines of creation; for *time* he immersed himself in Elizabethan sermons—all of which spiralling investigations he pursued in a spirit of 'hopeful doggedness' (1962: p. ix). In the case of *honest*, William Empson tells us, historical circumstances made '[t]he fifty-two uses of [it] in *Othello* . . . a very queer business' because, at the time of writing the play, the word 'was in the middle of a rather complicated process of change, and . . . what emerged from it was a sort of jovial cult of independence' (1951: 218). In all Shakespeare's uses of it in the play 'he never once allows the word a simple hearty use between equals' (218).

Words like *honest*, *honour*, and *time*—threading their iterative way through their plays—accrue heft and significance without any need of the esoteric knowledge supplied by Jorgensen or the etymological changes described by Empson. By the time we come to the tenth or eleventh iteration of *honesty* or *honest* in *Othello* the nightmarish gap between its denotative meaning and the situation of its speakers gives it a metaphoric intensity.[2] We don't have to read morality plays to experience this kind of radiation. (Reading and thinking about these earlier works may indeed be a positive distraction from the impact of Shakespeare's words-in-context.) S. L. Bethell makes the case that 'direct reference is poetically as important as the oblique reference of a figure, and, moreover, since there is less likelihood of its being unconscious, it is more likely to be directly relevant to the main theme' (1952: 62). James Calderwood talks about the way commonplace language in Shakespeare is transformed by him: 'the language the poet uses comes . . . drab and gross from the everyday world . . . but it has been transformed by the poetic imagination into a self-enclosed complex of meaning that abandons its referential dependence on the world out-side' (1971: 13). The twentieth century, especially under the impact of modernism, has responded avidly to the variety of language in Shakespeare—the drab and the gross as well as the orotund and the poly-glot—that 'miraculous, written vocabulary' (1995: 194), as Alvin Kernan extols it—a use vocabulary of 29,000 words, compared with

Dante's approximately 15,000, Petrarch's 4,500, and Marlowe's 11,500. (Those 29,000 words, it has been claimed, have provoked over six billion in response.) We are fully alive now to the difference that L. C. Knights urged us to see when he said that '[t]he thing "which shackles accidents, and bolts up change" is *not* the same as "[t]he deed which puts an end to human vicissitude"' (1963*b*: 48).

Shackling accidents and bolting up change are perfectly ordinary words bolted together in an extraordinary way, and twentieth-century critics have revelled in the transformative process. At the same time, the plangent force of plain, unbolted words in Shakespeare has also exerted an uncommon fascination for twentieth-century critics, so that the poignancy of Lear's 'Pray you undo this button' and his helpless five nevers 'Never, never, never, never, never' has aroused much admiration in the critical literature. And yet, despite the six billion words already spent on Shakespeare's words, the elusiveness of Shakespeare's genius as a writer continues to plague critical invention, so that at the end of the twentieth century a major critic, Frank Kermode (1999), can announce that he intends in the near future to write a book on Shakespeare's words, especially on their capacity to reveal character in the act of thinking, because, he says, this kind of analysis hasn't been done often enough or well enough.

Lear's nevers do not require the kind of bemused attention that Shakespeare's frequently difficult, obscure, and sometimes invented words require, singly or in combination. At the same time it should be remembered that criticism has been alive to what has been seen as the intentional duplicity of Shakespeare's use of plain words; they do not necessarily convey plain feeling, John Russell Brown argues, for Shakespeare's 'plain, everyday words cover, rather than reveal, the true force of feeling' (1996: 24), though Lear's clearly do not. Obscure words, and their combinations, cover the true force of meaning as well as of feeling in Shakespeare, and critics in the twentieth century have spent much time probing them. Dr Johnson's famous lament that Shakespeare's style was 'in itself ungrammatical, perplexed and obscure' has become in the twentieth century something to celebrate rather than to condemn, though it is in this century's last month that we can read Kermode's Johnsonian piece taking Shakespeare to task for the fact that his 'intellectual power is sometimes used in excess of the occasion . . . where words obscure the meaning' (1999: 7). Kermode instances Helena's 'I have felt so many quirks of joy and grief/That the first face of neither on the start/Can woman me unto't' (*All's Well that Ends Well*, 3.2.49–51) as sufficiently problematic to suggest that Shakespeare was not taking the writing here seriously. And in a play like *Henry VIII* (and elsewhere) there is complexity in excess of value. Kermode cites Shakespeare as his own best critic: 'O, it is excellent / To have a giant's strength, but it is tyrannous / To use it like a giant' (*Measure for Measure*, 2.2.109–11). Dr Johnson and Frank Kermode have their supporters but they tend to come at the beginning of the century rather than at its end, as in the case of A. C. Bradley, for instance, who believed there to be passages in Shakespeare that are 'obscure, inflated, tasteless, or "pestered with metaphors"' (1904: 73).

Shakespeare's twentieth-century critics by and large applaud his using his giant's strength like a giant and pestering his work with metaphors. They relish lines like Macbeth's 'The crow makes wing to th' rooky wood' (3.2.51 – 2) upon which, sparked by the cadenzas on it by William Empson, a disproportionate number of those six billion words has been expended. The passage in which this line appears prompts R. A. Foakes, however, to the despairing conclusion that '[p]ages of commentary would not exhaust the possibilities of interpreting the sense of these lines' (1980: 81).[3]

More representative of this century, perhaps, is Russell Brown's admiration for Shakespeare as a munificent word-spender: 'Words were infinite riches in the mind of Shakespeare: in possession of this treasure he lived like a lord, and was noble, generous, and free' (1996: 29). Even if the munificence comes in the form of incomprehensibility, no matter; the incomprehensible for many critics in this century has its own kind of poetry, is a kind of poetry, as the title of an essay by Stephen Orgel intimates, 'The Poetics of Incomprehensibility' (1991). T. G. Bishop asks: 'Why would a play deliberately, as it seems, cultivate obscurity as an aspect of its texture? What is the dramatic function of this sense of sense as veiled or layered in too much possibility?' (1996: 202). At one time the question could never have been asked, would probably never have even been thought of. For Bishop the cultivation of obscurity has psychoanalytic ramifications. Sense is veiled because characters like people in real life conceal the harsh reality of themselves from themselves (and from others) in a poetry of incomprehensibility.

In a work like *Hamlet*, so James Calderwood argues, the play of language deliberately obscures meaning so that 'the go-between of speech is so compacted by ironies, ambiguities, figurations as to become an impenetrable barrier to communication' (1983: 128). But this in *Hamlet* is a good thing, an artistic accomplishment. In the comedies the bulky materiality of the words sometimes takes over the sense completely (and this too is a good thing). As Susan Snyder observes, language in Shakespeare seems sometimes to have 'escaped human control entirely, . . . the words have taken over the situation and on the strength of their "auditory friendship" are dictating quite unreasonable and unlikely connections' (1979: 50).

If the incomprehensible can be poetic, so too, in twentieth-century criticism, can the defiantly unpoetic. Or, rather, the unpoetic can be successfully dramatic; the unpoetic on the page good drama in the theatre. T. J. B. Spencer observes—wryly I think—that 'it has taken almost until modern times to demonstrate that Shakespeare's bad poetry is just as good in its badness as his good poetry is good in its goodness' (1964: 158). H. W. Fawkner doesn't want to go this far. We should not 'generously translate what is bad in Shakespeare into goodness' but should allow that 'what is "bad" in a writer as complex and remarkable as Shakespeare fails to be bad in any simple way. Badness itself is rich in Shakespeare' (1992: 14).

A case in point—to return to *Macbeth*—may well be Macbeth's raptly bad poetry about his having murdered sleep as well as Duncan (2.2.34–8). Macbeth's stunned series of appositional clichés to 'sleep' is interrupted after five of them by Lady Macbeth's bewildered 'What do you mean?' (2.2.38), an interruption on her part that manages to return Macbeth to the urgent present. Otherwise—such is the effect on us of the speech's structure and the negative force of its clichés—we feel that he might well have gone on hatching these appositional common-places for ever. As literary critics we might therefore be inclined to agree with Lady Macbeth's judgement of her husband's performance: 'You do unbend your noble strength to think / So brain-sickly of things' (2.2.43–4).[4] As critics of the drama we think otherwise.

The notion of the aesthetic success of the brain-sickly gets the support of William Empson when he talks about the pantomimic tradition that enabled Shakespeare to think that 'gods in plays ought to talk in bad rhymes, like the fairy queen in the panto' (1987: 236). And in the course of his disquisition on *honest* in *Othello* Empson argues that one of the passages in which the word occurs 'is a bad piece of writing unless you are keyed up for the shift of the word' (1951: 222).

Words are Very Rascals

It's not surprising in this climate that Dr Johnson's puritanical view of the pun as Shakespeare's fatal Cleopatra should now be thought to be misguided. The homely pun in the hands of the modernists and others has taken on the force of revelation. Martin Green, for one, tells us that his book on the Sonnets was written in the firm belief that the pun 'can be a key to actual truth' (1974: 1). Michel Grivelet, for another, is convinced that punning 'irradiates meanings' (1963: 73), that when it descends into the nonsense of the comedies, when Feste, for instance, does impeticos Sir Andrew's gratility in *Twelfth Night*, its nonsense 'makes for better sense; it is a remedy, not a poison' (72).

On the other hand, the pun and its offshoots in the tragedies, according to Grivelet, contribute to our sense of the tragic world's vast confusions in the way they mingle (and mangle) meanings to help 'place darkness at the heart of bright vision' (73). For Grivelet a 'verbal power is released in the tragedies which has something of the evil growth in the "unweeded garden"' (72). James Calderwood follows the same line as Grivelet in adopting the metaphor of incest from *Hamlet* for its words' unnatural activity and their relation to the themes of the play: 'Between incestuous sheets Hamlet discovers the unnatural couplings of Claudius' oxymorons and the perverse unions of funeral and marriage, uncle and father, aunt and mother, and nephew and son. There too, it seems, are engendered his own incestuous abuses of words: his puns, riddles, equivocations' (1983: 71).

Critics like Calderwood, Green, and Grivelet see puns and equivocations everywhere in Shakespeare in a variety of forms: homophonic, semantic, orthographic. In our Freudian age the pun does not have to be consciously intended, though, of course, a lot of them are, especially those in the mouths of the professional corrupters of words who inhabit the comedies. In the tragedies, however, in particular, characters are often not aware that their puns are, in M. M. Mahood's words, 'involuntary and work[ing] below the level of consciousness' (1957: 38). Sometimes, Shakespeare himself is not aware of them, or so some critics claim; he like his characters is an unintentional punster, his words working like theirs as an outlet for his own repressed impulses. As is frequently the case in twentieth-century criticism of Shakespeare, the insights gained from this new understanding of the ways of words are matched by new absurdities and exaggerations in interpretation. M. M. Mahood warns us against over-reading: 'A generation that relishes *Finnegans Wake* is more in danger of reading non-existent quibbles into Shakespeare's work than of missing his subtlest play of meaning' (1957: 11). It is a warning we should bear in mind when reading her own well-known book, *Shakespeare's Wordplay* (1957).[5]

Particularly enticing for some twentieth-century wordsmiths are Shakespeare's forays into the greasily anatomical, the obscene, and the scatological. Now that the obscene pun is no longer off-limits to the critical literature, it threatens hegemony. Twentieth-century criticism, buoyed by its new-found freedom from moral censorship, from the bowdlerization involved in Dr Bowdler's nineteenth-century edition of Shakespeare for comfortable family reading, rushes in where prudes had feared to tread, taking great pleasure in muddying what had been thought to be the clear, pure waters of the Castalian spring. Taking Shakespeare's language down a peg or two often involves doing the same for its speakers of course, and Shakespeare's heroines, especially in the tragedies, have been the beneficiaries of this process, their covert unruly language hinting at an independent spirit otherwise severely constrained. (In the comedies the women are usually as verbally aggressive as the men, if not more so.)

Eric Partridge's 1947 dictionary of Shakespeare's off-colour terminology, *Shakespeare's Bawdy* (1968), limited in its first edition (for some reason) to a thousand copies, has become enormously popular, reprinted, revised, and enlarged several times since its original parsimonious printing. I suppose 1947 is a little early for the kind of matter-of-fact recording of Shakespeare's obscene wordplay with which we are now familiar, but, whatever the reason, Partridge's introductory essay through all the editions of his book strikes me as being an uneasy document, unnecessarily tender of Shakespeare's reputation and defensive at times about the very material the book is supposed to be being candid about. And so Partridge is at pains, on the one hand, to tell us that Shakespeare may have had a dirty mind, 'yet he certainly had not a filthy mind' (9), that it is ludicrous to think of him as a homosexual, and that though Shakespeare describes the dirt (without wallowing in it) he also praises 'that to which he aspired: the true, the beautiful, and the good' (6) (in case we hadn't noticed). Shakespeare, Partridge says, 'is never filthy: he is broad, ribald, healthily coarse, unsqueamishly natural, and unaffectedly humorous' (11). On the other hand, despite the candour of the words in the dictionary proper, in his introduction Partridge declines to mention what seems still to be the unmentionable in polite introductions, referring evasively to cunnilingus (I think) 'as being more insanitary than amorous' (25), and suggesting that Shakespeare, practising an artifice 'that I cannot becomingly mention here' (25), could have taught Ovid something.

Partridge acknowledges in a footnote that it is more than likely that he has—unbecomingly—missed some of 'Shakespeare's witty scabrosities' (9). But he would undoubtedly have been amazed at just how many he had overlooked were he to consult a more recent count of them. Frankie Rubinstein's 1984 update—with an engorged second edition in 1989—of Partridge's own frequently updated dictionary identifies (perhaps misidentifies would be nearer the mark in many cases) 'the hundreds upon hundreds of still unnoted [sexual] puns' (p. ix) in Shakespeare. Rubinstein has the grace to warn us that '[s]ome of these puns may seem outrageous', but Shakespeare's wit, like his genius—and Rubinstein's imagination—'is unbridled' (p. ix). Not surprisingly, she disagrees with Partridge in his disinclination to grant Shakespeare an interest in scatology, homosexuality, or lesbianism, and she may well be right here. But what seems to me unfortunate about her determination to squeeze every unlikely sexual connotation out of the hundreds of examples she offers is the way that such a single-minded insistence on the scabrous so frequently up-ends the poise and balance of the dramatic situation in which the alleged obscene word-play occurs.

One example of the dozens of instances I could adduce of Rubinstein's tin ear comes from her extended treatment in her Introduction of the lines from the Musician's song in *Cymbeline*: 'With everything that pretty is, my lady sweet, arise, /Arise, arise!' (2.3.24–5). Rubinstein pounces on 'arise' as bringing 'to mind a phallic erection' (p. xiv), especially in the light of Cloten's introduction to the song in which he talks of the Musician's ability to penetrate Innogen with his fingering. But it is precisely on the contrast between the aubade's delicacy and Cloten's lubricity that the scene's balance rests. 'Arise' should not suggest to us (though I suppose it might to Cloten) anything other than the beauty and innocence of the sun's and Innogen's awakening at the beginning of the day. To read the song as Cloten might have done is to miss the whole point of it.

It's only fitting perhaps in these circumstances that Rubinstein should open her Introduction with an epigraph from T. S. Eliot: 'About anyone so great as Shakespeare it is probable that we can never be right; and if we can never be right, it is better that we should from time to time change our way of being wrong' (p. ix). More pertinent warnings about the reading of sexual puns in Shakespeare come from Hilda Hulme and E. A. M. Colman. The former writes:

> The more skilfully the improper sense is suggested, the less likely it is we can prove that such a sense is present. The art of the speaker and of the dramatist will be shown ... by concealment, in the exactness with which the innocent and less innocent meanings can counterchange, the preciseness with which one sense fits the space taken by the other. (1962: 118)

Colman sums up the moral of his own level-headed investigation into the dramatic significance of Shakespeare's bawdy and it could serve as a more general one for all devotees of Shakespeare's wordplay: 'One result of this whole inquiry into indecency has been my own growing conviction that the golden rule is to be slow in *assuming* ribald significance anywhere in Shakespeare—above all when reading or directing the plays in the sex-conscious and irony-loving atmosphere of the later twentieth century' (1974: 21). Words of caution that have fallen largely on deaf ears.[6]

As I mentioned at the beginning of this book, twentieth-century criticism of Shakespeare is particularly alive to the indeterminateness of Shakespeare's meanings in the plays as well as in the poems. It's not just a question of the inevitability of indeterminateness because of the aporias, ambiguities, slippages, cracks, and fissures of language in its 'natural' state but a recognition that Shakespeare in particular (and other seventeenth-century writers too) relished what might be called the poetics of evasion. 'Surely', James Shapiro writes, 'in the hands of a talented dramatist, the less easily definable the social and psychological currents a play explores, the greater its potential to haunt and disturb' (1996: 121).

And haunting and disturbing are the manifest functions of the most talented of all dramatists. William Empson talks about Shakespeare's deliberate withholding of a clear intention—is this the eighth kind of ambiguity?—as in the case of Falstaff and the killing of Hotspur: 'Shakespeare is deliberately *not* telling us the answer, so an ingenious argument which forces an answer out of the text only misrepresents his intention' (1987: 45). Lachlan Mackinnon reveres Shakespeare's bountiful duplicitousness: 'This doubleness [in *The Winter's Tale*] can be described as duplicitous because it is all a result of artistic method. Shakespeare clearly set out to complicate and divide our responses, and his work is unusually hospitable to interpretation' (1988: 157). Shakespeare's doubleness induces a corresponding one in us: 'His purpose is to come down on neither side, but to divide us between aesthetic pleasure and doubt, to give us the mingled pleasure and pain which are the hallmark of the sublime' (158). More often than not Shakespeare doesn't seem to be deliberately not telling us the answer (such an assertion is obviously very difficult to prove in any case) so much as using words in such a way that grammar and word order conspire to withhold a clear intention, perhaps unbeknownst to the writer. There is, after all, a general tendency for the rich language of literature to refuse directly to answer the question, 'What is a poem's meaning?' The impulse of criticism, Stanley Fish argues, is 'to probe ever deeper the incorrigible duplicity of assertion even as it presents itself as univocal and single' (1995: 34).

One such incorrigible duplicity of assertion in Shakespeare, among scores of them, has intrigued modern criticism. When Lady Macbeth invokes the spirits that tend on mortal thoughts to 'take my milk for gall...' (*Macbeth*, 1.5.47), Janet Adelman, among others, suggests that the usual meaning 'exchange my milk for gall' does not preclude the more startling suggestion that 'for' here means 'as', so that her offspring would 'nurse from her breast and find in her milk their sustaining poison' (1996: 112). Adelman finds this equivocation enormously portentous: 'In these lines Lady Macbeth focuses the culture's fear of maternal nursery' (112). The milk nurtures the evil spirits: 'Lady Macbeth and the witches fuse at this moment, and they fuse through the image of perverse nursery' (112).

We could multiply this instance many times over in Shakespeare where a single preposition—in this case 'for'—could lead us in two different directions depending on our different but entirely legitimate readings of it. The simplest of words in the most straightforward-seeming of phrases in Shakespeare can open up contrasting interpretations, though the one need not necessarily cancel out the other (or others). In twentieth-century criticism of Shakespeare, despite the abuse noted above, the flowering of multiple meanings is a notable development, a democratizing of semantics that parallels the more general democratizing tendencies of our times.

A perfect case in point where a simple phrase suggests two contrasting but not mutually exclusive interpretations is the subtitle to *Twelfth Night. What You Will*, Shakespeare's only subtitle incidentally, is generally taken to mean, in the festive spirit of the main title, 'Whatever You Like', or 'As You Like It' perhaps. But the other meaning of *will* as voluntary effort, willed assertion, anticipates *Twelfth Night*'s need for a stranger from the sea, Viola, with her determination and sense of urgency, her agency in contrast to the passive languor of her employer, Orsino, to bring about the happy resolution where all the Jacks get their appropriate Jills. Without her Orsino would still be languishing on beds of flowers, Olivia immured still in her house of mourning. *What You Will* is both a throwaway phrase and one that tells us that comedy is not simply a matter of giving yourself over to a beneficent destiny, though it is that too.[7]

There seems then to have been a fiercely renewed attention paid to Shakespeare's words in the twentieth century. To all of them, as Mahood insists, to 'the immediately affective power of the words spoken and of the stage action that the words imply. *All* the words ... as spoken by *all* the characters' (1993: 134). And this determination to chase after and pin down—verbs suggestive of the necessary endurance and mental fortitude that Jorgensen described as hopeful doggedness—the affective and implicatory power of words might run counter to the notion that their author is dead or doesn't exist. The reasons for this new direction of interest on the part of modern critics, why formalist criticism, as Viswanathan claims, should be '*the* trend of twentieth-century Shakespeare criticism' (1980: 2), are not difficult to understand. Modernism itself was intensely formalist. Between the world wars the difficult, densely metaphoric poetry of the

Metaphysicals was rediscovered and celebrated; the word-drunk poetry of Gerard Manley Hopkins was first published in 1918 and by 1930 had become popular; Imagism in poetry, with its emphasis, as its name implies, on the single striking image, flourished between 1912 and 1917.

By 1945 the product of modernism, the New Criticism (as it came to be known when it was no longer new)—*the* criticism that responded to the excesses, ambiguities, and paradoxes of literature's words—had shouldered aside its rivals from history and traditional literary scholarship as a method of reading. We live still in the wake of its intense commitment to the enclosure movement it practised on poetry in particular, where considerations outside the boundaries of the works themselves were thought to be a distracting irrelevance, where the writer's intentions and the reader's emotional responses were both deemed fallacious in the pursuit of true understanding. The practice of New Criticism relies on native wit and aesthetic judgement and, as such, in the disenchanted words of Mark Krupnick, offers 'academic literary studies examples in the artful dodging of contemporary history' (1986: 8).[8]

If it is important to concern oneself with *all* the words in Shakespeare's plays, it is vital to do so when dealing with them in his non-dramatic poetry. Twentieth-century criticism, the New Criticism in particular, has been at its most inventive in its readings of lyric poetry, Shakespeare's above all. Helen Vendler observes that in lyric poetry the actors are the words, so that 'the introduction of a new linguistic strategy is ... as interruptive and interesting as the entrance of a new character in a play' (1997: 3). In her opinion an emphasis on theme in the poetry by those theme-hunting critics in the twentieth century 'loses almost all of [the words'] aesthetic richness' (7). To talk of the content of a Shakespeare poem, of any poem by any good poet, is to miss the point: 'A set of remarks on a poem which would be equally true of a prose paraphrase of that poem is not, by my standards, interpretation at all' (40). Grammar, syntax, the shapes and sounds of words, their obtrusive materiality, are just as important for an appropriately sophisticated reading of the poetry they transmit as the words' semantic richness, their polysemy. In Helen Vendler's view more important perhaps—and despite the enormous amount of formalist analysis in the twentieth century, at the end of it she, like Frank Kermode, believes that the criticism of this century has not been as diligent as it should have been in the exploration of Shakespeare's words.[9]

Taffeta Phrases, Silken Terms Precise

The New Criticism supplies, in R. B. Heilman's words, an account 'of the ways in which certain words and combinations of words affect the reader' (1963: 6). It was—and is—particularly sensitive to the workings of imagery. Its hegemony in Shakespeare criticism until, say, the 1960s can in fact be traced to the ground-breaking studies in Shakespeare's imagery around 1930 by Caroline Spurgeon as well as the 1933 essay by L. C. Knights with its provocatively anti-Bradley title, 'How Many Children Had Lady Macbeth?'

The first part of Knights's essay more or less states the credo of the New Criticism in expressing his belief that 'the total response to a Shakespeare play can only be obtained by an exact and sensitive study of the quality of the verse, of the rhythm and imagery, of the controlled associations of the words and their emotional and intellectual force, in short by an exact and sensitive study of Shakespeare's handling of language' (1963*a*: 10). It's Shakespeare's use of language that enables us 'to obtain a total complex emotional response' (6).

The second part of Knights's essay—an 'essay in elucidation' (18) of *Macbeth*—switches the emphasis from the means to the end to that of the end itself, from the use of language in the play to its outcome as 'a statement of evil' (18), a statement not of a philosophy but of 'ordered emotion' (29). Knights's exfoliation of this statement of evil in *Macbeth* consists in discovering a number of 'themes' in the play: (i) the reversal of values; (ii) unnatural disorder; (iii) deceitful appearance and consequent doubt, uncertainty, and confusion. The move from language to theme, from an intense concern for the specificity of language in its various verbal units to what is essentially a reduction and abstraction of that language into such a popular 'theme' as, say, (iii) above, has been both highly exploited by critics (pandemically one might say) and attacked by a smaller number of them for its frequent crudeness, tendentious argument, and ignoring of contradictory evidence.[10]

The New Criticism's obsession with the performance of language has been stimulated by and has relied upon Caroline Spurgeon's cataloguing of Shakespeare's imagery. In 1930 she gave a lecture to the Shakespeare Association called 'Leading Motives in the Imagery of Shakespeare's Tragedies', and she followed this in 1931 with her British Academy lecture on iterative imagery in Shakespeare: 'that is the repetition of an idea or picture in the images used in any one play' (1964: 171). This repetition, 'born of the emotions of the theme' (171), acts as an 'undersong' in the plays and is the touchstone of Shakespeare's work. It is peculiarly Shakespearean.

Spurgeon was by no means alone in the 1930s in responding to Shakespeare's use of imagery as the great strength of the poetry in the plays. In 1930, a year before her lecture to the Shakespeare Association, F. C. Kolbe published *Shakespeare's Way: A Psychological Study* which anticipated the strains of Spurgeon's undersong: throughout each play, he writes, 'at least one set of words or ideas [are] in harmony with the plot. It is like the effect of the dominant note in a melody' (87). And in 1935 M. C. Bradbrook signalled the general shift away from Bradley and his successors: 'The essential structure of Elizabethan drama lies not in the narrative or the characters but in the words. The greatest poets are also the greatest dramatists' (1935: 5). In the same year Spurgeon produced her enormously influential full-length work, *Shakespeare's Imagery and What It Tells Us.*

Since the 1930s Caroline Spurgeon's work has been used and denigrated by later commentators on Shakespeare in about equal proportions, suffering, that is, the fate of many of Shakespeare's major critics in the twentieth century. On behalf of the denigrators, Arthur Eastman writes: 'The simplicities and crudities are clear enough to a modern eye: the card indexing, the statistical egalitarianism, the rigid classifications, the cataloguing by figure to the exclusion of idea, the failure to explore the dynamics of images' (1968: 281–2). These adversarial critics argue that Spurgeon makes unwarranted biographical inferences, is inconsistent in applying her statistics, and unaware of the proverbial and the commonplace in Shakespeare's imagery, is unresponsive to the imaginative force of ordinary words, and unable to see the difference between the unconscious and conscious in his use of figuration. And yet, despite the litany of complaints about her shortcomings, Spurgeon focused attention on an aspect of Shakespeare's creativity that continues to inspire a sophisticated response. Perhaps she deserves something a little more affirmative than Kenneth Muir's damning with faint praise: 'It is difficult to believe that the sickness imagery in *Hamlet*, the cooking imagery in *Troilus and Cressida*, and the clothing imagery in *Macbeth* are quite without significance, even if we disagree with Miss Spurgeon's interpretation of them' (1965: 53).

In 1938 Derek Traversi published his *Approach to Shakespeare*, the first version of a book that, revised and expanded, continues to be widely read, particularly by students. In 1950 the second edition doubled the original book's number of words and by 1969, the year of its third revised and expanded edition, the 151 pages of the 1938 book had mushroomed to an amount that could not be contained in a single volume.[11] What is the aim of the modern critic of Shakespeare, Traversi asked in the 1938 volume. His answer in that book and in its variations over the years and in his other works on Shakespeare continued to be twofold: 'His aim is, as far as possible, to isolate and define the experience which sought expression in the plays, and which makes them individual and valuable. It seems obvious that this experience will find its most immediate expression in the language and verse of the plays' (13). On the one hand is the written word—'the written word [is] our unit' (1938: 15); on the other is what that unit leads us to, Shakespeare's 'experience' or, at other times, his 'emotions'.

Traversi traces this interanimation throughout Shakespeare's career:

The development of Shakespeare's versification is revealed in a growing flexibility of response to the increasingly complex needs of the individual word. The poet's continual effort to master his experience, to project it fully into his plays, is most easily traced in this continual adaptation of verse structure to the growing pressure of his emotions. (14)

Traversi's emphasis on the word as the gateway to the inner Shakespeare, to the 'fullness of [his] particular experience' (30), to the 'organization of experience' (88)—phrases like these are everywhere in his work—leads him to make the same kind of spurious biographical speculations that mar the work of critics like Caroline Spurgeon (and A. C. Bradley). And so—echoing T. S. Eliot—he writes: 'Hamlet's speculations on action proceed from a flaw in Shakespeare's personal experience which he was unable to project into a dramatic sequence adequately corresponding to it' (58).

Exploring the dynamics of images in ways neglected by Caroline Spurgeon (and Derek Traversi), for whom in Robert Heilman's

1. William Blake's watercolour of *Pity* (*c*.1795).

assessment imagery was 'merely... a kind of soft music in the background' (1963: 8), marks the criticism of later investigations of Shakespeare's imagery in this century. Under the influence especially of the New Critical concern for the organic unity of the literary artefact, critics have focused on the binding properties of Shakespeare's use of recurrent images in his plays.

A famous if controversial essay in a famous (if controversial) book of them by Cleanth Brooks, 'The Naked Babe and the Cloak of Manliness' in *The Well-Wrought Urn: Studies in the Structure of Poetry* (1947), traces the dynamics of two images in *Macbeth*, that of the saintly infant and ill-fitting clothes, as they, dolphin-like, appear and reappear above the element they live in. In a moment of poetic epiphany, Macbeth compares the pity that Duncan's murder will arouse in the Scottish kingdom to 'a naked new-born babe, / Striding the blast, or heaven's cherubin, horsed / Upon the sightless couriers of the air...' (1.7.21–3), and in the next act describes the daggers of the murderers as '[u]nmannerly breeched with gore' (2.3.115–16). Brooks then pursues the different re-manifestations of these powerful, strange images in the rest of the play in his attempt to read *Macbeth* as though it were a poem from the school of Donne. Both passages, he says, especially the second, are 'about as strained as Donne is at his most extreme pitch', but each 'contains a central symbol of the play' (31). In the case of those indecorously dressed daggers, '[t]hey are not honest daggers, honorably naked in readiness to guard the king, or, "mannerly" clothed in their own sheaths' (38) but unmannerly drenched in the blood of the man they should be protecting; in the case of the naked babe, it 'signifies the future which Macbeth would control and cannot control' (45), so that pity is like the helpless human babe and also like the angel that rides the winds: 'it is strong because of its very weakness' (48). Brooks concludes his imaginative depiction of Shakespeare's poetic imagination at work with an awed assessment of it that the reader may feel has almost as much pertinence for his own essay as it has for *Macbeth*: '... with a flexibility which must amaze the reader, the image of the garment and the image of the babe are so used as to encompass an astonishingly large area of the total situation' (49).

For a while in the 1940s especially there was excited talk of the usefulness of studying images that came in clusters, which might give evidence by their association of Shakespeare's psychology or even of his authorship of suspect passages. E. A. Armstrong pursued this line of enquiry for these reasons and also to identify what he called 'submerged themes' (1946: 1). Like Caroline Spurgeon before him, he was particularly interested, as the title of his book *Shakespeare's Imagination* intimates, in the way particular concatenations of images give us an insight into the working of Shakespeare's mind, and perhaps, seeing as we are all human, into the working of our own minds. His approach, in response maybe to the exigencies of his own times, clearly has a therapeutic intention. Shakespeare's plays, Armstrong believed, 'have captivated audiences throughout the centuries for many reasons, but fundamentally because they enable people to understand themselves better and to interpret life as it has to be lived more adequately' (2). In

1946 anything that might help us live life more adequately in trouble-some times would have to be welcomed.

Later exponents of the pursuit of clustered imagery are much more interested in the light an investigation of them might throw on the plays themselves, their 'submerged themes' especially. Hence Meredith Skura in the 1990s investigates clusters of images and the notion of flattery. She considers the cluster *dogs, licking, candy, melting* (first noticed by Caroline Spurgeon). This cluster widens out to embrace other ones and all of them are 'informed by a player's sense of being surrounded by a fawning audience who might at any moment turn on him—an audience conceived both as intimately maternal and danger-ously fickle' (1993: 167). What we're dealing with here is a hugely important topic for Shakespeare, flattery, in both the political and private worlds: 'The political language of flattery is also the private language of the nursery' (178).

Despite the dramatic quality of Donne's verse, so much of it begging to be read aloud, Donne did not of course ever write for the public (or private) stage, although his magnificent sermons filled St Paul's and were intrinsically a theatrical event. Criticism dealing with Shake-speare's imagery after the 1940s is much more cognizant of the gulf separating Shakespeare from Donne in ways unattended to by Cleanth Brooks; on the one hand there is the professional dramatist writing for the public stage, on the other a poet and preacher whose poetry, however dramatic, was intended for the solitary reader. In other words, if Shakespeare's plays continue to be read as poetry in the later twentieth century, they are read as plays in poetry rather than as poetry *tout court*. It is the dramatic as well as the poetic significance of Shakespeare's imagery that critics now examine.

Brian Vickers neatly encapsulates the essential evolution : 'Shake-speare's plays are not "dramatic poems" but "poetic dramas", and although that seems a small re-adjustment much is involved in it' (1968: 3). S. L. Bethell sounded an early note of caution, with perhaps the naked babe in mind: 'unless a method is followed which brings imagery into due subordination to other aspects of dramatic expres-sion, it can lead only to the construction of individual fantasies' (1952: 62).[12] We need to discriminate between 'those images which have no significance outside their immediate grammatical and rhetorical func-tion in the sentences in which they occur, and those which have a further significance either in relation to character or theme' (65). And in the same year Raymond Williams broadened the argument in a typically sensible manner: 'to consider plays simply as literature, without reference to their function on the stage, is part of the same fallacy as to say that plays need not be literature at all. No separation of drama and literature is reasonable' (1952: 18).

W. H. Clemen studied Shakespeare's images very much in the context of their plays, arguing, as perhaps Brooks would have done, that the connecting function of their images is much more important to the drama than to the novel or the epic poem: '... there exists a subterranean continuation of the same idea ... which may then produce a sequence of imagery long after the original image has been forgotten' (1951: 13). He calls this a symbolical interpretation of Shakespeare's imagery. But he stresses the need to take other things into account, 'to show the interdependence of style, diction, imagery, plot, technique of characterisation and all the other constituent elements of drama' (231). As M. Weitz maintains, Clemen reverses Spurgeon's thesis: '*Hamlet* (or any other Shakespearean drama) should not be interpreted in terms of its imagery; the imagery should be interpreted in relation to the whole play' (1964: 137).

The following year an influential article by R. A. Foakes amounted to a manifesto of the new movement: 'For the study of drama a new definition of imagery, one derived from drama, is needed' (1952: 85). Thinking of imagery in exclusively poetic terms, Foakes argues, tends to miss the way it is used dramatically for differentiation of character or in relation to plot, 'to situation, for special functions, to relieve tension, to close a scene, to provide information, to create a setting, or to show powerful emotion on the part of the character...' (89). There is in fact a wealth of different kinds of dramatic imagery Brian Vickers (1968) wants us to respond to, and he lists some of the major ones: thematic; situational; stage (visual effects in terms of grouping or movement); atmospheric; subjective; objective (where a character is consistently described by other people in the same terms);[13] and forensic (that is manipulative).

In his 1961 study of the Roman plays Maurice Charney, following Foakes's example, deals with them as poetry of the theatre. He makes the point that the paucity of imagery in *Julius Caesar* doesn't make it a lesser play than the image-ridden *Antony and Cleopatra*, just a more

.oman one. He also asks us to consider the importance of non-verbal imagery in these plays (the asp, for instance, in *Antony and Cleopatra*). Books dwelling on the linguistic image still continue to appear— witness Ralph Berry's which asks us to think of his selected plays from Shakespeare in terms of the metaphoric idea that organizes each one: 'One holds the play up to the light, and views it via that single angle of incidence' (1978: 1). Single angles of incidence may seem too restrictive amid such a plethora of metaphorical vantage-points.

Well into the 1970s and 1980s critics continued to worry about the pursuit of the unmoored image abstracted from the play itself and also from any connection with the historical circumstances of its production. It's this abstraction and autonomy that worries Robert Weimann, for example, who argues that we should make a connection between this tendency to grant such an authority to metaphor and the practice of modern poetry. The outcome of this approach, Weimann concludes, is to see metaphor as some kind of autonomous entity: 'For, no matter how subtly and elaborately these critics have read, they have not considered the theatrical functions of dramatic speech and the way it is correlated to non-verbal means of expression' (1974: 158). The fact of the matter is that we cannot regard metaphor as existing outside of time and space (or the theatre), 'a notion that can best be refuted by studying the referential and expressive functions of metaphor more closely' (164). And he then analyses the idea of the 'sea-walled garden' in *Richard II* in terms of its historical contingency: 'there is behind it the idea of a modern nation as a cultivated, ordered, and productive unit, an idea which conceives of the island boundaries as a protective as well as a unifying moment in a way which is really unthinkable in the fourteenth or early fifteenth centuries' (1974: 164).

The Swelling Scene

What is the structural angle of incidence most appropriate for the study of Shakespeare's plays? This is the question that in various guises dogs twentieth-century formalist criticism of Shakespeare. Is the essential formal unit a collocation of words, as we saw in the previous sections, or is it something more representatively dramatic, intrinsically theatrical, the scene, the act, the play as a whole? Of course all these are made up of words anyway but they are words shaped by the exigencies of the drama rather than simply by linguistic criteria. Undoubtedly the dominating formal unit as far as twentieth-century Shakespeare criticism is concerned is the play itself, in its entirety, but there have been other investigations throughout the century of the play's various bits and pieces seen to some degree as detachable units available for analysis (as were the words themselves).[14] Some of these units are not exclusively, predominantly, or inherently dramatic as we saw in the case of Shakespeare's imagery, and the same can be said for many of the units analysed in rhetorical and metrical studies.

The study of Shakespeare's use of rhyme in his plays, however, is almost always seen in twentieth-century criticism in terms of its dramatic function, partly because there's not enough of it to stand on its own and partly because of the old-fashioned, homespun quality of its language.[15] (This is obviously not the case with Shakespeare's non-dramatic poetry.) In fact it's difficult to think of 'rhyme' in the plays untethered from its hyphenated moorings, as in Frederic Ness's catalogue (1969) of them: speech-end rhyme; speech-pause rhyme; speech-beginning rhyme; speech-link rhyme; end-of-scene rhyme; end-of-act rhyme; and exit-and-cue rhyme.

A popular topic in twentieth-century criticism addresses rhyme's gradual disappearance over the course of Shakespeare's career. Some critics have suggested that Shakespeare simply came to feel the inherent impropriety of rhyme in drama; others that his increased mastery of blank verse rendered it nugatory. Yet other critics see in its disappearance the influence of Shakespeare's contemporary dramatists or even that of the new king who was known to dislike rhyme. What rhyme there is in Shakespeare's late career has sometimes been assigned to other (inferior) writers or blamed on floating remnants of dilapidated sources or, as a last resort, as fodder for the general. The most likely reason for Shakespeare's cutting back on the use of rhyme, however, was his growth as a writer, leading him to reserve rhyme for particular effects as other ways of writing, more sophisticated ones, took precedence.

A work such as Sister Miriam Joseph's *Shakespeare's Use of the Arts of Language* (1947) examines Shakespeare's plays in terms of their use of standard rhetorical structures which she sees as their basic building blocks. Although such an approach fell by the wayside in the latter part of the century it has never gone out of favour entirely. After all, as Brian Vickers observes in his useful book on Shakespeare's prose, the 'rhetorical' structure is 'the arrangement of prose into the patterns taught and practised by traditional rhetoric, patterns of symmetry and balance, a tradition with distinguished antecedents' (1968: 35).

Such a structural arrangement is not of course limited to prose and can be found 'used with fertile invention throughout Shakespeare's plays, endlessly adapted to character, situation and mood' (36). From this rhetorical tradition Shakespeare inherited a philosophy of language and a doctrine of decorum which was as much moral as rhetorical. It was a tradition that embraced the principles of copiousness and free invention, and its figures, as Marion Trousdale informs us, 'grow out of an understanding of language that is based primarily on sound' (1982: 56). Copiousness is controlled by affinity and opposition: there would be the 'appropriate commonplaces and then the fables, apologues, exempla, strange occurrences, *sententiae*, witty or unusual expressions, adages, metaphors, or parables gleaned from reading' (58). In employing all of these and more Shakespeare does not, however, 'fall into a kind of futile and amorphous loquacity' (59). But we need the Elizabethan poetic to know Elizabethan dramatic art, based, as it was, on the rhetorical ideal of oral persuasion. As Trousdale notes in some astute commentary on *Othello*, 'Iago persuades Othello as Shakespeare persuades us' (167). Othello's defect is 'to lack "those soft parts that chamberers have"... [and thus] to lack their defenses' (168).

Despite the Herculean labours of T. W. Baldwin (1947), no one now takes very seriously the notion that the most important structural unit in Shakespeare's plays is the act. We have to bear in mind in fact that dividing the plays into acts and scenes was the idea of later editors, beginning of course with the 1623 Folio. Apart from the 1622 quarto edition of *Othello* none of the quartos of Shakespeare's plays is divided into acts or scenes, and it is arguable that the division of all of Shakespeare's plays into five acts actually obscures the structural lines of the plays, or of some of them anyway. If the act then has been neglected in twentieth-century formalist criticism of Shakespeare, this is not so much the case for another promising candidate for the basic structural unit of the plays, the scene (the unit of action before and after which the stage is cleared), though even here some critics find scenic division an unwieldy affair obscuring oftentimes some other more fluid notion of the play's architecture. Recently there has been an interest expressed in the idea that Shakespeare composed his plays in a structural unit more pliable than either the scene or the act, namely the sequence. A book by the Halletts, Charles and Elaine, argues that there's often a difference between 'Shakespeare's units of place and time [and] his units of action' (1991: 2). There may indeed be more than one unit of action or sequence in a single scene and the book goes on to explore this phenomenon showing us how these sequences form a more plausible structural unit than anything larger than them. Things get a little cloudy when critics use sequence and scene interchangeably as A. R. Braunmuller does when, following Schücking, he asks us to consider the dominance of the scene as a structural unit, arguing that the English Renaissance dramatists composed in scenic units, 'in short stretches of sequential actions and speech' (1990: 68), with little thought beyond the effect of the immediate 'sequence'.

For many critics the scene is unquestionably the primary dramatic unit. Emrys Jones, for example, argues that Shakespeare is 'a poet of dramatic scenes, an artist in scenic form' (1971: 4). Shakespeare composes in units of a powerful simplicity, unpredictability, and versatility that exhibit much 'formal energy' and 'powers of enactment' (1971: 18). (Shakespeare's scenes are certainly unpredictable in length—*A Midsummer Night's Dream* has nine, *Antony and Cleopatra* thirty-six.) Shakespeare's scenes, Jones adds, are severely economical, purposefully shaped, and they maintain an audience-pleasing rhythm and tempo. Mark Rose concurs and adds that each scene is 'a single speaking picture' (1972: 26), its internal proportions similar to the play as a whole.

Much interesting work in the century has been done on the interrelationship of scenes within a given play. Often, Mark Rose observes, a scene will comment on the one preceding it, '[e]ven as image echoes image in the poetic structure of a play, so scene often echoes scene' (1972: 68). Graham Bradshaw calls this phenomenon Shakespeare's 'dramatic "rhyming"' (1993: 63) and suggests that it promotes an interesting intractability, 'richly and recalcitrantly contrapuntal' (1993: 110). If we fail to respond to the rich recalcitrance of this technique we do an injustice to the play as a whole. And so, to take one of Bradshaw's examples, Shakespeare's dramatic rhyming, where-by the experience of one scene problematizes and enriches that of another, makes the polemically anti-Prospero readings in *The Tempest* as inadequate as the polemically pro-Caliban readings. 'Is the problem', Bradshaw asks rhetorically and with some hauteur, 'that Shakespeare is so alarmingly simple, or [is it] that all these critics simplify what Shakespeare has made problematic?' (108). Making things problematic often depends upon a parodic relationship between the scenes. More complex than travesty or burlesque, the parodic scene, according to Joan Hartwig, 'asks us to see the "serious" action replayed in reduced terms: it also asks us to rethink both actions in light of each other's values' (1983: 6).

The Play's the Thing

The interplay between scenes, their mutual animation—parodic or not—suggests that the whole may be greater than the sum of its parts and this truism can be said to lie behind what is easily the most popular of all the candidates in this century for the essential structural unit of Shakespearean drama, namely the play itself in its entirety. (Though what that entirety precisely consists of has sparked some entertaining discussion.) An early piece pointing the way to much twentieth-century practice can be encountered in R. G. Moulton in his defence of the Shakespeare play as uncontaminated by outside forces:

In literature and art the term 'law' applies only in the scientific sense; the laws of the Shakespearean Drama are not laws imposed by some external authority upon Shakespeare, but laws of dramatic practice derived from the analysis of his actual works. Laws of literature, in the sense of external obligations limiting an author, there are none: if he were voluntarily to bind himself by such external laws, he would be so far curtailing art; it is hardly a paradox to say the art is legitimate only when it does not obey laws. (1966: 33–4).

What we have in essence here is the notion of the self-sustaining work of art; if we want to understand what is going on in a Shakespeare play we merely have to obey the laws of its creator, laws created presumably only by him, though Moulton's phrase 'laws of dramatic practice' suggests the possibility that they may come—as many of them obviously do—from a tradition of theatrical practice and dramatic convention external to and antedating the individual playwright.

Moulton's concern to stress the uniqueness of Shakespeare as an artist, to present him as *sui generis*, anticipates in its own way the twentieth-century obsession with the play as a poem obeying the laws of its own being, its parts all contributing to an overall purpose, a singleness of design. In the new terminology the play replaces Shakespeare as the supreme legislator. The modernists, Eliot, Yeats, Pound, read the plays in the way they read and wrote poems, and formalism, in Chris Baldick's words, became 'the theory of which the modernist movements provide the practice' (1996: 11). Renaissance plays, Shakespeare's in particular, came to be seen in terms of music and rhythm, the logic of the imagination, imagery, thematic patterns, and a realization of moral values in terms of poetic structure, metaphor, symbol, myth, and ritual.

In the 1930s the Shakespeare critic who most uncompromisingly rejected everything that Bradley stood for (despite his own belief to the contrary) and embraced with religious fervour the doctrine of the play as poem was G. Wilson Knight who, in book after poetic book, tries to take us as close as possible to 'that burning core of mental or spiritual reality from which each play derives its nature and meaning' (1930: 14). The intensity of Wilson Knight's engagement with the poetry of Shakespeare's plays, his conviction that each play is 'an expanded metaphor' (15), leads him to write in expanded metaphors himself in what at times seems an almost desperate attempt to convince us of Shakespeare's greatness. It is as though we are dealing here with a critic who does not have the critical vocabulary at his disposal to do what it is he wants to do with Shakespeare's poetry, and, instead, substitutes for it a 'poetry' of enthusiasm, a rhetoric of laudatory incantation, leading to the vagueness and impressionism of passages like the following: 'The *Othello* style is diffuse, leisurely, like a meandering river; the *Macbeth* style compressed, concentrated, and explosive; often jerky, leaping like a mountain torrent' (1930: 101).

None the less, despite meandering rivers and leaping mountain torrents, *The Wheel of Fire* (1930) and *The Imperial Theme* (1931) begin a long engagement on Wilson Knight's part with Shakespeare that impresses us with its persistence, conviction, and affection. And there is no doubt that Wilson Knight had considerable influence on the future of Shakespeare criticism, teaching us, for example, to see Shakespeare's plays, especially the tragedies, in 'spatial' or 'atmospheric' terms (for him the terms are interchangeable, but 'spatial' is the more helpful). Louis Marder focuses our attention on Wilson Knight's essential contribution to twentieth-century reading of Shakespeare: 'For Knight the atmosphere or space in which the play existed was more important than intentions, causes, sources, characters, or ethical outlook' (1963: 142).

Following the logic of the imagination, a spatial reading frees us from a sometimes hidebound dependency on narrative and chronology. In Wilson Knight's own words, each play must be regarded as 'a visionary whole, close-knit in personification, atmospheric suggestion, and direct poetic-symbolism' (1930: 11); we need to attend to 'groups of imaginative themes, poetical colourings' (1931: 22), to 'the symbols and symphonies of dramatic poetry' (22), to 'poetic splendours' (24). In the 1949 edition of *The Wheel of Fire* Wilson Knight himself thought that in 1930 he might have sacrificed too much to atmospheric suggestion. His observation about Shakespeare's characters—'The persons, ultimately, are not human at all, but purely symbols of a poetic vision'—can be found in the 1930 edition but not in the 1949 revision of it. Had he persisted in this kind of self-censorship over the years much else in his work would have had to have been deleted. Wilson Knight joins the ranks of those critics in the twentieth century—notably A. C. Bradley and Caroline Spurgeon—whose approval ratings lag far behind their influence on the shape of critical things to come.

C. S. Lewis followed Wilson Knight's lead in downplaying the importance of Shakespeare's characters in order 'to surrender oneself to the poetry and the situation. . . . For the poetry, the clothes, and the stance are the substance; the character "as it would have to be in real life" is only a shadow' (1964: 208). In this respect, Hamlet is not so much a man who has to avenge his father as one who has been given a task by a ghost. Surrendering oneself to the situation means surrendering oneself, like Hamlet, to the fear of being dead. The play's true hero is 'man—haunted man—man with his mind on the frontier of two worlds, man unable either quite to reject or quite to admit the supernatural, man struggling to get something done as man has struggled from the beginning, yet incapable of achievement because of his inability to understand either himself or his fellows or the real quality of the universe which has produced him' (215–16). But it's all finally mysterious because *Hamlet* 'is a mysterious play in the sense of being a play about mystery' (216). And here Lewis's resignation in the face of the mystery at the heart of things echoes A. C. Bradley's and Wilson Knight's.

The late 1940s and 1950s saw the influence of the New Criticism at its height in Shakespeare studies, especially in its persistence in unveiling the ways in which in a work of art the whole is greater than the sum of its parts. As Robert Heilman maintained: 'All the constituent metaphors must be related to the large metaphor which is the play itself' (1963: 12). In his popular books on *King Lear* and *Othello* he argues that the job of the critic is to trace 'patterns of meaning' (18) in order to reach the overarching, culminating one of which the patterns are a constituent and constitutive part. Heilman uses the word pattern 'to denote a combination or system of poetic and dramatic elements which can be shown to work together in encompassing a body of meaning that has a place in the over-all structure of the play' (24). This involves the mutual illumination and animation of the dramatic and poetic elements which while 'interdependent in the manner of the parts of an organism; together they form rich and stimulating patterns of meaning' (25).

What do these patterns of meaning mean, say, in *King Lear*? Essentially, they issue in a set of 'profound' interrogations: What is man's nature? What is nature? What in the nature of things may man depend upon? What is reason? What is folly? What is wisdom? What kind of thinking about experience is man's salvation? Rather in the manner of L. C. Knights, the end-product of Heilman's patterns of meaning is somewhat anti-climactic: 'For the evidence will indicate, I believe, that *King Lear* is finally a play about the ways of looking at and assessing the world of human experience' (28).

A phrase like 'assessing the world of human experience' could easily have been penned by F. R. Leavis and the Cambridge school of formalists (of which L. C. Knights was a member), and might well be found in their journal *Scrutiny* (established in 1932). The Cambridge critics were, like Heilman, and in the tradition of Matthew Arnold, moralists of a high order who as much as anything pursued Shakespeare's plays as poetry in order to excoriate the philistinism of

British culture, particularly in the postwar years (*Scrutiny* died in 1953).[16]

This helps to explain—but not entirely—the tone of Leavis's writings on Shakespeare. Critics can't deal with *Measure for Measure*, Leavis typically pronounces, because of 'that incapacity for dealing with poetic drama, that innocence about the nature of convention and the conventional possibilities of Shakespearean dramatic method and form, which we associate classically with the name of Bradley' (1952: 160). *Othello* '(it will be necessary to insist) is poetic drama, a dramatic poem, and not a psychological novel written in dramatic form and draped in poetry' (1952: 136). Leavis has good reason to find it necessary to insist on the poetic nature of *Othello* as his well-known essay on the play, 'Diabolic Intellect and the Noble Hero', strikes us as more psychologically than poetically oriented as though he were in fact, despite his best intentions, dealing with a psychological novel in dramatic form.

It is impossible to discuss Shakespeare's plays as perfect, poetic wholes, as we may see from the above discussion, without discussing what these wholes are all about. The New Criticism (in particular) marries its linguistic analyses to the plays' 'themes' even if the latter only amount to not very helpful generalities of the assessing-the-world-of-human-experience kind (an infuriating favourite is the contrast-between-appearance-and-reality).

Themes run amok in the criticism of Wilson Knight and the adventitious quality of his discovery of them in Shakespeare's plays underlines the dangers of searching for them in the first place. In decreasing order of credible worth, Wilson Knight moves from the unexceptionable proposition that *Troilus and Cressida* dramatizes the opposition between intuition and intellect, through the ho-hum discovery that in *Measure for Measure* '[e]ach person illumines some facet of the central theme: man's moral nature' (1930: 74), to the less than gripping notion that the hate-theme pervades *Hamlet, Troilus and Cressida, Othello, King Lear,* and *Timon of Athens* (alleviated by periodic injections of 'life-themes, health-themes' (1931: 25)), to the bizarre-sounding claim that somehow or other characters themselves turn into themes—hence the Iago-theme in *Othello*, the Brutus-theme and the Cassius-theme in *Julius Caesar*, and the Gloucester-theme in *King Lear*.

At this point in the criticism we may well feel that the word has lost any meaning it may once have had. And although Wilson Knight may be the extreme representative of the irresponsible thematist, the situation may have got sufficiently out of hand to justify Richard Levin's campaign against what he sees as the widespread collapse of rigorous thinking in the application of thematic criticism to the plays of Shakespeare (and to Renaissance drama in general).[17] In the words of Patrick Murray: 'From being the mirror of life, reflecting human sentiment and transactions with remarkable fidelity, Shakespearian drama has been transformed into a vast and inhuman metaphysical structure designed to illustrate abstract propositions' (1969: 68).

It's possible to argue, in fact, as some critics have done, that all kinds of inadequacies in the works themselves can be explained away in the name of the New Criticism's quest for poetic unity. A search for unity will inevitably produce it, much of the time enlighteningly, but crassly at other times. Ania Loomba denounces the wrong-headedness of the unity-seekers: 'Throughout the history of English studies, texts have not only been interpreted, evaluated and re-written to satisfy this demand for unity, but . . . even mutilated if they are seen to be defective' (1989: 65).

Shakespeare's occasional indulgences in the rash and the slipshod often get swept away in the fervour of any deeply held belief about the justice of any critical approach. It would be hard to imagine, for example, a committed New Critic being able to swallow the authenticity of Gary Taylor's discovery of a possible new poem by Shakespeare, its manifest rankness, for many, automatically prohibiting Shakespeare's authorship. Why is it so difficult, Stephen Orgel (1988) muses, for people to believe Shakespeare capable of writing a dud? Orgel makes the mischievous suggestion that the putative missing plays, *Cardenio* and *Love's Labour's Won*, were perhaps too bad to get collected in the 1623 Folio. Richard Levin goes a few steps further in the satiric presentation of the zealous thematist: 'If through some mix-up in Jaggard's shop a scene from *Coriolanus* had been printed in the middle of *Cymbeline*, a resourceful thematist would have no trouble showing how it contributed to the play's thematic structure' (1978: 176). And a similar kind of credulity can be found, according to Terence Hawkes, in the eagerness of present-day audiences to take in, or 'close with', any bizarre bit of contingent circumstance thrown up by

a play's production and render it part of an overall interpretation—
even pimples on the noses of the actors. Even 'no performance at all,
with a statement that the entire company had been brought low by
sudden sickness, might rank as an "interpretation"' (1981: 356).

We don't have to wait until the revolutionary year 1968, or the onset
of postmodernism, to hear other voices from other rooms. Although
A. C. Bradley saw in Shakespeare a combination of inspiration and
'considerate workmanship' (1904: 68), he, like Jonson and Johnson
before him, worshipped Shakespeare well this side of idolatry. Bradley
would never have submitted to the tyranny of the unified artefact: he
was well aware of Shakespeare's untidinesses, his digressions, inconsistencies, and contradictions, and those 'questions . . . to the reader
which it is impossible for him to answer with certainty' (1904: 73).
Shakespeare, it must be said, finished off his comedies negligently,
carelessly, 'as if it mattered nothing how the people got married, or
even who married whom, so long as enough were married somehow'
(76). But, when all is said and done, Shakespeare's imperfections were
'the sins of a great but negligent artist. He was often, no doubt, over-
worked and pressed for time' (75).

Some seventy years later T. J. B. Spencer echoed Bradley's concern
for Shakespeare's perfunctory endings and talked of the offensiveness
of 'instant happiness' (1973: 119) at the close of *As You Like It* and
Measure for Measure. 'Were Shakespeare's plays', he asks 'written to
"abide the most curious perusal"' (1973: 116)? Spencer doesn't think so;
in fact the truth of the matter is that 'Shakespeare is not writing nearly
so carefully or alertly as some of our sensitive literary analysts try to
demonstrate' (134). Alfred Harbage too believes that 'the plays cannot
be treated as if they were machine-tooled mechanisms, with each
word, image, or symbol meshing perfectly with all other words,
images, and symbols, as in a series of well-lubricated cogs' (1966:
34–5). In a play like *Hamlet*, so James Calderwood argues, there are
all kinds of examples of poor lubrication, of recalcitrant strangenesses,
and while the formalist seeks answers in the text for them, the more
appropriate, richer response is to accept them for what they are and
give them the same kind of welcome Hamlet asks Horatio to give to
the strange and to strangers.

After 1968, according to Chris Baldick, the unassimilable strangenesses in all of Shakespeare's plays were more than welcome, were

actively sought after, and positively proclaimed. The text's 'deformity and internal breakage' became a thing of beauty: 'the text was to be seen as polyvalent, multivocal, polyphonic, dialogic, multi-accentual, and preferably convulsed in schizophrenic babble' (1996: 165). And if the plays ended on an indeterminate note, so much the better. Terence Hawkes relishes the plays' inconclusiveness: 'Texts are never accurate or finished or concluded. They are endlessly, like language itself, in free play: wholly and permanently productive, referring to other texts, other uses of language, rather than to a limited range of reference imposed from outside themselves' (1986: 292).

But it is difficult to keep a good kind of reading down. At the end of the century in this instance as in a number of others, the (never entirely) superseded critical methodology seemed to be re-igniting. In the 1970s James Calderwood was alive to the anarchic dangers of the text at free play:

Sometimes we seem in danger of claiming that Shakespearean drama is such a deep and dangerous labyrinth of thematic passageways, each concealing minotaurine fallacies awaiting the unstrung critic, that its entrances should be posted 'Abandon Hope All Ye Who Enter Here.' Abandon hope, that is, of emerging again with anything like a declarative sentence on your lips, let alone a statable message. (1971: 18)

Nearly twenty years later Ernst Honigmann declares open season still on the problem of reading the play as a whole: 'After four centuries criticism is still largely defeated by a procedural problem, how to grapple with the play as a whole' (1989: 148), and returns to the notion of everything in the drama joining 'on to everything else' (149). Stephen Booth's pugnacious 'The Function of Criticism at the Present Time and All Others', addressed to secondary school teachers, asks them to ask their students to ask themselves 'what Romeo and Juliet or Hamlet have that their stories, other tellings of those stories, other plays in verse, and so on, do not' (1990: 267). And Graham Bradshaw in his sustained attack on the cultural materialists resurrects the notion of the purposive, meaning-driven author 'with the play as a highly organised matrix of potential meanings, rather than as a chaotic site' (1993: 31), particularly to be discovered in the 'strikingly purposive—creatively purposeful—departures from what Shakespeare found in his sources' (32).

We seem at the end of the century to be returning to positions taken nearer its beginning. And so Barbara Everett, in flagrant disregard of current orthodoxies, reanimates the notion of the play as a poem. (*Julius Caesar*, for instance, is 'less a political drama of types than a poem' (1998: 217)). She asks us to be careful of limiting Shakespeare, especially these days, to the theatre of the theatre and not to the theatre of the mind. And as she says, each Shakespeare play 'is also a poem to the degree that it is, at its deepest, a reasoned dream: an experience of the individual mind embodied as never before' (229).

What *Romeo and Juliet* or *Hamlet* have that other versions of their stories don't have is their quality as reasoned dreams: they are, in other words, aesthetic objects, and it is the concept of the aesthetic that is behind all formalist criticism. It is, of course, an evasive category but under its large umbrella a variety of defences operates against the cogent incursions of historicist and materialist criticism. Fighting this sometimes rearguard action in the cause of an untrammelled hedonism has an ancient and modern history. It flourished at the end of the nineteenth century in Shakespeare studies, for example, in the feud between Swinburne and Furnivall.

We might consider here Terry Eagleton's eloquent definition of the sublime, alluring pointlessness of the aesthetic's *raison d'être*: ' ... what the aesthetic imitates in its very glorious futility, in its pointless self-referentiality, in all its full-blooded formalism, is nothing less than human existence itself, which needs no rationale beyond its own self-delight, which is an end in itself and which will stoop to no external determination' (1992: 30). (In another piece he talks of the glories of Shakespeare's 'libidinal excess' (1988: 204)).

More succinct is Samuel Goldwyn's defence of the pointlessness of his art: 'If I wanted to send a message, I'd use Western Union'. If Shakespeare's works are not merely 'empty signifiers freely available for opportunistic appropriation' in Michael Bristol's words (1996: 26) then some version of 'self-delight' must prevail as it does overwhelmingly for Harold Bloom. Bristol feels that 'Shakespeare's plays really do represent a significant reserve of literary value and I suspect that most Shakespeare scholars, including many of those whom Harold Bloom would consign to the "school of resentment" have a similar belief' (131). The notion of the aesthetic fuels Gary Taylor's impatience with interpretation: 'Criticism too often consists in filtering out pleasure in the pursuit of meaning, in reducing poems to their lowest common denominator... in counting how many images had Lady Macbeth' (1985: 1). Lachlan Mackinnon tells us that he is trying 'to deal with the plays as objects without meanings, to analyze their appearances as aesthetic artifacts, and it is in this direction that I have tried to move' (1988: 158). And Norman Rabkin, speaking of *The Merchant of Venice*, asks us why it is that the experience of the play escapes so many good critics. His guess is that 'our troubles stem in good part from the value we have put on reductiveness. We have been betrayed by a bias toward what can be set out in rational argument' (1981: 19) and 'its consistent suppression of the nature of aesthetic experience' (21). We need now 'to consider the play as a dynamic interaction between artist and audience, to learn to talk about the process of our involvement rather than our considered view after the aesthetic event' (27)—there is simply an 'existential complexity' (32) which 'undercuts thematic paradigms' (33).

After Mackinnon has outlined his desire to engage with the plays as objects without meaning his following sentence concedes that '[i]t is ultimately an impossibility...'. And it is important to emphasize the degree to which late twentieth-century criticism of Shakespeare eschews the notion of an inherent aesthetic quality in a work of art, even in one by Shakespeare. As Isobel Armstrong says: 'A permanent ethical and aesthetic value does not reside inherently in literary works or objects of beauty... but is *deemed* to belong to them by cultural consensus' (1989*b*: 15). It simply isn't the case in her view that pleasure in something we designate the aesthetic experience takes place in some corner of the brain cut off from contingency. Nor is it the view of Mary Beth Rose who points out that 'literary forms and artistic conventions do not constitute static rhetorical paradigms that are transmitted without alteration through history; they are themselves social and ideological constructs whose varying patterns, sudden appearances at distinct historical moments, and shifting dominance served as significant registers of cultural transformation' (1991: 291).

Critics like Ania Loomba, Armstrong, Rose, and Stephen Greenblatt emphasize the need to *historicize* pleasure. There is aesthetic pleasure, for instance, in discovering in the plays something illicit and subversive in opposition to the world of social regularity. And it is noticeable in the late twentieth century just how pervasive the notion is in some influential critical quarters that aesthetic pleasure in Shakespeare's plays must needs be defined by their expressions of nonconformity and social rebellion that the main thrust of the plays is trying to contain. But aesthetic pleasure I suspect is more complicated in its circumstantiality than this. The pleasure of the subversive can be matched by the pleasure to be gained from expressions of social allegiance: the pleasure, say, that some of us might get from giving way to another driver as opposed to beating him to the lights. And we might bear in mind here what John Fiske says in his essay 'Searing Towers': 'There are pleasures, even for the most subordinated, in aligning oneself with the system that subordinates one' (1989: 214)—the pleasure that the shrew takes in being tamed perhaps.

An Army of Good Words

Some critics in the twentieth century believe that no Shakespeare play can be read in isolation from his other works (including the poems). Their angle of incidence, then, from which to view Shakespeare's achievement, takes in the broad sweep of Shakespeare's works as a whole. The essential formal unit for them cannot be found within the boundaries of a single work; the unified artefact embraces all the plays and non-dramatic poems. The most influential critic to promulgate this critical position was T. S. Eliot who argued famously that 'the full meaning of any one of his plays is not in itself alone, but in that play in the order in which it was written, and in its relation to all of Shakespeare's other plays earlier and later: we must know all of Shakespeare's work in order to know any of it' (1950: 170).

Wilson Knight believes that the whole of Shakespeare's work makes up one poem and that the plays from *Julius Caesar* (about 1599) to *The Tempest* (about 1611) follow a significant sequence, an 'evolutionary progress', which he calls the Shakespeare Progress. The title of Barber and Wheeler's book on Shakespeare, *The Whole Journey: Shakespeare's Power of Development* (1986), encapsulates this bird's-eye view of Shakespeare's work, but one of the things that this book emphasizes—as do many others of course—is the strikingly multifarious nature of Shakespeare's achievement, the manner in which groups of plays do not lead smoothly into other groups. Connections there may be; but there are also breathtaking changes in direction as, for instance, in the transmogrification of the final tragedies into the late romances. In his book, *Shakespeare and the Confines of Art*, Philip Edwards focuses on what he believes to be the restless changes of form throughout Shakespeare's career. Shakespeare at the turn of the century, he says, exhibits an astonishing array of different kinds of dramatic endeavour: 'the idyllic or Illyrian comedies, *As You Like It* and *Twelfth Night*; the Roman tragedy, *Julius Caesar*; the revenge-tragedy, *Hamlet*; the bourgeois-farce, *Merry Wives*; the category-defying *Troilus and Cressida*; the folk-tale tragicomedies, *All's Well* and *Measure for Measure*; and the marital-tragedy, *Othello*' (1968: 10–11). Edwards concludes: 'We just do not have the sense of an exhibition in a gallery by one painter' (11). But, as he also points out, there is reiteration in this heterogeneity. And it would be inadequate, of course, to respond to any of the groupings we may care to establish for Shakespeare's works without taking into account the stunning differences between individual members of them. David Young writes a whole book in awed response to the differences between the four major tragedies. We should consider, he says, how 'daring' the leap from one play to the other, how 'exhilarating' (1990: 138).

There are many different ways of exploring the pattern in Shakespeare's carpet. One is to consider the growth of entire plays from earlier ones, to notice, as Emrys Jones does, for instance, how the three parts of *Henry VI*, *Richard III*, and *King John* 'became rich repositories of structural paradigms' (1971: 88) for the later tragedies. Or how Shakespeare in his tragedies, as Brian Vickers points out, uses a version of the comic prose he wrote for his comedies: 'The move from comedy to tragedy is only the sharpest sign of Shakespeare's ability to re-create old forms and to pull initially external devices into the closest and most meaningful relationship with character, mood and situation' (1968: 431). Both Leslie Fiedler (1973) and John Gillies (1994) argue that the situation in *Othello* continues the plot of *The Merchant of Venice* where Portia elopes with Morocco, the thwarted fathers of Portia and Jessica merge into Brabantio, and Graziano becomes Iago. Other critics find significant signs of fertilization within groups of Shakespeare's plays, as Sherman Hawkins does with the history plays, the second group taking their artistic cues from the first, the first play of the first tetralogy linked to the last one of the second:

'*1 Henry VI* and *Henry V* are ... clearly parallel and antithetical' (1991: 38).

Yet another way of exploring the pattern in the carpet is to consider, as Susan Snyder does, Shakespeare's intermingling of genres. Was Shakespeare, she asks, dissatisfied with *Romeo and Juliet*? This tragedy, unlike any of his others 'becomes, rather than is, tragic' (1979: 57). Similarly, until the first scene of the second act, *Othello* is a perfect comic structure: 'Iago is a clown without good humor' (79–80). And in *Hamlet* the graveyard scene is a 'comic-absurd challenge to heroic individuality' (129). In the final analysis, Snyder believes, 'Comedy's world must be seen not as completely elsewhere but a possible starting point, or a running accompaniment, or even a constituent element, of Shakespeare's tragic vision' (55).

Shakespeare's artistic licence here (and elsewhere) exemplifies Pope's famous observation that 'Great wits sometimes may gloriously offend'. And as a final comment on the boldness of Shakespeare as an artist we might consider how his restless experimentation resembles the methods of postmodernism. According to Todd Gitlin, we're living 'hip-deep in debris' (1988: 35), for postmodernism is indifferent to consistency and continuity: 'It self-consciously splices genres, attitudes, styles. It relishes the blurring or juxtaposition of forms (fiction-nonfiction), stances (straight-ironic), moods (violent-comic), cultural levels (high-low). It disdains originality and fancies copies, repetition, the recombination of hand-me-down scraps' (1988: 35). How different, one wonders, is this from Shakespeare's practice?

Shakespeare in the Theatre (and the Theatre in Shakespeare)

This Wooden O

In the twentieth century an enormous amount of first-class research went into the investigation of Shakespeare's theatre as a material and cultural institution: on one level, its buildings, actors, and audiences; on another, its financial and regulatory infrastructures; on a third, its stage traditions and conventions, and, in the wider contexts of its institutional setting, its place in the local (and national) economy, and its social impact on different strata of society. Critics in this century pursuing these kinds of interests had to have at least a nodding acquaintance with disciplines not immediately associated with literary criticism: archaeology, law, anthropology, economics, architecture, and the like. Truly, in this area if in no other, the twentieth-century obsession with scientific method and exactitude would seem to have found its perfect hunting-ground. Here, one would have thought, Moulton's and Dowden's 'rich feelings for positive concrete facts' would have found the ideal material for a prolonged love affair. And the late nineteenth-century ambition for a steady and reliable evolutionary progress in literary criticism would seem also to have been realized by the patient accumulation of evidence of a satisfyingly confirmable kind about the physical features of the theatres. So it's not surprising that critics working this vein of literary criticism—if literary criticism it is—should lay claim to a scientific accuracy that their colleagues can only envy. A prominent twentieth-century historian of the stage, J. L. Styan, certainly thinks so, with his conviction that real progress in dramatic criticism lies not so much on the literary side but in scholarship 'more directly related to the practical business of staging a play' (1977: 4), and he instances the work done on the London and provincial playhouses by the Malone Society after 1906 and also the investigations of the Elizabethan and Jacobean stage by such luminaries as J. Q. Adams, A. H. Thorndike, W. J. Lawrence, and, pre-eminently, E. K. Chambers and G. E. Bentley.

Some idea of the evolutionary, building-block nature of this kind of research can be gleaned from the publishing career of a standard work on Shakespeare's theatre, Andrew Gurr's *The Shakespearean Stage, 1574–1642*, which first appeared in 1970. A second edition twelve years later produced minor corrections and added new photographic and factual material. A third edition another decade later—in 1992—takes into account 'shifts in priorities which have appeared in the last decade' (p. xiii), but is largely concerned 'to incorporate new evidence that has appeared since 1980' (p. xiii). In reissuing his book at ten-year intervals, Gurr only changes the basic text each time in a number of minor ways: he notices a handful of new trends, incorporates some new evidence, adds the odd photograph or two, corrects minor errors, shifts emphases, and generally tidies up. No process could be more satisfyingly rational, accumulative, and verifiable; it's 'scientific' criticism at its most transparently accountable.

But as we know from the twentieth-century's understanding of Darwinian theory such a smooth transition from point to point on the evolutionary trail is a chimera: evolution moves in mysterious ways, with sudden unaccountable leaps into the future and bizarre disappearances of species. A recent new discovery in the evolutionary story of the Elizabethan playhouse manages to overturn much previous thinking. In 1989 the remains of the Rose Theatre in London were discovered and R. A. Foakes tells us that as a result 'our concept of what E. K. Chambers called "The Elizabethan Stage" has been changed out of recognition' (1996: 10).[1] In 1990 a collection of essays, *New Issues in the Reconstruction of Shakespeare's Theatre*, edited by F. J. Hildy, specifically addressed this new age in the understanding of Shakespeare's theatre, as did John Astington's collection, *The Development of Shakespeare's Theatre* (1992).

Although Foakes may be correct in his large claims for the Rose discovery, it's obviously not the case that the four volumes of E. K. Chambers and the seven of G. E. Bentley are now otiose. Scholars of the theatre continue to use all eleven volumes on an almost daily basis, such is their authors' formidable acuity in the gathering and arranging of a mass of information about everything to do with Shakespeare's stage. In any case, as we have already seen, the one consistent feature of twentieth-century Shakespeare scholarship and criticism is the way the definitive almost always eludes entrapment. Even in matters as straightforward and basic as the dimensions of the Elizabethan theatre, the conjectural continues to outweigh the certain: hence C. Walter Hodges in the most recent of his many considerations over the years of the physical dimensions of the Elizabethan theatre—his first, *The Globe Restored*, was in 1939—still has to admit that his drawings contain 'exploratory variations' (1999: p. ix); they are not 'final or definitive solutions to outstanding and still unresolved problems' (p. x).[2] Besides, even research so fundamentally factual and positivistic cannot escape being buffeted by the prevailing shifts in paradigms. William Ingram tells us that theatre historians like their literary colleagues 'now stand at a Kuhnian juncture where neither old nor new paradigms command general assent' (1992: 14). The old certitudes now seem remarkably fragile, constructs even of the imaginations of their twentieth-century proponents, and hence, like so much else in this century, labile, vulnerable, and culture specific.

As the century progressed, the notion of the materiality of the Elizabethan theatre took on exciting new dimensions. The Elizabethan theatre became, in T. G. Bishop's words, 'an active site of cultural reflection in the moment of performance' (1996: 71). Less a physical object of bricks, wood, and mortar, the theatre became more a source of study as an economic and cultural phenomenon of its (and later) times. The cultural geography of the theatre district in London, for instance, in the sixteenth and seventeenth centuries—the area known as the Liberties—has been investigated fruitfully and imaginatively by a number of works in the twentieth century of which Stephen Mullaney's (1988) and Michael Bristol's (1985) are two of the more significant. 'For the first time', Douglas Bruster comments, 'acting companies began to enjoy the use of semipermanent, pur-pose-built structures for the marketing of dramatic entertainment, staging productions in playhouses that would become regular fixtures in the urban geography of Renaissance London' (1992: 1). We need to see London's playhouses therefore as centres of production and consumption of an aesthetic product; after all, between 1580 and 1642 fifty million visits were paid to the London theatres, engendering over that time an enormous amount of profit for their investors and encouraging the growth of ancillary enterprises. It's no wonder that contemporary critics frequently compared London's theatres to London's money marts, Gresham's Royal Exchange and the New Exchange.

Twentieth-century interest in the materiality of the theatre does not of course confine itself to its Elizabethan manifestations. How Shakespeare's plays were presented, in what theatres, under whose auspices, with what effects on the local and national economies, are some of the material questions that can be addressed for any century. But it is, of course, the twentieth century with its extraordinary efflorescence of different kinds of opportunities for the presentation of Shakespeare's plays—now no longer restricted to wooden o's or their modern-day equivalents—that has commanded the attention of many theatre critics. And so nearly all research into the materiality (and the immateriality) of Shakespeare's theatre takes the English Renaissance theatre and the twentieth-century world theatre as its fields of choice. Critics writing on the theatre's materiality in twentieth-century Britain have had a wide range of subjects to choose from.

Back in 1906, for example, Sir Sidney Lee made a case for the establishment in England of a municipal theatre, something that is commonplace in Europe. For him, the municipal theatre was as important as the municipal anything else: 'the municipal theatre is the natural complement of the municipal library, the municipal musical entertainment, and the municipal art gallery' (133). It would be a theatre which would bring Shakespeare to the wide audience he should enjoy. Lee explained the lack of such a theatre to the fact that 'England is the only country in Europe in which theatrical enterprise is wholly and exclusively organized on a capitalist basis' (1906: 124).

If not a municipal theatre, then a national one with Shakespeare as its national poet. Dennis Kennedy traces Granville Barker's life-long involvement with such an ambition: 'Harley Granville Barker was everywhere that drama mattered in England in the first sixteen years of the century, but nowhere was his power of thought and action more evident than in his fight for a national theatre' (1985: 190).

Recently, critics have turned their attention to money matters and Shakespeare's theatre. Susan Bennett, for example, takes on the arts funding system in Britain: 'What I think is particularly needed (indeed long overdue) in order to understand in more complicated ways the operation of various categories of theatre in Britain is an account of the theory and practice of the arts funding system and its relationship to audience and venue development' (1996: 170); while Peter Holland thinks that the economic pressures on theatrical organizations like the Royal Shakespeare Company should be investigated now by academic writers: 'Marketing Shakespeare and measuring response to marketing is a precise indication of the cultural placing of Shakespeare in late twentieth-century Britain' (1997*a*: 11). Literary criticism needs to get its hands dirty in the real world of profit and loss.

The Swelling Scene

Aside from studying the archaeology, sociology, and the economics of the physical theatre, the practical business of staging a Shakespeare play is clearly the most compelling subject in the twentieth century for critics of the theatre. We now call such criticism—somewhat inadequately considering the scope of the subject—performance criticism. Critics of the stage have long been intrigued by the possibility of recuperating Elizabethan performances. John Russell Brown asks the vital question: 'Did [Shakespeare] indicate, by any recoverable means, the manner in which his plays should be staged and performed?' (1996: p. vii).

The title of a book by Alan Dessen, *Recovering Shakespeare's Theatrical Vocabulary*, published the year before, suggests that those means have now been recovered. What did a play-goer at the original production of a Shakespeare play actually see, Dessen asks, and gets his answer from an analysis of the stage directions in the approximately 600 English professional plays performed before 1642. What Dessen is providing, he believes, are 'pre-interpretative materials' (1995: 2), and his analogies for what he is doing are to philology, iconography, archaeology, and other discursive and signifying practices. His book focuses 'on potentially meaningful "images" and configurations

generated in Shakespeare's theatrical vocabulary by means of Elizabethan staging practices, especially when those images and practices
are sufficiently different from today's procedures that the original
effects are concealed and blurred' (111). In other words, Dessen is
dealing here not so much with a book written by Shakespeare intended
to be read (there is indeed little evidence that Shakespeare ever
thought of his plays as enterprises in reading) but with a playscript
intended for the professional stage.

The study of Shakespeare's plays as playscripts is a distinctively
twentieth-century phenomenon. And one way to approach them as
predominantly theatrical constructs is to think of Shakespeare as the
plays' director rather than as their author. Hence Anne Pasternak Slater
in 1982 published a book with the optimistic title *Shakespeare the
Director*. She writes: 'This book is a study of Shakespeare's direction
of his plays, analysing the implications of theatrical effects specifically
engineered by him' (1). (As opposed, I imagine, to those effects—
largely unrecoverable but undoubtedly mixed in the brew—engineered
by the actors or any other personnel of the company, apart from
Shakespeare himself, who had a creative hand in the production of
the plays.)

There is now much talk, in Jean Howard's words, of Shakespeare's
'purposeful management' (1984: 2) of 'the aural, visual and kinetic
dimensions of stage production' (2), of the way the dramatist 'controls
the temporal continuum of impressions flowing in upon the spectator'
(2). We're dealing here with 'tempo, kinetic effects, visual happenings,
tonal shifts' (14). It's a question of contrapuntal asides, speaking
silences, counterpoint, let's say, whereby there is 'a sustained juxtaposition, within a scene, of two separate lines of stage speech that unfold
concurrently and prevent the audience from focussing its undivided
attention on either' (52). In a word, 'Shakespeare's meaningful choreography of stage spectacle' (102).[3] And in meaningful counterpoint
to the directorial Shakespeare, another biographical-cum-theatrical
approach is to think of Shakespeare not so much as the choreographer
but as one of the participating dancers of the production, hence
Meredith Skura's book *Shakespeare the Actor and the Purposes of Playing*
(1993).

To consider Shakespeare as actor and director, rather than strictly
speaking as writer, can only be possible if the stage conventions and

traditions of the day have also been recovered. So later / grateful to the ground-breaking work of earlier theatric who brought our attention, on, it seems to me, a more basic ˎ interpretative level than Dessen's, to the marshalling stage conventions of the time, the basic underpinnings of all professional Renaissance plays not just Shakespeare's.

The most well-known of these pre-interpretative interpreters is E. E. Stoll whose work is still in circulation and had at one time a considerable influence. Stoll has critics like G. Wilson Knight firmly in his sights in his attempts to understand the plays in the no-nonsense ambience of the theatre, as opposed to the fancifulness—as he fancifully imagines—induced by fine frenzies of critical speculation. 'Mr. Knight', Stoll charges, 'has made a popular poet, writing for the stage, as dark and unintelligible as an esoteric "modernist", a Sitwell or a Hart Crane, writing for print' (1933: 31). What Stoll stresses time and again is the necessity for the 'mechanical' in art, 'its superiority in these regards to the psychological formula offered, with its claptrap and legerdemain' (21). In _Othello_, he scolds, it's claptrap to speculate on the reasons why Othello succumbs so precipitously to Iago's dubious logic; Othello has to succumb in the way he does simply because he is at the mercy of 'the convention, not infrequent in tragedy and comedy, as in myth and legend, of believing at the critical moment the detrimental thing that is cunningly told' (1933: 6).

Later theatre critics like Slater and Skura do well to concentrate more on the cunning of the telling of the detrimental thing rather than on its convention's capacity to induce a barely willing suspension of disbelief. One of the charges that can be brought against Stoll's pugnacious reductionism is the way it short-changes Shakespeare's capacity to rise above the convention he is exploiting. In the theatre— ironically enough—Othello's abrupt and total disintegration in the face of Iago's presentation of the detrimental thing has never seemed to me to be unconvincing (unless it's badly acted). Stoll's reliance on the formulaic here seems as much a piece of legerdemain as anything dark and unintelligible from Wilson Knight.[4]

Truth to tell there is no dark divide between Stoll's down-to-earth investigations of Shakespearean theatrical convention and, let's say, Wilson Knight's poetic exuberances. S. Viswanathan has a point when he argues that formalist criticism, New Criticism in particular, owes a debt to investigators of theatrical convention like Stoll and Schücking who lead to the more nuanced and formally inflected theatrical criticism from critics such as M. C. Bradbrook and S. L. Bethell. Bethell's book in particular is exemplary in its careful consideration of the way ordinary language and theatrical convention combine. As Bethell says: 'From time to time and from place to place the drama varies its position on a scale between two extremes of absolute conventionalism and absolute naturalism' (1944: 13). As opposed to Stoll's dogged insistence on the primacy of convention, Bethell suggests that in Shakespeare's time there was a dual awareness in his audiences, an understanding that the drama was a mixture of conventionalism and naturalism that demanded 'a dual mode of attention' (27). Shakespeare's 'popular audience, uncontaminated by abstract and tendentious dramatic theory, will attend to several diverse aspects of a situation, simultaneously without confusion' (28).

Later critics, such as Maurice Charney (1971), with one eye on what happens in the theatre and another on what happens on the page, can be considered as the descendants of this line of thinking. Charney talks, for instance, like Stoll, and like Bethell, of the dubiousness of psychoanalysing a character like Desdemona. And there is no cause, Charney says, despite Othello's later threnody on that word, for Othello's suspicions about Desdemona's fidelity other than Iago's conventionally irresistible farrago of nonsense about Desdemona's need for change—she must have change, she must. Equally we must believe, we must, in the absolute innocence of Ophelia in *Hamlet*, the absolute malevolence of Iago in *Othello*, and the absolute natural evil of Caliban in *The Tempest*. In the case of Caliban, if we accept the absoluteness of his natural evil, we must also accept what Charney describes as a necessary (and absolute) 'discontinuity' in his character: we can't reconcile his poetic and sensitive isle-is-full-of-noises rapture at the beauty of the natural world with his lust to kill and rape. (Some critics might beg to differ here, but that's another story.)

Comparisons are Odorous

Recuperating Renaissance performance attracts archaeologically inclined critics; those with historically shorter attention spans focus on the history of twentieth-century productions of Shakespeare.

2. A scene from Beerbohm Tree's production of *Twelfth Night* (1901).

Another bountiful harvest, this. In Edwardian times gorgeous Shakespeare productions, the legacy of the nineteenth century,[5] were the norm. 'It was an age', writes Dennis Kennedy, 'of conspicuous consumption; Thorstein Veblen could have used Tree's *Twelfth Night* (1901), with real fountains and famous grass carpet, as an example of the irresponsible show of wealth' (1985: 149). By the end of the nineteenth century the theatre on the economic level had changed with the times and could be compared with industry and commerce as a capitalist enterprise, but, despite these changes, its aims were not very different from those of the 1830s, namely, the achievement of pictorial realism in staging and of psychological verisimilitude in acting. Shakespeare's theatre was considered at this time in the critical literature to be a primitive version of what had replaced it rather than something entirely different.

It gradually became apparent to twentieth-century critics, however, that Shakespeare's stage amounted to little more than an unlocalized platform with a limited 'above', and a discovery space. Even more gradually the advantages of such a 'primitive' staging seeped into the understandings of both literary critic and theatrical activist, but it wasn't until 1973 that Alan Dessen (see Dessen 1980) could lay claim to the superiority of such bareness for the symbolic power of the single property or the distinctive figure. For the famous writer-director, Harley Granville Barker, the unlocalized, uncluttered stage placed an appropriate emphasis on the characters: 'Ignoring whereabouts, letting it at most transpire when it naturally will, the characters capture all attention' (1957: 11).

Whereabouts in fact has captured a great deal of critical attention from writers on the theatre in this century. According to Dennis Kennedy, *the* twentieth-century question with regard to staging, and one constantly asked by critics and directors alike, is: 'What is the appropriate setting for Shakespeare's plays?' (1993: 3). It is the theatre's variety of answers to this question, its visual history in the twentieth century, its scenography,[6] that fascinates many critics, perhaps because, as Kennedy alleges, the visual history of performance tells us so much about the relationship between Shakespeare and the culture at large. When we think back to the Edwardian revolt against the opulent scenography of Beerbohm and Tree, we see that, as Kennedy argues, '[t]he most radical implication of the movement was that a visual approach to Shakespeare should be derived, not from the taste of the time, but from attitudes inhering in the scripts themselves' (1993: 35).

So the return to Shakespeare's theatre involved a return to Shakespeare's scripts and a new orthodoxy loomed—about which more later. But we should also bear in mind that a number of Shakespeare productions, particularly in the latter part of the century, were designed deliberately to run counter to what the director understood to be the orthodox interpretation of the text (about which also more later). As Russell Jackson reminds us: 'Among theories of directing, the notion that a valuable production takes issue with the text it starts from has an honoured place' (1996a: 228). And there are connections to be made of course between the larger culture and unorthodox interpretations of the plays. After the First World War, as Dennis Kennedy points out, '[u]nprecedented slaughter, the dislocation of the old order, and a breakdown of traditional moral values, which brought political turmoil and revolution to so much of middle and Eastern Europe, also brought extreme artistic experimentation and reevaluation of the classics' (1993: 82). Extreme experimentation does not inevitably produce something either excitingly new or newly valuable. Max Reinhardt's reliance upon theatre technology 'provoked fastidious over-production' (59) just as in the nineteenth century. And Peter Holland describes a moment in watching the murder of Cinna the Poet in *Julius Caesar* done so graphically that he felt physically sick (1997a: 80). Harley Granville Barker suggested some time ago that '[m]an and machine ... are false allies in the theater, secretly at odds' (1957: 7).

A Little Brief Authority

Performance criticism in the century can be broken down into criticism of a number of different performances: those of the director, the actor, and the somewhat more elusive one of the audience. Without doubt this century can be thought of as the century of the director, or as he or she—overwhelmingly he, sad to say—used to be known, the producer. W. B. Worthen comments on the position's modernity: 'The director is a distinctly modern figure, arising in the late nineteenth century to impose a newly desired representational unity on stage plays' (1997: 45–6). And he goes on to investigate the new need for such a controlling influence: 'in one sense, the director arises as a functional necessity of the convergence of two theatrical aesthetics: environmental naturalism and historical picturalization' (46). Much critical work has been done on—and sometimes by—marquee directors, who often were/are also famous actors: William Poel, Harley Granville Barker (a critic of course in his own right, as well as an actor), Laurence Olivier, Peter Brook, Joseph Papp, Buzz Goodbody, Charles Marowitz, Michael Bogdanov—to name but a few (and—representatively proportional—only one of them, Buzz Goodbody, a woman).

Critics of the theatre like Stanley Wells send us back to the afternoon of 16 April 1881 as the moment when the directorial era virtually began, with William Poel's determinedly Elizabethan production of the first quarto of *Hamlet* at St George's Hall in London, using a bare, draped platform and Elizabethan costumes—not a piece of scenery in sight, not even a helpful placard. This was the performance that introduced the play-going public and the critics to a foretaste of the next century's unromantic, de-sentimentalized Hamlet, and heralded the obsession—sometimes a pernicious one (as numerous critics point out)—with giving modern-day audiences an authentic Elizabethan theatrical experience. Poel's by and large good influence on modern-day acting survives in the importance today's actors still give to his belief in the necessity for the actor to develop what he called an interior stillness, and to his conviction that the speaking of Shakespeare's verse needs an 'exaggerated naturalness' and 'tuned tones', as though Hamlet's naturalistic-sounding advice to the Players were to be stiffened with a touch of Marlovian declamation. Poel's seriousness and persistence as a reformer in the theatre can be sampled in his two volumes of collected papers, *Shakespeare in the Theatre* (1913) and *Monthly Letters* (1929).

There's something very engaging about him as a critic of the theatre. Poel reminds us in his high-mindedness, persistence, and a certain kind of ascetic aestheticism of a theatrical William Morris. Russell Jackson notes that Poel attacked realism 'as inimical to plain living and high thinking' (1996*b*: 124), and in his Fabian-sounding pamphlet *What's Wrong with the Stage?* Poel espoused a progressive system of theatre government whose model was the People's Theatre in Berlin, with its membership of 5,000 workers. His life, however, was a series of splendid disappointments. Robert Speaight tells us that 'he was angered, but he was not embittered, by the chaos of vulgarity that surrounded him' (1954: 209). And it is Poel who took up the strife-ridden cause of a National Theatre whose establishment, he believed, would at last accord Shakespeare the theatrical dignity he deserved and whose very existence would help promote high standards for the theatre as a whole.

But perhaps Poel's most important contribution to Shakespeare's theatre in the twentieth century was as mentor to Harley Granville Barker, arguably the most influential of the writer-directors in the first half of the twentieth century. Barker's well-known *Prefaces* to Shakespeare's plays, scene-by-scene analyses of them that marry literary criticism with the concerns of the man of the theatre, still have a flourishing readership among literary students and theatre directors.[7] His was the art of *rapprochement*. In the Introduction to the *Prefaces* he writes: '... the Procrustean methods of a changed theater deformed the plays, and put the art of them to confusion; and scholars, with this much excuse, have been apt to divorce their Shakespeare from the theater altogether, to think him a poet whose use of the stage was quite incidental, whose glory had small relation to it, for whose lapses it was to blame' (1957: 1).

Making the stage less incidental went hand in glove with re-establishing the primary importance of the text. Envisaging a marriage between the theatre and the text in this manner anticipated (maybe instigated) much later work in this century on Shakespearean performance, both theoretical and practical. Barker imagined that his *Prefaces* examined Shakespeare's plays 'in the light of the interpretation he designed for them' and 'the production he would have desired for them' (1957: 4). Although the confidence expressed here may be risible, the notion that the director of a Shakespeare play acted as caretaker for the reputation of the dramatist was a novel one—not that it has been universally followed; nor, perhaps, should it be.

Such a concern for Shakespeare's integrity did not prevent Barker—indeed, quite the reverse—from being the most exciting innovator in the English theatre in the first years of the century. Dennis Kennedy sends us back—with a due sense of occasion—to a date in 1912 for the equivalent for Barker of Poel's 1881 production of *Hamlet*: 'It is 21 September 1912, the Savoy Theatre, Granville Barker's *The Winter's*

Tale, and Shakespearean production will never be the same' (1985: 123).[8] Summing up his significance for the operation of Shakespeare criticism in this century, Kennedy focuses on Granville Barker's influence on the radical shift from study to stage: 'Barker was the man most responsible for the shift away from the literary-historical approach in Shakespearean criticism to the theatrical approach that has begun to flower in recent years' (153).

Poel and Granville Barker were the first in a line of famously benevolent—and not so benevolent—dictator-directors in the English theatre in the twentieth century. For better or worse, the director, previously of little clout in the era of actor-managers, has emerged as the focal point in this century of virtually all productions of virtually all plays, not just those by Shakespeare, in more or less every country on the globe. Some critics have questioned the desirability of such a monopolization of power. Is it necessary? Is it a good thing? Does it produce the best interpretations, the best performances?

Over twenty years ago John Russell Brown in a provocative little book with the provocative title, *Free Shakespeare*, excited us all with the idea that perhaps a production of Shakespeare hammered out in the democratic free-for-all of a group effort with no one actor—no one anybody—in charge (rather like, perhaps, the brain-storming sessions of writers for a television series) would come up with a much more exciting night in the theatre than that produced by a single controlling intelligence. 'Are Shakespeare's plays,' he asks rhetorically, 'best performed when actors and audience submit to a simple overall conception and point of view arrived at by the director after private study of the text?' (1974: 40). Most critics perhaps would still answer in the affirmative, but not much, to my knowledge, has been done to give us the evidence for any answers to the contrary.[9]

In England, even more perversely, as Robert Smallwood grimly notes, 'Shakespeare production in this country in the last third of the twentieth century has been in the hands of male graduates of university English departments' (1996: 178), with Cambridge predominant.[10] Like Brown before him, Smallwood questions the desirability of such sexist inbreeding and asks us to take a long and sober look at the power these graduate directors have; not only do they get to choose the actors, but it is they who appoint a freelance designer, a lighting designer, a composer, and any other specialists they may need.

The power of the director is even greater in film and television as there is no chance of anything changing over the course of a long run. (There is no such thing as a run in television.) In the theatre, at least, something creatively untoward might happen after the director has left the production; the mice might feel free to play a little.[11] One might have thought that the tendency these days to present plays in smaller venues—other places—would have encouraged director-free productions; oddly enough, the reverse is the case as 'studio' or 'chamber' Shakespeare seems to attract the services of famous directors.

There is no doubt, however, that some famous directors in the twentieth century have given us hugely exciting, memorable, sometimes controversial, renderings of Shakespeare's plays in performance. This needs to be freely acknowledged. Books and articles have been written in this century that have been largely anthologies of directorial (and architectonic) *coups de théâtre*. For Robert Smallwood these comprise 'the most valuable feature of "directors' Shakespeare", [the] stimulus to think afresh about the play' (1996: 196), and he instances as one such the jolt he experienced in the theatre when Sam Mendes has Ariel spit on Prospero at his moment of freedom in Mendes's production of *The Tempest* in 1993: 'It is a challenging and disturbing reading of the relationship, defiant of nearly everything in the theatrical tradition of performing it, hugely controversial . . .' (196). (Hugely controversial, maybe, but not without grounds for the justice of it in the text of the play.)

Sometimes whole productions of a play amount to a sustained *coup* and remain embedded in the memory, as many critics fondly remember. Peter Brook's 1970 Stratford production of *A Midsummer Night's Dream* was such an experience for many critics as was his production of *King Lear* in 1962. For those people lucky enough to have seen Deborah Warner's Swan Theatre 1987 production of *Titus Andronicus*, Robert Smallwood writes, 'it will never again be possible to dismiss *Titus Andronicus* as a minor example of its author's theatrical art' (1996: 182). It's a specific reminder of Stanley Wells's more general proposition 'that any work of art written to be performed is as great as its performers can make it' (1994: 76). This was certainly true for A. D. Nuttall in his response in particular to an actor, Richard Pascoe, in the 1980 production of *Timon of Athens* at Stratford's Other Place. For Nuttall Pasco's performance was extraordinarily moving and opened his eyes to the affective possibilities of 'this harsh, mannered play' (1989: p. xxii).

Examples like these are legion in this century as any reading of anthologies of theatre reviews will amply demonstrate. Smallwood notes that directors are drawn to 'the alluringly vague area between the houselights going down and the first word of dialogue' (1996: 192) and to the play's final exeunt. Sometimes the houselights don't even have to go down, as in Michael Bogdanov's saucy version of *The Taming of the Shrew* in Stratford-upon-Avon in 1978, where the play 'begins' with a fracas in the audience that spills over onto the stage with stage-hands involved in an increasingly balletic struggle with an apparent intruder (the actor who played both Christopher Sly and Petruchio), tearing down in the process a stuffy Victorian stage-setting to reveal the real one, in steel and ultra-modern.

An ultra-modern looking Shakespeare brings home the new importance in this century of the various designers of any production. Fashions in design change bewilderingly, critics note. In the 1980s, for instance, the Royal Shakespeare Company moved away from the minimalism of its previous style to something more like the plush effects of West End musical productions. Peter Holland believes that criticism should now be as much concerned with the designer as with the director or the actor. Since, Holland says, 'the directors tended to work with the same group of designers the RSC's style was defined directorially and visually, rather than through a performance ensemble' (1997a: 25). What disturbs Holland is the extravagance of designers: 'There are times when I wonder whether designers have ever read the play they are working on' (34), and as a general principle Holland praises simplicity over what he calls directorial excess. Innovation and imagination are all very well, he believes, but not at the expense of 'the adequacy of the text' (74).

At first blush the typical twentieth-century Shakespeare production might strike us as being, like many of the productions of twentieth-century literary criticism, not only innovative and imaginative, but belligerent and confrontational, sometimes confronting Shakespeare, more often confronting us as audience with a version of Shakespeare that is as implacably driven by twentieth-century concerns as anything by Brecht or Genet. And that is why untypical Shakespeare plays like *Timon of Athens* and *Titus Andronicus* appeal to our bloody-minded century both as theatrical and reading experiences. Who would have imagined fifty (ten?) years ago that *Titus Andronicus* would have been a box-office success as a movie? It seems likely, as I write this, that the movie version of the play starring Anthony Hopkins will be as success-ful in the twenty-first century as his *Silence of the Lambs* was in the twentieth, and for the same reason. Just like literary critics, theatre and movie directors want to make Shakespeare their own, and they usually do so by giving him a twentieth-century pedigree, often a blood-stained one.

The book of literary criticism in the 1960s that most affected the thinking of directors along these lines—theatre directors, that is—was of course Jan Kott's *Shakespeare Our Contemporary* (published in Polish and French in 1962 and in English in 1964) which turned Shakespeare into a twentieth-century European writer (Polish specifically—see Chapter 5 for more details) rather than a seventeenth-century English one. This, the most widely read book on Shakespeare since A. C. Bradley's *Shakespearean Tragedy* (1904), reads Shakespeare by the searchlights of a police state. Kott saw Shakespeare in Genet-like terms as a dramatist of pain. Dennis Kennedy tells us that '[i]n the histories he saw the "Grand Mechanism" of implacable human cor-ruption, in the comedies a dark and bestial vision of sexuality, in the tragedies a kindred comic grimace reminiscent of Samuel Beckett' (1996: 139).

University trained, influenced by the literary criticism they read there, many twentieth-century directors feel compelled to make Shakespeare our contemporary. If he was, as Jonson believed, for all time then he must be—indubitably—for our time. Hence the vogue for what Peter Holland calls the analogue production whereby direc-tors attempt to find 'the precise analogy in recent history to serve to explicate the Shakespearean text as if the play had no function in relation to its own time and, more significantly, could only be made popular by the recreation of the play as modern parable' (1997a: 95).[12]

Even though there was in the United Kingdom during the 1980s a swing in theatrical fashion away from Kott—he has come to be considered a rather old-fashioned pessimist—the lure of the analogue remains all-powerful. Michael Bogdanov, for instance, asks us to think of *Hamlet* as both the perfect Watergate play and the perfect Falklands War play: 'The government was sending the same number of men,

20,000, to fight for a barren piece of ground so poor that, for five ducats, I would not farm it' (Elsom 1989: 2). Politicizing Shakespeare in this way, as far as the director, Charles Marowitz, is concerned, celebrates the malleability of a classic not just its age, but it is a celebration, like Bogdanov's, with a distinctly tendentious trajectory.[13] No doubt a number of British theatre directors have been influenced by the left-wing politics of the cultural materialists, and vice versa. At all events, as H. R. Coursen puts it, '[p]roduction gets trapped in the sign-systems of its decade' (1993: 178).

Although American productions of Shakespeare are by and large not as heavily inflected politically as their British counterparts, they are just as likely to be trapped in their own sign-systems. What American directors do in particular is to fill their productions with American popular imagery; and this has been going on since the 1950s when, for example, Katherine Hepburn starred in a Texan *Much Ado About Nothing* (1957). Amy Green writes: 'Action painting, Beat poetry, Happenings, rock music, and new kinds of dance contributed to the development of an aesthetic that valued spontaneity and juxtaposition over method and unity' (1994: 40). So American productions of Shakespeare, as the critics remind us, are often a rag-bag of miscellaneous twentieth-century allusions to life in the maelstrom of American popular culture. Green considers the work of Joseph Papp, especially his production of *Hamlet* in December 1967: 'Hamlet appeared at different points in the production as Ramon, the Puerto Rican janitor; as a peanut vendor, tossing bags of nuts to "customers" in the audience; as one of a pair of vaudevillian comics; and as a ventriloquist's dummy' (77). This production raised the question—one among many—as to whether the play belonged to the American avant-garde which tended to value 'image over word, disjuncture over synthesis, and instinct over intellect' (82). And the twentieth century over Shakespeare perhaps.

Such Seething Brains

If nothing else a director's Shakespeare reminds us of just how unmoored, improvisatory, and malleable the plays' texts are, how open to suggestion. As Dennis Kennedy suggests (1993: 182), in this century the director's 'take' on a play's text is little different from its interpretation by a literary critic (except that the director has no need to convince an editorial board of the justice of his or her reading). We can therefore study their work as though they were honorary literary critics. Stanley Wells considers the enormous divergences between different productions of the same play: 'Two different productions of the same, unadapted text of one of [Shakespeare's] plays can create an effect as different as if the events had been narrated by, say, Dickens on the one hand and D. H. Lawrence on the other hand' (1994: 28–9).

A director's version of events can sometimes almost change attitudes of a lifetime. Peter Holland, for example, comes close to such a major reassessment: 'I had always thought that *The Taming of the Shrew* was a play about gender-conflict. Bill Alexander's production nearly convinced me that the play is instead about class and that male subjugation of women is only an example of masters' oppression of servants' (1997*a*: 129). (Not that the oppression of servants is missing from Shakespeare's text, we should remember.) So the history of theatrical production in the twentieth century can act as a kind of safeguard against an overly confident belief in the accuracy of any one critical interpretation.

It's arguable given these circumstances that the very ephemerality of Shakespeare in the theatre is one of the theatre's great strengths.[14] One might look with some dismay therefore on those gilded monuments of video and film. And many critics do, James Bulman, for one: 'Because film and video allow us repeated viewings of a single performance, they encourage us to assimilate that performance to the condition of a literary text—a stable artifact rather than a contingent, ephemeral experience' (1996: 2).

Peter Reynolds explores the live theatre's exciting range of possible interpretation by inventing three directors who describe their very different productions of *As You Like It*, all equally plausible: one as an optimistic romance, another as a political scandal, and a third as a feminist tract exploring the nature of homosexuality. Reynolds draws a liberating moral for the reader from his theatrical invention: 'Lay claim to the text on your own behalf, as *you* like it' (1988: 113).

In praise of theatrical production, theatre critics remind us time and again that so much of any play is inevitably missing from the printed text of it. As Jonathan Miller points out: 'Playwrights do not include— and cannot, because of a shortage of notation—all those details of prosody, inflexion, stress, tempo and rhythm. A script tells us nothing about the gestures, the stance, the facial expressions, the dress, the weight, or the grouping or the movements' (1986: 34). And the greatness of a great play rests in its 'capacity to generate an almost infinite series of unforeseeable inflexions' (34–5).

Is it a case then of anything goes? Not according to Peter Holland for whom Robert Lepage's production of *A Midsummer Night's Dream* is beyond the pale (as it was for many critics): 'Different is not better and the result, visually magnificent, vocally catastrophic, was a production in which the play-text was not even the pretext, only a curious encumbrance to the theatrical poetics of the director's imagination' (1997*a*: 140–1).

Despite the ephemerality of a theatrical production of a Shakespeare play, for the time that we are in the theatre that production, if it is successful, has the force of holy writ—far more so than any piece of literary criticism. There's something very focusing about a theatrical production in fact in terms of its intense commitment—for however brief a period—to a particular point of view. If, say, at the end of *Measure for Measure* Isabella refuses to take the Duke's proffered hand (there is no stage direction one way or the other in the early texts and she says nothing in fact for the rest of the play), she will do so as the climax of an interpretation of her behaviour—perhaps a feminist one—that stresses her unwillingness to be a mere pawn in the Duke's game of political reparation.

There's no possibility here of that wavering in interpretation that so often comes from the experience of reading. (Though in this particular case it is more likely that as readers we would simply assume that she acquiesces.) A. C. Bradley talks sensibly about this: 'The actor who plays the part of Hamlet must make up his mind as to the interpretation of every word and deed of the character. Even if at some point he feels no certainty as to which of two interpretations is right he must still choose one or the other. The mere critic is not obliged to do this' (1904: 152).[15]

At the same time, the theatre's intractable materiality undermines a conceptual reading. Each performance may well generate uncontrolled interpretations, as may each venue. Anthony Dawson instances a performance of *As You Like It* where the erotic charge between Rosalind and Orlando simply cannot be reproduced in words, either in his or in Shakespeare's: 'Here was something that no amount of reading could produce, something totally unconceptual, a demonstration once again that theatre is a physical art' (1991: 325).

That physical art has produced extraordinary theatrical occasions, often in unexpected places, away from the easy seductions of centres of traditional interpretation. In her analysis of some seventeen productions of *King Lear* in the 1980s, Susan Bennett finds that, unlike the legendary one by Peter Brook in 1962, only a handful of the seventeen can be considered truly original. The opportunity for radical innovation best comes about, she says, when the play is more or less rewritten (though that wasn't the case with Brook's). And so, for instance, the 1987 play *Lear's Daughters* by the Women's Theatre Group is radically innovative. So too is Barrie Keeffe's *King of England*. What this last version of *King Lear* does, Bennett argues, is to 'take up the global cultural awareness of Shakespeare's plays and resituate it in the specific experience of a community audience' (1996: 55).

There are two other productions of *King Lear* that are directed at community audiences and that merit attention as true originals. One is by Footsbarn, a company of British theatre professionals based in France; the other is a play called *The Tragedy of King Real*, produced by Welfare State, another of Britain's alternative theatre groups with a long and radical history. What these productions demonstrate is 'the attainment of socially responsible criticism through the production of site-specific community-relevant art' (60). Site-specific and undoubtedly community-relevant was a performance of *King Lear* given to the inmates of England's secure psychiatric hospital, Broadmoor. Peter Holland highlights the work of Northern Broadsides, a regional company based in the North of England. He writes: 'Where some productions seem almost to be apologizing for doing Shakespeare at all, Northern Broadsides showed why he was the English Renaissance's most popular dramatist and why he should continue to be the centre of vitality in our theatre culture' (1997a: 154).

Exciting regional theatre of this kind is a phenomenon of the twentieth century. At least in the United Kingdom. Indeed, the history of the theatre in this century in this country in particular can be seen in terms of an ongoing struggle between a predatory metropolitan theatre, of a usually rather conventional crowd-pleasing kind, and a provincial theatre, community based, where the accents are regional rather than RADA, and the productions likely to be harder edged.[16] No evolutionary law applies here if Jonathan Miller (1986) is to be believed. He argues that the 1960s were a flourishing time for working-class actors but that in the last twenty years the theatrical focus has shifted heavily in favour of London rather than the provinces, and much spontaneity and flamboyance have been lost because of the bureaucracy.

An end of the century state-of-the-theatrical-nation address from Russell Jackson is much more optimistic. He applauds the use of the thrust stage, which thrusts the actors out among the audience, and the disappearance of upper-class accents and mysogyny: 'The audience in the 1990s will have seen...warriors who are suspect, fairies with unresolved sexual problems, and clowns who might have been conceived by Dostoievsky and trained by Beckett' (1996a: 230). We are enriched, he says, by a wide range of theatrical experiences from the lavish to the Spartan, and morally stimulated by the theatre's healthy scepticism about heroism and the easy achievement of human happiness. At the end of the twentieth century Shakespeare's theatre, in his view, has never been more various or more spirited.

Put on the Destined Livery

Directorial excess cannot conceal for some critics, however, a certain hollowness at its heart's core. For them the emperor has no clothes. In a version of the anxiety of influence, Susan Bennett's discussion of the seventeen *King Lear*s acknowledges 'the tenacious web of nostalgia and tradition that has Shakespeare as performance in its grip' (1996: 40). Most of the productions she considers echo or are reproductions of earlier performances, earlier productions. Directors, like critics and writers, chafe under the work of their predecessors. They are also, according to some critics, more timid in their work than may at first appear to be the case.

W. B. Worthen, in fact, argues that it is a mistake to think that the director is a liberated interpreter. The director comes into being, Worthen believes, 'at the moment that "drama" gains an independent existence as literature, a mode of being and a cultural authority independent of theatrical production' (1997: 47). Many directors tend to subscribe to that cultural authority and echo its presuppositions:

'Describing performance, performers, scholars, critics, teachers, and directors invoke surprisingly literary valuations of a stable text, and an intending author' (1997: 3). One strain of theatre criticism in this century, theoretically inflected, tackles the symbiotic relationship between literary criticism and Shakespeare in the theatre. Are directors, W. B. Worthen asks, 'faithful servants or egomaniacal traducers of the unprotected word'? (49). In nine cases out of ten, Worthen argues, they are more likely to be, or consider themselves to be, faithful servants of Shakespeare's words which they feel have been handed to them as a sacred trust. And so, Worthen again,

despite the 'death of the author' (Barthes), or the author's functional absorption into the systems of cultural and ideological production (Foucault), 'Shakespeare'—sometimes coded as the 'text,' its 'genre,' or the 'theater' itself—remains an apparently indispensable category for preparing, interpreting, and evaluating theatrical performance, at least as much for practitioners as for scholars and critics. (3)

But Shakespeare's words do not of course come unmediated into the minds of these practitioners; they come heavily freighted with everything to do with the twentieth century, not least the directors' own experience of it, through education, class, politics, family, and the thousand and one ways the prevailing ideology grafts itself onto the unconscious. As Robert Smallwood argues, 'most current professional productions of Shakespeare are not direct, unhampered encounters between actors and texts' (1996: 177). On the contrary, they take the stage 'in a general climate of critical thinking about Shakespeare and cater for audiences which include many who are well aware of the play and its recent critical and theatrical history' (177).

These audiences include professional critics, both academic and popular, and they too, like the plays' directors, do not come virginally to productions of Shakespeare. For this reason—and for others— Anthony Dawson resists 'claims about the necessity of reading Shakespeare's plays as "dramatic scripts" rather than literary texts' (1991: 319). Dramatic scripts are only thinly disguised literary texts, or literary texts at one remove. They can even be postmodern literary texts, or at least texts refracted anamorphically through postmodern critical eyes. This is the burden of Samuel Crowl's interesting work, *Shakespeare*

Observed: Studies in Performance on Stage and Screen (1992), which emphasizes the links between performance event and postmodern literary criticism: 'For example, as criticism undertakes to deconstruct ideology and discover marginal voices and perspectives, so performance criticism directs our attention to silences and subtexts' (1992: 12).

At all events, it would be unwise, many critics now argue, to divorce literary criticism *per se* (if it now can ever be considered to exist *per se*) from performance criticism. In his discussion of the struggle between performance criticism and close reading in the twentieth century, Richard Levin argues for restraint on both sides: 'it is evident that either mode of criticism, when left to itself, can be pushed too far, and that they could both benefit if they interacted with each other and, one would hope, restrained each other' (1986: 545). One of the new claims by performance critics, Levin goes on to say, is that the Renaissance thought of the plays as existing only in performance not in printed texts. But this is not the case. It is clear that the playwrights thought of their readers as reading with the performance in mind; and it is equally clear that the playwrights thought of a good performance as increasing the value of the play. So it is a question of 'an ideal of mutual animation' (556).

Mutual animation has quite a history in twentieth-century Shakespeare criticism. Unsurprisingly, directors still conceive of Shakespeare's plays largely in terms of characterization. For them character is god, as was the case with literary criticism until relatively recently, and even now, as we have seen, in criticism characters refuse to take a final curtain. Cary Mazer investigates Edwardian theatrical practice to show us the cultural bond between the criticism of A. C. Bradley and the theatrical production of the time. Mazer talks about the necessity for the integration of the actor into the stage picture, and tells us that this was achieved mainly through the employment of 'strictly pictorial, compositional values' (1981: 19). There was also a widespread use of the tableau, and Mazer notes that '[t]he curtain tableau implies that the life of the play continues behind the curtain without the audience's participation or perception' (23) just as Bradley's endnotes do for the readers of the play. Mazer instances a famous tableau sequence from Tree's *Tempest* (1904):

Caliban creeps from his cave, and watches the departing ship bearing away the freight of humanity which for a brief spell has gladdened and saddened his island home, and taught him to 'seek for grace.' For the last time Ariel appears, singing the song of the bee... The voice of the Sprite rises higher and higher until it is merged into the note of the lark—Ariel is now as free as a bird. Caliban listens for the last time to the sweet air, then turns sadly in the direction of the departing ship. The play is ended. As the curtain rises again, the ship is seen on the horizon, Caliban stretching out his palms towards it in mute despair. The night falls, and Caliban is left on the lonely rock. He is a King once more. (1981: 28)

No Edwardian novelist could have better milked the scene for its pathos.[17]

And We'll Strive to Please You Every Day

The performance of the actor has come under intense scrutiny in the twentieth century. It shouldn't come as any surprise, given the enormous number of productions of Shakespeare throughout the world over the last hundred years or so, that there is a considerable body of work on acting Shakespeare in the twentieth century. But acting him at other times has of course drawn the attention of the archaeologists of the theatre, and, again not surprisingly, it is speculation about the acting of Shakespeare in Shakespeare's time that has exerted the greatest fascination. The bedevilling question about acting in Shakespeare's time has been to what degree the actors acted from convention or from nature. How trippingly did they speak Shakespeare's language? Just how much did they saw the air with their hands?

The consensus of criticism seems to agree on two things: one is that the actors were much more likely to have been approved of by Hamlet than not (despite what he says in his play); the other that during the course of Shakespeare's career the acting would have tended to hold the mirror up to the play's language. We would in other words expect *Henry VI, Part 1* to have been acted differently from, let's say, *Hamlet*. The acting in the early history play might well have been closer to the acting of *Hamlet*'s play-within-the play than to that of *Hamlet* proper. Hamlet might not have approved. Anne Pasternak Slater puts it this way: Shakespeare progresses 'from the ritualized and formulaic use of stage action, to the lively realism of the middle plays and the uneven but often sophisticated mannerism of the last plays' (1982: 14). She argues that we can glean at least this much from studying the bad quartos—those condensations now thought to be playscripts—particularly their stage directions.

Shakespeare's actors have been pursued biographically in this century, and sociologically. We now know much more than we used to about their status in society, how much they earned, how schooled, trained, where they came from, how they ended up. From what we now know it seems that Shakespeare was one of the lucky ones, one of the few to have made a good living and cut something of a figure in society. Anne Pasternak Slater's book, for instance, is at pains to demonstrate the lack of power that actors had. On the other hand, the professional player might well be considered the bell-wether for the changing social realities denounced in the Homilies. And John Russell Brown speculates that Shakespeare's image of the 'cry of players' 'suggests that actors in a theatre company have a corporate strength; and that they physically strong [*sic*], specialized, energetic, instinctive, trained, and cruel' (1996: 12).

A more fanciful speculation, in some ways typical of the tendency to narcissism in twentieth-century criticism, comes from Meredith Skura's pursuit of the important connections to be made (with appropriate reservations of course) between the profession of actor in Shakespeare's time and the profession of actor in our own time. She asks us to ponder the similarity in the trajectory of their lives, in both the seventeenth and twentieth centuries; how frequently, for instance, in both centuries actors have uneasy relationships with their fathers, or how frequently they're deserted by their fathers. In both eras, actors are praised for their mimetic skills, but are praised more highly for their ostentatiousness as actors. In these terms we might consider that Bottom could stand for actors in general in his childishly narcissistic exhibitionism. Or perhaps Richard III: 'Richard's story almost parodies the modern actor's history of narcissistic wounds, subjective crisis, and dependence on the mirroring response of others, all of which make performance an ambiguous achievement' (1993: 71).

For someone like Martin Buzacott, to take an even more extreme version of this position, most modern-day actors are narcissistic Richards—Bottom is too genial a model—and their only competition in this regard comes from performance critics who, Buzacott says, put on deplorable performances of their own in the way they idolize actors while plying their 'actor-centric' criticism. But actors cannot do anything but offer us a 'mutilated Shakespeare' (1991: 24). They terrorize the text: 'through brutal coercion, the text is rendered subservient to the human appearance and voice which seeks to embody it' (30). The actors are losers, full of vanity, strutting and fretting, responding nauseatingly to the 'most extraordinary power' of the theatre 'to immortalize and deify even the most pathetic of society's losers' (38).

Reading Buzacott is like reading a more amusing William Prynne, his book the modern-day critic's version of *Histriomastix*, Prynne's venomous attack on the seventeenth-century English theatre. And Buzacott seems to me to be so much part of the tradition of a puritanical anti-theatrical hysteria[18] that Jonas Barish would seriously have to consider including him in any update of his popular work, *The Antitheatrical Prejudice*, a prejudice, Barish says, at its height when the theatre was at its height—in ancient Greece, Renaissance England, and seventeenth-century France: 'The bright day of Aristophanes and Sophocles brings forth the anxious Platonic reaction, the generation of Marlowe and Shakespeare calls forth the vituperations of the Puritans, and the triumphant artistry of Racine and Molière bring down the anathemas of the sternest moralists in the French religious community, the Jansenists' (1981: 191). And, we may say, the triumphant commercialism of Shakespeare in the twentieth century awakens an equally strident moralizing from the self-elected guardians of our own secular high culture, the literary critics (or some of them anyway).

This is a far cry from Russell Brown's encomium on the life-giving qualities of the twentieth-century actor: 'Very literally it [the play-script] comes alive onstage (and then in the minds of an audience) by means of what the actors do, their thinking, feeling, looking, their physical actions and reactions, their breathing, intelligences, and individual imaginations, their very being' (1996: pp. vii–viii). And the reactions of many other critics to moments of intense pleasure in the theatre, as we have seen, attest to the power of the actor to overcome implausibilities in the script.

A notoriously difficult episode psychologically speaking for both actors occurs in *Richard III* when Richard woos Anne over the body of her dead husband lying in state. She moves in a few lines from expressions of extreme revulsion for Richard, her husband's murderer, to a kind of passionate acquiescence in his proposal. Shirley Garner describes a production of *Richard III* where the extraordinary acting of Byron Jennings as Richard overcame the awkwardness of the circumstances of Anne's conversion, not least because 'Jennings, as Richard, was an incredibly attractive figure, physically and intellectually' (1996: 289).

In any case, Stephen Booth (1985) argues in a witty *jeu d'esprit*, it's not so much the actor's fault if he or she fails in the role, it's the role's fault, or Shakespeare's. And Booth instances what he considers to be four characters in Shakespeare who have a built-in failure component for actors, deliberately, not to say painstakingly, contrived by Shakespeare: Antony, Cleopatra, Brutus in *Julius Caesar*, and Hal in *Henry IV, Part 1*. In each case, Booth alleges, Shakespeare succeeds only too well in drawing an impossibly wonderful or contradictory character that his actor simply cannot live up to or contain.[19]

One of the by-products of this actor-centric age is the contribution actors and directors have made to the huge body of writings on Shakespeare or his plays. This is clearly a twentieth-century phenomenon. W. B. Worthen (1996*b*) notices that in these books (whether or not they're on Shakespeare) the actors reveal their eclecticism in the construction of their characters, and in this respect, Worthen argues, they resemble the new historicist use of the episodic, anecdotal, contingent, exotic aspects of the historical record. If we want to make a connection, then, between actors' conceptions of their roles and literary criticism we would give the nod to the work of Stephen Greenblatt, say, rather than to that of Dover Wilson. The most influential book by a director is Peter Brook's *The Empty Space* (1968). Even voice coaches get into the act. Richard Knowles (1996) goes so far as to claim that a book by one of them, *Voice and the Actor* by Cicely Berry, was as pivotal an influence on Shakespearean performance as Peter Brook's famous production in 1970 of *A Midsummer Night's Dream*. And there have been a number of books by film directors that have made useful contributions to our understanding of the hazards of transcribing scripts designed for the theatre into film scripts.[20]

In this century when all the world is its stages there has been a fair amount of discussion not only about the obvious difficulty of acting Shakespeare in languages other than English, but also in other kinds of English. It may well be easier, in some ways, to act Shakespeare in

French or in Russian (or in Urdu, for that matter) than in Australian or Canadian English. (Or in the English of Newcastle upon Tyne or Glasgow.) For most of the century the dominant accent in the English theatre has been a refined one from the Home Counties. I would wager that in 1950 most people in England would have thought that the voice of Laurence Olivier or John Gielgud was the 'natural' Shakespeare voice, aside, that is, from those descents into the vernacular by the clowns and other assorted homespuns. Later in the century it became a little more usual (but only a little) to hear regional inflections in the voice of a Hamlet or an Anthony (a Scottish Macbeth, however, became almost *de rigueur*). And so we still have the odd phenomenon of listening to a star of American films, Mel Gibson, speaking Hamlet as Christopher Plummer might have done (a further irony here is that Plummer is a Canadian and Gibson an Australian)— odd because it's more than likely that Gibson's natural Australian voice is closer to the way Shakespeare's major actors spoke in his time than the way Plummer does (let alone Olivier or Gielgud).

Dennis Salter argues that in Canada at least actors find the Shakespearean text and language estranging, and that they have to realize that Shakespeare can never be their contemporary. After all, Shakespeare's connotations 'often remain elusive, and might never in fact get into the bloodstream' (1996: 116). In any case, what does it mean to speak Shakespeare naturally? 'Natural by what standard? Natural in what ways? Natural to whom? Natural when and where?' (117). The fact of the matter for Salter is that natural speaking is never natural; natural acting is never natural. It is always artificial; it only seems natural by tradition, and Canadian actors have to establish their own tradition of speaking Shakespeare naturally; they have to find their own way of injecting him into their bloodstream.[21]

Some Quantity of Barren Spectators

The performance of the audience seems always to have generated more heat than light in twentieth-century Shakespeare criticism (and in the criticism of other centuries). This is particularly true in the case of work done on the audiences in Shakespeare's time whose behaviour can only be glimpsed second-hand through partisan accounts and, in this century, political agendas. At the beginning of the century,

Samuel Johnson's notion that Shakespeare's audiences were 'gross and dark' had many more advocates than it does now. Robert Bridges, for one, waxed as irately as Johnson himself on the subject. Bridges would like all editions of Shakespeare to come with a warning label that some of their contents might be harmful to the mental health of the young:

Shakespeare should not be put into the hands of the young without the warning that the foolish things in his plays were written to please the foolish, the filthy for the filthy, and the brutal for the brutal; . . . if out of veneration for his genius we are led to admire or even tolerate such things, we may be thereby not conforming ourselves to him, but only degrading ourselves to the level of his audience, and learning contamination from those wretched beings who can never be forgiven their share in preventing the greatest poet and dramatist of the world from being the best artist. (1927: 28–9).

Bridges was practising a particularly insidious form of Shakespeare idolatry in exculpating Shakespeare from his lapses in judgement by blaming not him but his audiences for them. (Although it doesn't say much for Shakespeare to have to imagine him unable to prevent himself from writing foolishly, filthily, and brutally.) Writing in the same year, and expressing similar sentiments, Wyndham Lewis talks of the 'sad compromises and shifts' in Shakespeare's works 'necessitated by the stupid and mean egotisms of his audience (whose tastes or lack of taste it is his unpleasant duty to learn by heart and have at his fingers' ends)' (1966: 172). A. C. Bradley manages to avoid the heated tone of these pronouncements, but his view of a bifurcated audience is just as condescending: 'In *Hamlet* Shakespeare gave his audience plenty that they could not understand, but he made it up to them in explosions' (1965: 371). And so is Granville Barker's: 'doubtless many of the audience for Shakespeare's new version of the old play [*Hamlet*] only thought he had spoiled a good story of murder and revenge by adding too much talk to it' (1957: 8).

Bridges and Lewis, Lewis especially, tend to weave Shakespeare's audience out of whole cloth. Bradley and Barker take a more caviare-to-the-general view of it by dividing Shakespeare's audience into the cognoscenti and the benighted. It's only for the latter that Shakespeare dropped his standards (and his aitches). This notion of a double-barrelled audience in Shakespeare's time, one part that knew its caviare and the other that didn't, continues to find adherents and could be described as the standard one for the twentieth century. Versions of it continue to flourish in the work, for instance, of Rene Girard and Harry Berger Jr.

And yet precisely because the facts about Shakespeare's audiences are so meagre, other countermanding views of them can also get a sympathetic hearing. Back in 1906 indeed Sir Sidney Lee argued that the theatrical audiences of his day were not as receptive and capable as they were in Shakespeare's time as twentieth-century audiences simply lacked the imagination to ascend the bright heaven of Shakespeare's invention. Such a defence of the spectators in Shakespeare's theatre usually insists on the superiority they must have had over audiences from later crasser eras in the way in which they were accustomed to hear difficult language spoken in public. They lived in an aural and oral culture; even if they were illiterate they could still absorb the cut-and-thrust of spoken argument however complex. Their ears were tuned to poetry.[22] S. L. Bethell can say in 1944: 'the average Elizabethan play-goer would seem, both from the plays themselves and from external evidence, to have been in many ways better educated than the average play-goer today' (43). And Bethell is one of a number of twentieth-century critics to use the audiences of yester-year as a club with which to beat modern-day audiences: '. . . materialism, middle-brow psychological drama, the craze for scene-painting, and the cinema's habitual use of natural settings, have all tended to undermine the creative naivete of the popular audience' (25).

It may be a wartime-induced nostalgia that drove critics in the 1940s to look back at Shakespeare's theatre and find it populated with a respectable and colourful citizenry. Here's Alfred Harbage in 1941 imagining himself transported back to the Globe: 'Surrounding me would be cheerful and decent folk who had come singly, in mixed couples, in family parties, wearing their Sunday best' (1969: 158). Harbage insists on the representational nature of Shakespeare's audiences: 'But most importantly, Shakespeare's audience was socially, economically, educationally heterogeneous. It was motley, and for this we must be thankful' (162). It is but a short step from this laudatory view of such a motley assembly to the one that turns Bridges on his head by arguing that the audience 'must be given much of the credit for the greatness of Shakespeare's plays' (159). A glimpse into the collective mind of these audiences, so Harbage believes, would be like a glimpse into Shakespeare's mind. And this, surely, reflects well on audiences generally, including ones in 1941: 'If we withdraw the opprobrious terms and concede the audience a share in the merit of the plays, we add to our own stature and our right to glory in our kind. It is an opportunity not lightly to be dismissed' (164).

A laudatory view of Shakespeare's audience from a different perspective—one that would, I think, have horrified Harbage—can be found in Ann Jennalie Cook's controversial contribution to the debate, *The Privileged Playgoers of Shakespeare's London, 1576–1642* (1981). The playgoers of her title aren't so much privileged because they can see a Shakespeare play perhaps with Shakespeare in it (though that would have undeniably been a great privilege) but privileged because they come from the privileged classes. Cook would no doubt have scorned Harbage's notion of a theatre full of decent folk dressed in their Sunday best. Her theatre is filled with the aristocracy, the gentry, and the professional classes. There seems to be very little room (even standing) for groundlings. Cook's work hasn't just caused consternation politically; her methodology has also been severely criticized and David Margolies combines the two neatly in his belief that she uses her material 'illogically, anachronistically, insensitively and either naively or disingenuously' (1988: 53) and demonstrates 'the spirit of Reaganomics in theatre criticism' (53).[23]

There is a tendency in nearly all criticism in the century trained on audiences, Shakespeare's or ours, to talk about them as though they comprise same- or similar-thinking collectivities. Some criticism attempts to chart a course among them, describing how a certain age throws up a certain kind of collectivity, how it differs from the representative audience of a previous or later age. There have been attempts as well to discriminate among the collectivities in Shakespeare's own time. The argument here is that at a time of intense theatrical activity such as Shakespeare's, the expectations of the audience will change in line with the increasing sophistication of the plays' presentation in the theatre.

Andrew Gurr believes that the 1590s was one such crucible for change when '[w]hat the players now had to supply was plausible impersonation' (1987: 136), and he asks us to consider the term 'personation', a term that first came into use in the 1590s, as 'signalling not only the concept of a player pretending to be a real human being (as distinct from Magnificence or a king like Cambyses) but the arrival of stage heroes with whom many of the spectators could identify themselves and their wants' (136). M. C. Bradbrook offers us the inverse of this process whereby the play creates its audience when she says that '[t]he English History play must have been one of the great means of unifying the spectators and creating an audience out of a throng' (1964: 110).

Were Shakespeare's collectivities of spectators audiences or throngs? Recently there has been a renewed emphasis on the idea that his audience was myriad-minded. Playwrights, so argues Bradbrook, 'achieved something like the feat of conducting an orchestra as they wove together the variety of demands that the mixed audience exacted' (1976: 31). Jean Howard claims that 'the institution (the theater) could and did serve a variety of competing class and gender interests' (1994: 12). Anthropologically inclined critics like François Laroque see the Elizabethan theatre as a form of popular culture that was a 'complex, contradictory and virtually unclassifiable mixture, at once an art of living and a world vision, incorrigibly down-to-earth and materialistic, yet, at another level, haunted by superstition' (1991: 50). Its audiences were incredibly diverse, and that diversity included women for whom, as paying customers, the play should please; so that even though the ends of plays usually satisfied the desires of men, in the course of getting to that satisfaction there had to be pleasures in the play for women. In other words, just like any other professional writer, Shakespeare had to bear in mind his various constituencies without necessarily kowtowing to any of them. On the other hand, Meredith Skura argues that, as in the present-day, the Elizabethan audience identified with character and performer thereby fostering in them 'the ambivalence and regressive concerns typical of modern actors' (1993: 29). Indeed, the Elizabethan player 'was marked as the Other whose strangeness fascinates and repels, the charismatic transgressor who all too easily becomes a screen for the projection of the audience's disowned impulses' (37–8). Including, one might say, the playwrights' who, for instance, frequently complained about the alleged wealth of the players.

Criticism in this century has been at some pains to try to establish Shakespeare's view of his audiences. Are his and Hamlet's views of them one and the same? Would Hamlet's advice to the Players be

Shakespeare's advice to his players? This is a position that has often been taken by critics, especially in the absence of anything more authoritative. Louis Montrose begs to differ with the standard interpretation, however. In this, as in many other ways, Shakespeare is no Hamlet: 'The playwright's perspective on the purpose of playing is more capacious, popular, and equivocal than that of the Prince' (1996: 44). It has to be capacious enough at least to take in the audience at the Blackfriars as well as the one at the Globe. If Alfred Harbage (1950) is to be believed, the expectations of these two audiences differed considerably, though his compartmentalization of the repertory into one for the public theatres and another for the private has come in for a good deal of criticism. Alvin Kernan (1995) thinks that Hamlet's advice to the players probably does not reflect Shakespeare's theatrical credo, but it might very well reflect the court's, although Kernan argues that James himself was not much of an audience—he lost interest quickly, and his tastes were probably closer to those of Polonius than to those of Hamlet.

On the other hand, there is a line of critical opinion in this century that thinks Shakespeare out-Hamlets Hamlet in taking a dim view of the capacities of the average Elizabethan audience. Richard Wilson believes that the image of Shakespeare's theatre 'as a democratic forum, where citizens of England's supposedly organic pre-industrial community met in a classless mutuality which remains a glowing example to the world' (1993: 23) is a fabrication engendered in the twentieth century by the panic brought on by the European revolutions of 1917–20. Shakespeare himself doesn't demonstrate this classless mutuality, Wilson believes, in his at best ambivalent attitude towards the populace (and by inference towards his audiences), alive as he was to the dangers of the emergence of the city mob. Is Wilson's inference a reasonable one though? Would there not be a difference between a mob and an audience (or even a throng)?

Kowtowing to a particular constituency on Shakespeare's part is the burden of Alvin Kernan's consideration of the performance of the king—and the nobility—as audience in the early seventeenth century. Kernan's book talks about Shakespeare as a patronage dramatist and his hard-headed thesis flies in the face of the still popular notion of Shakespeare as a romantic artist writing primarily out of his own creatively free imagination. Between 1603 and 1613, Kernan tells us, the King's Men played before the court 138 times, an average of nearly fourteen performances a year, more than any other company, and far more than during the reign of Elizabeth where the average was only six plays a year. Kernan uses these statistics, among other arguments, to press the case for a Shakespeare who was 'a helpful royal servant, a propagandist for the monarchy, a radical conservative' (1995: p. xxii). Shakespeare was also, we should remember, 'upwardly mobile, acquisitive, patrician in his interests and aspirations' (p. xxii). Kernan here joins the ranks of the other twentieth-century sceptics who, as we saw in Chapter 2, cast a cold eye on Shakespeare as the writer with aspirations to social and economic grandeur. Kernan recognizes that he is swimming against the tide: 'Our democratic age will resist even a partial transformation of Shakespeare into a courtly servant and a recipient of patronage' (p. xxii).

What then of other audiences in other centuries? Critics seem to agree that by and large the typical theatre audience for Shakespeare in the twentieth century has had little of the verve and colour of Shakespeare's original audiences. Mute and inglorious, many in today's audiences attend the world's Stratfords more as an educational obligation than as a pleasure. Only in the cinema, perhaps, does Shakespeare reach out to that cross-section of the public that—*pace* Anne Jennalie Cook—flocked to the Globe. Only in the cinema, I suspect, would a production like Franco Zeffirelli's *Romeo and Juliet*—whatever its shortcomings as an interpretation of the play—cause teenage girls to swoon and weep.[24] And yet this is the audience—and *a fortiori* the one for televison—that is most derided by critics for its passive consumerism.

Television audiences in particular draw the ire of critics as some quantity of barren spectators indeed. But they are in the nature of the beast. Television creates us, so H. R. Coursen believes, as passive consumers: 'On television even our laughing is done for us. Our own participation is minimal and it is meant to be, the better to lull us into the robotism of consumption' (1993: 14). Just as robotically we consume Shakespeare. If Coursen's position sounds like an extension of William Prynne's or Martin Buzacott's, it is a view that is held by many influential critics; we must beware of an excessive reliance on video and film, Jay Halio warns, for 'without proper care the study of Shakespeare could degenerate into entertainment without insight, a joyful

but vacuous apprehension of the plays leading to, at best, a sophisticated appreciation of staging techniques or, at worst, a debased taste
for gimmickry' (1977: 273–4). At least there's joy involved here however
vacuous it may be.

The last word perhaps should be given to what in the end will be the
determining factor, the purchasing power of this much maligned
beast, the twentieth-century audience. David Edgar writes in a review
article on books on Noel Coward: 'The greatest change of the Eighties
and Nineties in the theatre—as in British culture as a whole—has been
a shift of power from the producer to the consumer: it's no surprise
that audiences have flocked back to a playwright whose stated purpose
was to give them a good time' (1999: 27).

Beastly Shameless Transformation

Until fairly recently, most books and articles written on film and
television productions of Shakespeare in the twentieth century concern themselves with questions of textual purity. Film and television
tend to take more liberties with Shakespeare's texts than the theatre
does. Harley Granville Barker had a famous argument with Alfred
Hitchcock in the 1930s about the pictorial indulgence of the cinema's
treatment of Shakespeare. As far as Hitchcock was concerned Barker's
position was that of the stuffy traditionalist defending his turf at all
costs—an irony considering Barker's own iconoclasm. John Collick
dismissively lays out the typical questions asked by writers on film:
'How should a Shakespeare play be filmed? What film techniques,
settings and methods of editing will ensure that the movie stays
faithful to the original text? Should Shakespeare's works be made
into movies at all?' (1989: 1).

Mutatis mutandis, the same questions are asked, with even greater
vehemence, about television. Whether or not Shakespeare should be
filmed at all seems a peculiarly redundant question considering that
between 1897 and 1989 over 200 films and countless television shows—
not to mention radio transmissions—have beamed Shakespeare into
places where at best he only ever existed as an unopened musty tome
next to the family bible. So we should be thankful to the technology of
the twentieth century for its role in the dissemination of Shakespeare's
plays even though they come perforce with a far greater number of the

explosions than A. C. Bradley condemned in the original production of *Hamlet*. Witness, for instance, the prolonged battle sequences in both Laurence Olivier's and Kenneth Branagh's film versions of *Henry V*, though they are inflected very differently: Olivier's, ceremonious and pageant-like; Branagh's, slow-motion studies in the grisly shedding of blood. None the less, as Anthony Davies argues, Olivier's 1944 *Henry V* was probably the first film that 'operates on too many levels to be patronizingly dismissed or glibly celebrated' (1987: 3).

Nobody now can patronizingly dismiss the cinema as a legitimate outlet for Shakespeare in the face of such masterpieces as Akira Kurosawa's *Throne of Blood* (1957), Roman Polanski's *Macbeth* (1971), Orson Welles's *Chimes At Midnight* (1966), Franco Zeffirelli's *Romeo and Juliet* (1968), Peter Hall's *A Midsummer Night's Dream* (1969), Grigorii Kozintsev's *Hamlet* (1964) and *King Lear* (1970), and Peter Brook's *King Lear* (1970). These and other films of similar worth are explored and celebrated in a number of books on Shakespeare and film by, for instance, Jack Jorgens in 1977 and Roger Manvell in 1979. Anthony Davies (1988) assesses the adaptations of Shakespeare's plays in the films of Laurence Olivier, Orson Welles, Peter Brook, and Akira Kurosawa (as does Peter Donaldson (1990) with additional considerations of Liz White's *Othello* and Jean-Luc Godard's *King Lear*.) The extraordinary number of silent films of Shakespeare's plays are the subject of a book by Robert Hamilton Ball (1968).

But if it is one thing to talk about Welles and Kurosawa (and even Zeffirelli) it's quite another, some critics argue, to talk about, say, Mel Gibson's *Hamlet*. And so a collection of essays such as Lynda Boose's and Richard Burt's *Shakespeare the Movie: Popularizing the Plays on Film, TV, and Video* (1997) worries about what Boose and Burt describe as 'the Hollywoodization of Shakespeare in the nineties' (8). Gibson's *Hamlet* and other Shakespeare plays produced or influenced by Hollywood at the end of the twentieth century 'construct a world even more obsessively masculine than did the *Hamlet*(s) that preexisted any articulated feminist critique of popular culture' (9) climaxing in the 1996 production of *William Shakespeare's Romeo and Juliet* starring Leonardo DiCaprio and Clare Danes (the title includes Shakespeare's name in case the film's hoodlum ambience à la 1990s Los Angeles might suggest it was written by someone else).

Critics, however, can still patronize the newer technology, television, and many still do, but the new use of video in the classroom has made a series like the BBC production of the complete plays, the BBC/Time-Life series, too valuable a pedagogic tool to be slighted, despite the antagonism of someone like Graham Holderness who thinks that the series 'was produced in the image of the Corporation itself: a classical monument of national culture, an oppressive agency of cultural hegemony' (1988: 181). (The broad brush-stroke of this criticism hardly takes into account the variety in quality, approach, and ideology of the individual productions.)[25]

Shakespeare on television is different from Shakespeare on film, as many commentators tell us, and Shakespeare on television is not really like anything else on television either, according to H. R. Coursen: 'Watching Shakespeare on television may not be like "watching Shakespeare," but it is not like watching television either' (1993: 27). The uniqueness of television may make it, oddly enough, uniquely appropriate as a medium for dramatizing Shakespeare: hence the question driving one of the sessions in *Is Shakespeare Still Our Contemporary?* (Elsom 1989), Session 6, Does Shakespeare write better for television? Some of his plays clearly work better on television than others, *All's Well That Ends Well* works better than *A Midsummer Night's Dream*, for instance. H. R. Coursen (1993) believes that the theatre works better on television than television does; that is, television translations of actual stage productions, like the Royal Shakespeare Company *Macbeth* and *Antony and Cleopatra*, are better than productions mounted especially for television. This is where the future lies, Coursen believes. (Hard to believe, really.) The 1960s and early 1970s did give us television adaptations of interesting stage productions: the Hall-Barton *The Wars of the Roses*, the Papp-Antoon *Much Ado About Nothing*, and Trevor Nunn's *Antony and Cleopatra*, for instance.

A number of critics, however, urge the case for radio. Radio, they say, can do things that film and television can't; it's intrinsically more receptive to the spoken word, and the use of radiophonics can produce an exciting aural experience that allows the listener's imagination to work in ways unknown to the other media. In this sense it is closer to the experience of the Globe audience—oddly enough—than the hyper-realism of this pre-eminently visual century.

The future of literary criticism with regard to film, television, and radio (and the theatre) may lie in exploring the ways in which twentieth-century productions in different media interanimate. Samuel Crowl notes that the success of the Royal Shakespeare Company and the National Theatre has shifted our interest away from film and video to the stage; but these stage productions are distinguished by their cinematic qualities:

The spare, sparse, monochromatic set and costume designs which dominated R. S. C. productions in the early Hall years were derived, I believe, as much from the influence of the great black-and-white films of Bergman, Welles, and Renoir as from the more obvious influence of Brecht and contributed to create a modern, anti-ceremonial anti-rhetorical approach to these plays. (1992: 22)

And while it is obvious that stage productions of Shakespeare have influenced the way Shakespeare appears on the screens of television and film, the nature of that influence is more elusive than that of the screens on the stage. More work needs to be done on this stage-to-screen trajectory of the interanimating process. One recent book that does so for Shakespeare's history plays is Ace Pilkington's which explores the relationships between the BBC television productions of the plays of the second tetralogy to Orson Welles's *Chimes at Midnight* and Olivier's *Henry V.* He concludes soundly enough: '. . . each new example of filmed, televized, or videotaped Shakespeare helps to rewrite expectational texts, helps to suggest more fully the contours of each play it presents and the medium it represents' (1991: 163).

To Double Business Bound

A strain of literary criticism in this century—formalist as much as anything—considers the idea of the theatre in Shakespeare. Shakespeare's plays, it is argued, are extraordinarily self-reflexive; they comment obsessively either directly or indirectly on themselves as theatre. They not only hold a mirror up to nature but also up to the lineaments of their own art. In the case of a play like *Hamlet*—if Hamlet's advice to the players is indeed a version of Shakespeare's—Shakespeare seems to stand aside from his play for a while in order to comment prescriptively on the nature of playing. Standing aside from the play, however, is a somewhat misleading description of an episode in a play that seems to be based on a series of standing-asides (as well as theatrical asides), insets, parentheses, and Polonius-like meanderings away from the point. We would do well to see Hamlet's advice to the Players then as exemplifying the play's structural pattern and meaning rather than as a self-indulgent digression into extraneous matter. None the less, it is one of the few moments in Shakespeare when the topic of the theatre takes central stage in the theatre. And as many twentieth-century critics have noticed, Hamlet, like many of his fellow protagonists, speaks the language of the theatre throughout the play.

In one of the first treatments of the metadramatic or metatheatrical—as theatre-speak has come to be called—in Shakespeare, Anne Righter lists the words that Shakespeare constantly uses metaphorically in their theatrical sense: act, scene, tragedy, perform, part, play, counterfeit, shadow, prologue, shape, applaud, show. She says: 'They remind the audience of the playlike nature of its own life, and they lend an ominous, portentous quality to the action on the stage' (1962: 92). Ominous and portentous? Not in the early comedies according to this same author: 'Shadows, dreams, a sense of enchantment and festivity surround the idea of the play in these early comedies' (104). And she later says that often the metaphor is used to glorify the stage: 'The actors, Shakespeare's own companions and friends, have become the chroniclers of man's great deeds' (158). After, and perhaps including *Hamlet*, things change. 'It is difficult not to feel, however, that some obscure but quite personal disgust with the London theatre and with the practice of the actor's and dramatist's craft also lies behind this change' (173). In the problem plays there is now a tendency to insult the theatre, even more so in the great tragedies. As for *Timon of Athens* it's 'marked by a curious strain of contempt for shadows, shows, imitations of all kinds, even for the clothes men wear' (186). In *Coriolanus* and in *Antony and Cleopatra* the stage denotes futility and shame. In the last plays, however, 'the bitterness, the sense of futility and pride' (192) attached to the image of the theatre vanish as the theatre becomes reality.

I quote from Anne Righter at some length because the two directions her metadramatic criticism takes are by and large the ones taken by most critics pursuing the representation of the theatre in Shakespeare's plays. They either look inward into the plays themselves and assess the contribution the play's self-referentiality makes to its meaning, or look outward to matters of biography or sociology. In a series of sparkling books, James Calderwood practises the first of these approaches.[26] He tells us that a Shakespeare play is, in some sense, about 'its materials, its media of language and theatre, its generic forms and conventions, its relationship to truth and the social order' (1971: 5), in a word, dramatic art itself. Of *Hamlet* Calderwood writes: 'Deconstruction, it seems to me, is built into the play, as it is in many literary works, to the extent that *Hamlet* repeatedly insists upon its own fictionality, or in this case theatricality, and addresses itself to the nature of dramatic illusion' (1983: p. xv). In the process of repeatedly insisting on its own theatricality, plot and aesthetic commentary interanimate, so that, for instance, 'Hamlet's inexplicably stalled revenge may be to some extent a metadramatic reflection of Shakespeare's resistance to the structural syntax of revenge tragedy' (27). What differentiates *Hamlet*, then, from other revenge tragedies is its exploration of form.

Metadramatic criticism's centrifugal exploration grapples with the problem of intention. Is the plays' indulgence in self-reference alienating, playful, celebratory, or all or any one of these at different stages in Shakespeare's career? We might take the metatheatricality of *A Midsummer Night's Dream* as an indication of just how malleable it can be from an interpretative point of view. For Anne Righter, it's a question of dream and festivity; for Robert Nelson, Bottom's play may be playful, but it serves by its ineptness to stress the social distinction between players and played-to: 'In the class-structured society of Elizabethan England only the most persuasive and sincere attempts at illusion could allow for identification between lowly actor and royal spectator' (1958: 14); for Louis Montrose, talking of Quince's prologue, playfulness almost disappears:

In this darker or more oblique sense, Shakespeare's metatheatrical Prologue is an interpretive challenge, immediately directed toward the regulatory authority of the Duke and his Master of the Revels; and, beyond them, mediately directed to the Elizabethan authorities—the Queen, the Master of the Revels, her Privy Council, to whose interpretive findings and takings the intentions of the players and their playwrights were always ultimately subject. (1996: 195)

Metadramatic criticism of Shakespeare's plays, then, parallels most other criticism of Shakespeare in the twentieth century in its tendency to muddy the waters while providing exciting moments of release and clarification.

Shakespeare in History and History in Shakespeare

The Thick Rotundity o' the World

Not even the most committed formalist would argue that Shakespeare's works could be satisfactorily understood with no concern for their place in history. After all, the very language the formalists practise their art on is a language from another historical era whose idiom—as the mass of commentary in most modern editions of Shakespeare testifies—often needs strenuous interpretation. One of the glories of twentieth-century Shakespeare criticism, as we have seen, is the inspired interpretations of those Shakespeare passages bristling with ambiguity and metaphor. Modernist poetic practice spurred on modernist critics to give full reign to their intense engagement with Shakespeare's imagination, and they could not do so without an understanding of the time-bound language and concepts with which he shaped his art. But this is the application of history at its most minimal, whereas for many twentieth-century critics history at its most interventionist is now the *sine qua non* of Shakespeare criticism—and of most other kinds. 'The systematic application of historical findings to the interpretation of secular literature', writes S. Viswanathan, 'is a characteristic twentieth-century development' (1980: 7).

History, however, is not a term that runs pure and clear. Twentieth-century Shakespeare criticism reminds us constantly that concepts like these are never innocently transparent; when we talk about *history* we are always talking about someone's history at the expense usually of someone else's (often Shakespeare's). Much of this chapter, therefore, will inevitably concern itself with an investigation of who those some-ones are in the twentieth century, and it seems only appropriate that the main Shakespeare texts that will be considered here are the Histories themselves, a group of plays which, as John Bromley says, has found its spiritual home in the twentieth century; we're more comfortable than our predecessors have been—more cynically com-fortable perhaps as Bromley's idiom suggests—with this 'record of the fratricidal brawling conduct for nearly two centuries over a crown which in retrospect was not worth getting because not worth having' (1971: 2).

Historical criticism, however, like its formalist compatriot, is not an invention of the twentieth century, though the large claims made for it undoubtedly is. In some form or other it has always been around and we can experience a version of it, for instance, in the criticism of John Dryden in the eighteenth century. Part of the industrial revolution in late nineteenth-century Shakespeare studies that Chapter 1 discusses was devoted to investigations of the background to Shakespeare and his works. J. W. Lever argues that a 'common fallacy would have it that Shakespeare studies in the late nineteenth and early twentieth century consisted mainly of sentimental biography, character-analysis and patriotic effusions on history plays' (1976: 79), but in fact, as he goes on to demonstrate, the groundwork—of a distinctly humanist cast— for understanding Elizabethan thought was laid during this time. Two papers for the New Shakspere Society in 1874, 'The Political Use of the Stage in Shakspere's Time' and 'The Politics of Shakspere's Historical Plays', written by a researcher called Richard Simpson, even anticipate the twentieth century's obsession with political history. C. H. Herford commends Walter Raleigh's *Shakespeare* (1907) for its attempt 'to interpret Shakespeare in terms of Elizabethan England' (1923: 37), and laments the influence of A. C. Bradley in encouraging students to turn their backs on Elizabethan history for 'historical' biographies of Shakespeare's characters of a far more speculative, fantastic, Bradleyan kind.

Much of the historical research of the 1920s and 1930s concentrated on Shakespeare's stage conventions, audiences, and theatre. If only we could think like the average Elizabethan play-goer, so the argument ran, most interpretative problems would be solved. In 1934 J. L.

Hotson, in assessing the direction of Shakespeare criticism, is convinced that '[t]he student's approach to Shakespeare, as the work of the last thirty years has planned it, will be something like a *contemporary* approach. He will try to make himself one with the audience of the Globe or Blackfriars' (1934: p. ix).

E. E. Stoll thought the matter commonsensical and straightforward, but vital: if we don't read Shakespeare in terms of Elizabethan England then he 'now is Dowden, Swinburne, Bradley, Raleigh ... no longer himself' (1927: 258). And despite the possibility, as Stoll himself acknowledges, that Shakespeare might not have been perfectly cognizant of his own intentions, 'to get at Shakespeare's intention is not hard' (262), for, once we are aware of the dramaturgical conventions he is following, he 'constantly sets us right' (263); it's just a question of reading him Elizabethanly. A knowledge of those theatrical conventions makes short work, for instance, of the problem of Shylock in *The Merchant of Venice*. Shylock has to be seen under Stoll's tutelage as a comic villain and his characterization has to be understood—it's unfortunate, but there you are—in the tradition of antisemitism that was Shakespeare's intellectual heritage from at least the thirteenth century. Stoll's Shakespeare is clarity itself, 'no abysmal irony undermines his solid sense and straightforward meaning' (1927: 298), and right to the end of his long working life Stoll persisted in his belief that the clue to understanding Shakespeare was an historical understanding of Elizabethan audiences and a knowledge of Shakespeare's 'primitive' stage conventions. His last book reiterates his working philosophy: 'The right and just conception of the work as a whole—which is the author's—can be obtained only through a knowledge of the conventions and traditions of the author's art, belonging to the author's time' (1944: 24).

Stoll's work was—and is—influential and led, for instance, to attempts by directors to stage Shakespeare in the light of a growing understanding of the Elizabethan stage conventions and conditions that Stoll explored. Hence R. W. Babcock's admiring judgement of Harley Granville Barker: 'The best theatrical study of Shakespeare's plays from the Elizabethan point of view appears in the late Mr. Granville-Barker's famous *Prefaces*, wherein a distinguished English critic shows brilliantly how the plays should be acted by Elizabethan standards and with reference to the Elizabethan triple stage' (1952: 18).

Despite Stoll's tireless advocacy, Elizabethan stage conditions and conventions obviously do not exhaust the possibilities for historical research though they remain a favourite area for researchers of a more practical bent. For most early twentieth-century historical critics, however, all the Elizabethan world was their stage and expeditions to it promised them golden returns in their pursuit of Shakespeare's meaning. Hardin Craig speaks for many of them in insisting that we need to get into Shakespeare's world without bringing to it the distorting baggage of our own beliefs and presuppositions; he is especially contemptuous of those 'surrealistic conclusions' (1949: 109) about Shakespeare that the Freudians ask us to swallow. We 'have to make ourselves at home in the Renaissance' (110), he avers. On the other hand, he warns us (as many other critics did, and still do) that we should not be bound by a 'rigidly systematized faculty psychology' (109) as were the Elizabethans. We need Shakespeare's meaning not theirs.

Despite his warnings, criticism still has an interest in arriving at Shakespeare's mind via some kind of historicized medical understanding of the *echt* Elizabethan mind. This particular historical approach to Shakespeare's plays—especially to the characters in them—in the light of the poet's own Elizabethan thought and psychology is largely a modern American development and its countervailing instructiveness to a twentieth-century critical commonplace is summed up neatly by Paul Gottschalk: 'Hamlet's emotion is not in excess of the facts as they would appear to an Elizabethan' (1972: 67). (Actually, I am not all that sure, despite the authority of T. S. Eliot, that Hamlet's emotion *is* in excess of the facts of the play as they appear to us.)

As the century wore on, twentieth-century Shakespeare criticism widened its historical horizons. Immersion in such areas as the social and economic conditions of Shakespeare's time, its intellectual and cultural climate, its religious beliefs, its literary and dramatic theories, its flirtations with pneumatology, demonology, and other superstitions, became *de rigueur* for critics attempting to parse Shakespeare's greatness. In a word, this was the heyday of the now suspect ideas-of-the-time approach to the study of literature. Critics like J. M. Robertson, E. E. Stoll, L. L. Schücking, Theodore Spencer, Lily B. Campbell, and E. M. W. Tillyard culled historical evidence from a variety of intellectual movements for a better understanding of Shakespeare's works.

For a while research into Shakespeare's religious background took centre stage. In a move that smacks of the twentieth century, J. W. Lever links our time with Shakespeare's to explain the postwar fashion for religious interpretation: 'A comparable passion for metaphysical assurance may explain the rise in the forties and fifties of a new school of Shakespearean exegesis, which reads the plays as repositories of Christian doctrine' (1976: 88). Lever perhaps exaggerates when he argues that T. S. Eliot reflected 'a widespread attitude amongst intellectuals of his generation' (80) in his rejection of secular humanism, but he doesn't exaggerate in arguing that, for many important critics, making themselves at home in the Renaissance entailed making themselves at home in the Middle Ages also as so much of Shakespeare's thought looked back nostalgically to medieval certainties. Critics thus followed T. S. Eliot in his tendency, in Lever's words, 'to minimize the significance of the Renaissance as a distinctive culture, to stress its continuity with the middle ages, and to explain any strains of skepticism as a kind of incipient "modernism" or even "Counter-Renaissance"' (80–81).

A number of useful books look back along these lines—among the more notable being H. B. Charlton's *Shakespearian Comedy* (1938) and *Shakespearian Tragedy* (1948), W. W. Lawrence's *Shakespeare's Problem Comedies* (1931), John Dover Wilson's *The Fortunes of Falstaff* (1944), and Willard Farnham's *The Medieval Heritage of Elizabethan Tragedy* (1956). Some of this kind of research into the ideas of Shakespeare's time, however, deserves the strictures it received from later critics. Wilbur Sanders believes that '[b]y the imposition of a static, schematic conception of the major epoch of our literature, the historicists have contrived to confine that literature within little closed compartments, so the living interests of the general reader cannot hope to achieve any vital engagement with it' (1968: 1). He describes the fruits of this kind of research as—in a pungent phrase—a 'gelded Elizabethanism' (2). And we may feel that Richard Levin's judgement on the inadequacy of the ideas-of-the-time approach is no more than just: '... Shakespeare can teach us more about the ideas of his time than the ideas of his time can teach us about Shakespeare' (1977: 137). He warns us to watch out for the 'dreary victory of the official ideas of the time over the plays of Shakespeare, and over the facts of our experience' (133).

In All Line of Order

According to many recent critics the dreariest victory over Shakespeare's plays by a gelded Elizabethanism in the twentieth century can be blamed on E. M. W. Tillyard, the sometime dean of the historical approach to Shakespeare, architect of the infamous Elizabethan World Picture, and rival to A. C. Bradley in the number of well-thumbed copies of his books on today's university library shelves.[1] The extent of the vehement denigration of Tillyard's work matches the degree of popularity of the work itself. In this respect (among others) Tillyard resembles Bradley (and Caroline Spurgeon) and it might be appropriate to ask the same question about him that I asked about Bradley in Chapter 2: what is the secret of his immense success with the readers of our time? The answer resembles the one I offered for Bradley in that Tillyard, like Bradley, gives his readers a fundamentally reassuring, and reassuringly accessible, account of the essential philosophy of Shakespeare's plays, and gives it to them at least initially—unlike Bradley—at a time when reassurance was most needed—that is, in the last years of the Second World War. In 1904 the necessity for that degree of reassurance was unimaginable.

In what follows I shall be concentrating on his most notorious book, *The Elizabethan World Picture: A Study of the Idea of Order in the Age of Shakespeare, Donne and Milton* (1943) and the one that he published the following year, *Shakespeare's History Plays*, but we should bear in mind that he wrote books on the problem plays (1949), the early comedies (published posthumously in 1965), and the last plays (1938), and that they mirror the kind of treatment of Shakespeare's plays discernible in the first two.

The Elizabethan World Picture, then, is an unpinning of what Tillyard thinks the average Elizabethan intellectual believed in, knowingly or not; beliefs, that is, 'which were quite taken for granted by the ordinary educated Elizabethan' (1943: p. vii), those that 'would have been present to the mind of every educated man in an Elizabethan audience' (72–3).[2] They were 'the average beliefs of the well-educated Elizabethan' (43) and they amounted to a 'supreme commonplace' (68) or a series of them 'more often hinted at or taken for granted than set forth' (26). One such supreme commonplace, 'peculiarly vehement in the age of Elizabeth' (75), was '[t]he battle between Reason and Passion, the commonplace of every age' (75).

In his book on Shakespeare's history plays the 'ordinary educated Elizabethan' becomes the 'plain man' (1986: 29), deeply suspicious of Machiavelli, who foreshadows the twentieth-century plain man, deeply suspicious of Oscar Wilde, the former 'turning Machiavelli's specific political remedies for Italy in the year 1513 into eternal principles' (29), the latter 'turning Wilde's homosexuality into the mainspring of his whole life' (29). Somehow or other Shakespeare and the Elizabethan plain man and by extension the twentieth-century plain man merge in Tillyard: 'the poet is most individual', he declares, 'when most orthodox and of his age' (1986: 108).

A plain man speaking about another plain man to other plain men obviously holds an attraction for readers—the men anyway—battered by the twentieth century's complexities and terrifying immoralities. And Tillyard's emphasis on Shakespeare's historiography is perhaps equally reassuring, though I think his position here has been somewhat oversimplified. Tillyard's view by and large is that Shakespeare followed the chief historiographers of the Tudor period, the chroniclers and the writers of the Homilies, who justified the Tudor dynasty's claim to the throne by an elaborate defence. Their careful construction of what has become known as the Tudor myth began with the work of Polydore Vergil (?1470–?1555), who saw the stretch of history from Richard II to Henry VII in a solemn moral light, and climaxed in the writings of Edward Hall (d. 1547) who even more solemnly recorded the providential triumph of the Tudor line of kings.

Tillyard argues that this is the pattern followed by Shakespeare in his history plays:

In the total sequence of his plays dealing with the subject matter of Hall he expressed successfully a universally held and still comprehensible scheme of history: a scheme fundamentally religious, by which events evolved under a law of justice and under the ruling of God's Providence, and of which Elizabeth's England was the acknowledged outcome. (1986: 324–5)

We can imagine the attraction for readers in 1944 of this 'fundamentally religious, still comprehensible scheme of history' in which a strong and united England justly and providentially triumphed over the machinations of wicked adversaries. Reason has triumphed here over

Passion again in the Elizabethan version of that commonplace struggle of every age, as perhaps it did in 1945. Shakespeare was responding essentially, Tillyard argues, to a triumphalist national sentiment, expressing 'the steadily rising pride in political accomplishment, in the growing awareness of having made good nationally, in having emerged against all odds from the hazards which had so beset the rest of Europe' (1986: 148). And all of these recent events of contemporary history 'were to him what the French Revolution and the doctrines that accompanied it were to Wordsworth, or Godwinism was to Shelley' (1986: 150).

These ringing words tend to locate the Elizabethan World Picture as much in the century of the second Elizabeth as in that of the first. But Tillyard becomes, perhaps, even more recognizably twentieth century in his awareness, first of all, of the foreignness of Hall's doctrine, and, secondly, of the degree to which the plays strain against the framework of the World Picture (something that recent excoriators of Tillyard conveniently ignore), and, thirdly, of just how political that straining is. We are fascinated by the political themes in the history plays, so Tillyard believes, partly because they are so 'remote and queer' (1986: 152). 'Queer' in fact becomes an indispensable word in his vocabulary to describe Elizabethan seriousness, and also acts as a bridge to the events of 1943: 'And, if we reflect on the habit, we may see that (in queerness though not in viciousness) it resembles certain trends of thought in central Europe, the ignoring of which by scientifically minded intellectuals has helped not a little to bring the world into its present conflicts and distresses' (1943: 109). Here, Tillyard hints that the Tudor myth of order resembles the German and Italian Fascist myth of order in the twentieth century. And throughout his books Tillyard, while maintaining time and again that for the Elizabethans 'the desire for order was there' (1943: 99), none the less just as frequently—especially in his discussions of the history plays—finds himself having to deal with a state of chronic anarchy, actual or threatening. No wonder there was a desire, then, for order. The world the Elizabethans 'lived in was becoming ever more difficult to fit tidily into a rigid order: the mathematical detail of correspondences became less and less apt; you could not base your faith on the endless accumulation of minutiae' (99); the 'fierceness' of the Elizabethan interest in the nature of man 'delighted in exposing all the contrarieties in man's composition' (1943: 76).[3] And these contrarieties are essentially *political* in nature, a word Tillyard uses frequently even in discussions of plays like *The Comedy of Errors* and *Titus Andronicus*.[4] As Paola Pugliatti observes, Tillyard was the first to 'direct our attention compellingly towards Shakespeare's history plays as a corpus of political texts' (1996: 10). She acknowledges that, despite his 'doctrinaire monologism' (1996: 10), '[n]o work has been so vehemently confuted, none has been more radically demolished; nevertheless, all readings of the history plays take us back to Tillyard as a necessary starting point' (1998: 339).

It's not terribly surprising that twentieth-century critics of Shakespeare's history plays should seize with some avidity on Tillyard's notion that they comprise a corpus of political texts. The plays were written during interesting times, to say the least. The 1590s and early 1600s experienced among other uncertainties an intensified Recusant problem, the rapid rise of an aggressive Puritanism, the rebellion of Essex, the Gunpowder Plot, peasant disorders and riots against enclosures of common land. Works of art as intensely communicative as Elizabethan and Jacobean plays could hardly fail to allude in some way or other, however 'mystified', to the burning issues of their audiences. And this would be even more the case with plays that deal with history, whether British or Roman.

G. K. Hunter (1990) notes that many of the titles of the history plays have the word 'true' in them in contradistinction to the comedies or tragedies of the period as though to demarcate a special area of verisimilitude exclusive to their genre. True about what and to what extent is one of the burning issues of twentieth-century Shakespeare criticism. Part two of Lily B. Campbell's still popular 1947 study, *Shakespeare's 'Histories': Mirrors of Elizabethan Policy* (1965) is entitled 'Shakespeare's Political Use of History' (117), and in her introduction to this second part she notes that it stresses 'the traditional nature of Shakespeare's interpretations and of the effect of contemporary political situations upon the selection and alteration of historical fact in the plays' (125). She concludes her chapter, 'What Are "Histories"?', by differentiating between histories and tragedies in a style similar to R. G. Moulton's: 'Tragedy is concerned with the doings of men which in philosophy are discussed under ethics; history with the doings of men which in philosophy are discussed under politics' (1965: 17). In

1988 Alexander Leggatt ruffled no feathers by calling his book *Shakespeare's Political Drama: The History Plays and the Roman Plays*. Of all Shakespeare's history plays in this century, *Henry V* has the distinction of being considered the most politically controversial. Gary Taylor describes it as constituting 'a critical no man's land, acrimoniously contested and periodically disfigured by opposing barrages of intellectual artillery' (1982: 1). One such famous barrage claimed the play for the Tudors. E. M. W. Tillyard in his *Shakespeare's History Plays* (1986) saw it as perfect propaganda for *The Elizabethan World Picture* (1943). And according to Lily B. Campbell the play expresses 'a dominant political pattern characteristic of the political philosophy of the age' (1965: 6) in attempting to justify the ways of Henry to men.

For many critics the justification—if indeed there is one—is about as successful as Milton's for God. Taylor argues that the key to Henry's victory at Agincourt is his 'coldblooded murder of the defenceless French prisoners' (1998: 33). The king's character and the play's are co-extensive. Is *Henry V*, asks Jonathan Hart an 'heroic play or subversive war-pamphlet' (1992: 3)? Barbara Hodgdon asks in similar vein: is Agincourt bloody manslaughter or heroic myth—'homosocial fantasy' (1991: 193)? For Hart all this questioning makes the second tetralogy itself a long problem play, 'one that interrogates its own genre' (1992: 7). Norman Rabkin also insists that *Henry V's* 'terrible subversiveness' (1981: 49) makes it a problem play. Jean Howard and Phyllis Rackin find the terrible subversiveness of *Henry V's* political stance stretching out to embrace the politics of sexual relations. '*Henry V* is the only Shakespearean history play where male authority is demonstrated in modern terms, by the hero's sexual conquest of a desirable woman; and it is not surprising that modern critics have admired the wooing scene as a final demonstration of Henry's "humanity"' (1997: 196). But this in fact is a kind of rape on Henry's part; it's an aspect of 'performative masculinity'; it's a question merely of male heterosexual dominance.

The Hatch and Brood of Time

Reading Shakespeare Elizabethanly, making ourselves at home in the Renaissance, thinking like the average Elizabethan theatre-goer, all advocated in their different ways by historical critics like Stoll, Tillyard, and Lily Campbell, sound like simple injunctions to follow, but in practice they beg many questions. Historical research in the 1960s and 1970s—some time before the work of the so-called new historicism—has no such illusions about turning ourselves into Elizabethans. Making ourselves at home in the Renaissance is a strenuous task and Tillyard's 'doctrinaire monologism' comes under heavy fire. For one thing, Shakespeare was obviously not a 'plain man' in thrall to 'supreme commonplaces'. While it may be the case that these last commanded the assent of the silent majority it surely was not applicable to the likes of Raleigh and Fulke Greville or Jonson, Marston, and Chapman, or to the mature Shakespeare.

Robert Ornstein has some trenchant things to say about the tendency of many literary historians to appeal to the lowest common denominator: 'But the same assumptions about a dramatist and his cultural milieu which lead scholars to interpret Shakespeare by means of La Primaudaye, Charron, and Coefeteau should lead us to interpret *A Streetcar Named Desire* by reference to Norman Vincent Peale, a latter-day ethical psychologist no less influential than his Renaissance counterparts' (1959: 3).[5]

Just as naive an approach is a one-to-one topicality. John Dover Wilson sees a simple political process of identification at work in the history plays: for him the very 'body of the time, its form and pressure' has reference to real people and real events. So *Henry V* has a relevance to the Irish campaigns, and to the careers of Essex and Southampton, and *Troilus and Cressida* was Shakespeare's 'courageous, almost savage, attempt to goad the Earl into action' (1932: 101). Similarly, *Hamlet* 'is Shakespeare's effort to understand Essex, to understand him as a dramatist, not as a psychologist' (104).

This close association between the world of the plays and external reality—the old historicism as it is now dismissively known—comes to be seen as inherently unlikely, and Wilbur Sanders anticipates much later studies—especially those of the toilers in the new historicism—when he follows Croce's dictum that 'all history is contemporary history' in his claim that 'the best of our systematic knowledge of the world is no more than a mental construct' (1968: 4).[6]

The old historicism, Howard Felperin argues, operated 'as a late, empirical application of nineteenth century hermeneutics, it identified the meaning of the literary text with the author's intention and his or her historical culture's understanding of it, the adequation of the one to the other being assumed in a successful work' (1987: 264). For the old historicism language was not a problem. It considered itself objective: 'so it could yield authentic knowledge of the other, of the other *as* other, untransformed and unappropriated by the language of the self' (265). What the old historicism revealed was the truth; it was true because it was historical.[7]

The most quoted anti-Tillyard essay of these times, the essay that instigated much savage mauling of the Elizabethan World Picture—that 'hotch-potch of antiquated science, fancy, and folklore' (1987: 5), as J. W. Lever memorably describes it—is A. P. Rossiter's lecture on ambivalence in Shakespeare's history plays. In his view the history plays are much more mysterious than has hitherto been supposed; they proffer mixed messages at best, contradictions, and wavering moral judgements. It is a mistake—one generously indulged by the theatre during the 1940s and 1950s—to view them moralistically: 'Already semi-deflated Falstaffs are reaching the stage—Welfare-State Falstaffs, shrunk in the moral wash, or pre-conditioned for pricking before they have got so far afoot as Shrewsbury' (46).[8] What shrinks in the moral wash more generally is a necessary elasticity of understanding, one that can see the validity of two (or more) opposed viewpoints (Rossiter's definition of ambivalence), one that can follow the pattern of 'travesty-by-parallel' (46) and the process of 'retributive reaction' (42). We need to take a 'two-eyed' view of events in the plays, so that, for instance, Poins and Hal's comic robbing of the robbers in *Henry IV, Part 1* can be seen as a comic parallel to what Henry IV would do with Percy's Scottish prisoners. For Rossiter what goes on in the histories can be summed up by the Bastard in *King John*, 'Mad world, mad kings, mad composition!' (2.1.562). I don't think Tillyard would have been in essential disagreement with the necessity to take a two-eyed view of the plays but he certainly would not have given much credence to the idea that the madness of the times fatally compromised a subtending moral teleology.

Rossiter's lecture was followed by a spate of books pushing the same line. Norman Rabkin's masterly *Shakespeare and the Common Understanding* (1967) emphasizes the '[i]llogicality, irregularity, complexity, contrariety, complementarity, polyphony, doubleness, ambivalence, even *discoherence*' (46) of Shakespeare's plays. Arnold Kettle's largely

Marxist collection of essays, *Shakespeare in a Changing World* (1964), emphasizes the *changing* nature of both our world and Shakespeare's. His sensible introduction anticipates a concern of much later Shakespeare criticism when it asks us to bear in mind that '[w]e are all, Shakespeare and ourselves, characters in history. The better we succeed in seeing ourselves as such, the better we shall understand him. And *vice versa*; for no other literature can help us more than Shakespeare's plays to see ourselves as we are' (1964: 9). Kettle adds presciently: 'The changing world, then, is neither Shakespeare's or ours, yet it is both Shakespeare's and ours' (9).[9]

Wilbur Sanders (1968) talks of the confusing number of multiple perspectives that the history plays especially promote. In them the ambiguities of complex (and simple) words match the ambiguous positions towards their culture (and others) taken by the plays themselves. In similar fashion Tillyard's notion of a guiding providence behind the history plays takes a knocking. We should try, Sanders urges, to avoid the view as Elizabethan that 'history is the triumphal march of Providence toward universal beatitude' (1968: 110), and his position is supported in W. R. Elton's *King Lear and the Gods* published two years earlier. Sanders believes that Shakespeare's lack of conviction in *Richard III* 'seems to indicate that he never succeeded in believing in this external, meddlesome Providence in the way that is essential to a creative artist' (1968: 111). For H. A. Kelly '[t]he providential aspect of the Tudor myth described by Mr. Tillyard is an ex post facto Platonic Form, made up of many fragments that were never put together in a mental pattern until they felt the force of his own synthesising energy' (1970: 298).[10]

So what we're dealing with here is not so much *the* Elizabethan World Picture as Tillyard's version of the Elizabethan World Picture. Is the anti-Tillyard version of the Elizabethan World Picture closer to *the* Elizabethan World Picture? I think it probably is but the use of *version* as opposed to *the* here illustrates one of twentieth-century criticism's most formidable insights: the extent to which any attempt to characterize the past brings with it whether we like it or not the anachronistic intellectual baggage that Hardin Craig so deplored. Anachronistic but inevitable, and, for later critics, welcome. If it is inevitable for us that we should view Shakespeare's plays through the prism of the twentieth century it was equally inevitable for

Shakespeare that he would view the events and concerns of the 1400s through the prism of the late sixteenth century. Tillyard and his opponents would at least agree with each other—if about little else—that the presentation of Shakespeare in their work was as the analytic contemporary historian, the critic of his own times. As Phyllis Rackin says, Shakespeare's history plays 'tell us more about his world than the world of the Plantagenets' (1990: 36).

But post-Tillyard critics stress the *critic* in Shakespeare, and see the Elizabethan World Picture refracted adversarially through its greatest writer. Thus A. P. Rossiter's essay (1961) on *Troilus and Cressida* argues that the play was never really one about the ancient Greeks but a sceptical probing of contemporary values. Stanley Cavell goes much further in judging that all Shakespeare's works necessarily engage 'the depth of the philosophical pre-occupations of his culture' (1987: 2); in Cavell's view Shakespeare addresses the problems of his times with a far-reaching seriousness and an astonishing capacity to probe the pieties of his day. What that philosophical preoccupation was in Shakespeare's time was the advent of scepticism as manifested in Descartes's *Meditations*; the plays then explore 'the question whether I know with certainty of the existence of the external world and of myself and others in it' (3), and they 'find no stable solution to skepticism, in particular no rest in what we know of God' (3). Cavell suggests that Shakespeare's scepticism all but destroys the Elizabethan World Picture, not just Tillyard's version of it, but *the* Elizabethan World Picture: 'If there was an Elizabethan world picture, Shakespeare questions it, shatters it, as surely as the new science did. No "source," no received conception, survives its incorporation into Shakespeare without sea-change' (36).

Shakespeare may have shattered the Elizabethan World Picture but critics at the end of the twentieth century are still attempting to put it back together in some form or other with a view to revisiting it without Hardin Craig's twentieth-century intellectual baggage. Or, at least, the possibility of so doing remains a tempting rhetorical topic if nothing else. Phyllis Rackin's *Stages of History: Shakespeare's English Chronicles* (1990) wrestles again with the dilemma. Her opening sentence suggests that there is no problem: 'This book represents an attempt to historicize Shakespeare's historical practice—to situate his history plays in the context of Tudor historiography, in his theater, and in his world' (p. ix), but she then immediately acknowledges that '[t]he questions asked are the products of my own historically specific concerns' (p. ix). It's an impossible situation: 'The products of our own discursive framework, our interpretations of the plays inevitably become the mirrors for our own situations, even as we attempt to use them for windows into the past' (36).

Back in 1965 L. C. Knights, somewhat reluctantly perhaps, accepted the necessity for this imaginative transference:

> If we believe that the attempt to reconstruct the Elizabethan or Renaissance meanings of Shakespeare's plays is almost inevitably attended by the danger of obscuring their imaginative life, does this mean that we must simply accept the fact of different meanings for different generations, or indeed for different individuals living at the same time? I think it does. (145)

It's arguable that in his English history plays Shakespeare was, in fact, more concerned to shatter the medieval world picture than the Elizabethan. A minority of twentieth-century critics of the history plays believes that we need to take Shakespeare seriously as a historian of the English past, the past in which his major history plays were set. (A similar argument has been made about Shakespeare's credentials as a historian of the ancient Roman past, emphasizing the Romanness, that is, of the Roman plays.) Paola Pugliatti's *Shakespeare the Historian* (1996) juggles with both notions of 'historian' in her title—Shakespeare as the historian of the sixteenth and seventeenth centuries and Shakespeare as the historian of the fifteenth century. Although Michael Hattaway, the Cambridge editor of *Henry VI, Part 1*, believes the play to be almost as much about Shakespeare's time and our time as about the fifteenth century, he urges us to consider it above all as 'a complex essay on the *politics* of the mid-fifteenth century' (1990: 1).

Tillyard himself didn't think the politics of Shakespeare's history plays were necessarily Shakespeare's politics but those of an earlier time, and his position has gained support in some unexpected quarters. Graham Holderness, for example, a critic as unsympathetic to the views of Tillyard as it is possible to imagine, asks us not to make too much of the plays' relevance to late sixteenth-century events. Instead, they should be taken seriously as exercises in Renaissance historiography. So we should think of Henry V, for instance, as a feudal overlord—because this is how Shakespeare thinks of him—rather than as the monarch of a sixteenth-century nation-state. We should see him as someone closer to Hotspur than to Elizabeth I. Holderness goes on to argue that the plays embody a conscious understanding of feudal society though not in the scholarly antiquarian manner; he thinks it remarkable 'that we should find within Shakespeare's historical drama, alongside echoes of Christian providentialism and Italian humanism, a grasp of history more akin to a new historiography of the seventeenth century than to either of those older perspectives' (1988: 18). In *Richard II* and the other plays of the second tetralogy, Holderness believes, Shakespeare reveals 'a historically informed apprehension of the struggles of later mediaeval society; in particular the long struggle between monarchy and nobility which developed out of the contradictory nature of the feudal order, and was arrested by the accession of the Tudors' (19).

Christopher Pye argues that what we get in *King John* and the other histories is the representation of the absolutism of the sovereign in an attempt to preserve a feudal power structure in centralized form against 'the gradual emergence of mobile free labour' (1990: 6). Some light is thrown on all this discussion of Shakespeare as a respectable historian of the fifteenth century by Peter Saccio (1977) who examines the differences between medieval history as we now understand it and Shakespeare's versions of that history.

To Sound the Bottom of the After-Times

Janus-faced Shakespeare was not just the analyst of his past and present, however, but, for a number of twentieth-century critics, seems also to have had the gift of prophecy. His history plays in particular seem to look forward to, even comment proleptically on, the consuming events of the twentieth century. So too do his Roman plays. In his essay on *Antony and Cleopatra* Northrop Frye marvels: 'It's amazing how vividly Shakespeare has imagined a world so much more like ours than like his' (1986: 122). Looking before and after Shakespeare lays waste our powers.

We can trace this response to Shakespeare-as-Cassandra at least as far back in the century as Sir Sidney Lee in 1906 who wished 'to survey Shakespearean drama in relation to modern life, and to illustrate its living force in current affairs' (p. vii). As we have seen in Chapter 2, for him Shakespeare was a wiser, more potent Carlyle or Ruskin. In 1932 John Dover Wilson argued that though '[t]he modern world speaks a different language and has run a very different political course', none the less 'the mood of 1932 is almost exactly the mood of 1602; for, though our material conditions are better, the height of our spiritual fall has been greater' (1932: 36–7). G. Wilson Knight also celebrates Shakespeare as prophetic: 'I saw that Shakespeare's seemingly out-dated kings and barons with their rivalries and murders were, if we were prepared to see Shakespeare's persons as corresponding to contemporary parties or nations, not out-dated at all, but rather true reflections of the turmoils and tyrannies rampant across Europe' (1967: 4).

Another popular work, Una Ellis-Fermor's *The Frontiers of Drama* (1964), first published in 1945, while admitting that in Shakespeare what is celebrated by and large is the triumph of the individual, 'an inner aristocratic ideal' (53), goes on to celebrate that celebration as anticipatory of the situation in 1945 when the freedom of the individual was more a democratic concern than an aristocratic one: 'Shakespeare's final position is an uncompromising declaration of individual freedom and responsibility, that supreme virtue of which the Jacobeans knew so well the value' (54). Her essay on *Troilus and Cressida* is also heavily influenced by her times. She believes that we can now respond fully to the play because 'our actual experience of disintegration and disruption, so unlike that of any age between, has thrown fresh light upon the nature and foundations of what we call civilization' (57). She admires in particular the way that Shakespeare's art brings order out of chaos: 'The content of his thought is an implacable assertion of chaos as the ultimate fact of being; the presence of artistic form is a deeper, unconscious testimony to an order which is actually ultimate and against which the gates of hell shall not prevail' (73).

Even Tillyard can be seen as constructing the Elizabethan World Picture, if unawares, in the light of the twentieth century. Tillyard's aesthetic dimension, it has been argued, is essentially Modernist, his concepts of the Tudor myth and the Elizabethan World Picture, according to Hugh Grady, 'owe much of their force and much of their easy and quick acceptance in the post-World War II era to the anti-Romantic revolution in taste and aesthetic criteria associated with the Modernism of T. S. Eliot' (1991a: 178).

If Tillyard was blithely unaware of his modernist agenda, no one could be more aware, I suppose, than Jan Kott was of his. As Peter Brook says in his introduction to the English edition of *Shakespeare Our Contemporary*—the book that so heavily influenced the production of Shakespeare in the theatre of the next two decades—'Kott is undoubtedly the only writer on Elizabethan matters who assumes without question that everyone of his readers will at some point or other have been woken by the police in the middle of the night' (Kott 1964: n.p.).

Martin Esslin's Introduction spells out the implications of Brook's assessment of Kott's vantage-point: 'Daily proximity to civil war, brutality, ideological intolerance, conspiracy and its bloody repression determined the life of Shakespeare's time . . . as it did and still does the atmosphere of mid twentieth-century Eastern Europe' (p. xix). This is to argue, as Kott himself argues, that the Polish World Picture in the mid-twentieth century is the equivalent of the Elizabethan World Picture at the end of the sixteenth.[11] It's not so much a question then for Kott of applying, or interpreting, Shakespeare; it's more a question of reading Shakespeare in the light of his prescient capacity to read us.

Kott replaces the unshunnable authoritarianism of Tillyard's Elizabethan World Picture with what he calls the Grand Mechanism (the workings of which are just as irresistible). This Grand Mechanism is equally Elizabethan (and Polish) and expresses 'the conviction that history has no meaning and stands still, or constantly repeats its cruel cycle; . . . it is an elemental force, like hail, storm, or hurricane, birth and death' (37). It is a cruel and tragic farce. It's no wonder that *King Lear* is considered by Kott to be *the* twentieth-century tragedy. How close the play is, for instance, Kott argues, to the grotesque vision of Brecht, Durrenmatt, or Beckett: 'The theme of *King Lear* is the decay and fall of the world' (152). Kott goes on to say that in it '[t]here are no longer kings and subjects, fathers and children, husbands and wives. There are only huge Renaissance monsters, devouring one another like beasts of prey' (153).

In his juggernaut manner, Kott considers Shakespeare's comedies in the same way. He describes the spirit Ariel in *The Tempest* as 'an Angel, executioner, and agent provocateur' (214) and he believes *A Midsummer Night's Dream* to be 'a most truthful, brutal, and violent play' (222).[12] As we saw in the chapter on the history of Shakespeare in the theatre in the twentieth century, Kott has had an immense influence on the direction of Shakespeare productions in the second half of the century. To take just one representative example: John Elsom notes that in the nineteenth century (and before) in productions of *Hamlet* Fortinbras was considered the saviour at the end of the play. After Kott's *Shakespeare Our Contemporary*, he

became a leader of the dark and menacing forces hovering on the borders of Denmark, waiting until the nation is too weak and divided to defend itself, a model for Polish history as the Poles see it. Hamlet was no blond hero, but the agent of national self-destruction. Claudius was no devil, but a strong leader weakened by guilt and self-doubt. (1989: 2).[13]

But Kott's was not the only influence in interpreting the plays in the grim light of a depraved century. Brecht is a major factor here and so also is the homegrown naturalistic drama of the 1950s of which John Osborne's *Look Back in Anger*, first performed in 1956, was the most potent. The result of these destabilizing influences, as Russell Jackson explains, was to problematize the plays in the theatre, all of them, not just the histories: 'It is as though all the plays are now "Problem Plays", in the sense of being problematic, if not in the stricter Shavian meaning of expounding problems' (1996*a*: 223).

A fascinating variation on Stanley Cavell's position about an ultra-sceptical Shakespeare has recently been advanced by Lars Engle who agrees with Cavell that 'late sixteenth-century England and late twentieth-century America may be akin in that both cultures were hospitable to skepticism about the truths provided by certainty-producing institutions' (1993: 49). He says that we should remember that Shakespeare was writing in the period before Descartes and Galileo who 'launched the great certainty project of modernity' (8). Pragmatism is a reaction to this project: 'Pragmatism, as a philosophical movement, constitutes a reaction to what James and Dewey perceived as the excesses of theory or pure rationality in philosophy' (8). So his argument is that Shakespeare has more in common with James and Dewey than with Descartes or Galileo.

It's not surprising then that Engle finds contemporary concerns, our concerns, in Shakespeare's works (in this instance in the Sonnets): 'My own argument . . . backdates certain explicit modern philosophical issues by finding them implicitly treated in Shakespeare's sonnets'

(29). Engle therefore offers 'a Shakespeare who anticipates the pragmatism of late Wittgenstein or Richard Rorty' (30). And he also offers as similar endeavours to his the works of Fineman (1986) and Ferry (1983) who find Locke in Shakespeare and Lacan in Shakespeare. Shakespeare then in this view stretches to the crack of doom in a line of surrogates that includes—at the very least—William James, John Dewey, Wittgenstein, and Richard Rorty as well as Carlyle, Ruskin, and John Locke.[14]

Foul Subornation is Predominant

Most of the discussion in this chapter so far has concerned itself with the surge of interest in historical matters that we can find in twentieth-century Shakespeare criticism of the 1950s, 1960s, and early 1970s. How, then, do we explain Alvin Kernan's lament in 1986: 'Many teachers of Renaissance literature simply have grown weary, as I have, of teaching texts as ethereal entities floating above the urgencies and contradictions of history' (1986: 15)? For Heather Dubrow (1997) the age of historical enquiry runs from 1970 to 2000. In 1996 Susan Bennett considered the past to be 'a present-day epidemic' (1). Did they, then, not notice the existence of the 'new historicism' of the 1960s?[15]

Of course, my discussion of the history plays in the preceding pages in terms of historical criticism involves their necessary but misleading isolation from other critical movements of the twentieth century. The main critical focus during these years, as we saw in Chapter 3, was formalist. Historical enquiry during this time can be considered a minor tributary compared to the mighty rivers of the New Criticism.[16] So it's possible to argue that historical criticism during this time simply didn't beat a loud enough drum to get heard. For a more provocative explanation for the neglect by the new historicists and cultural materialists of Wilbur Sanders, Robert Ornstein, J. W. Lever, Jan Kott, A. P. Rossiter, Norman Rabkin, and so on—anti-Tillyard to a man—we might recall Chris Baldick's 'cut-throat intellectual bazaar of contending critical "schools" whose only point of agreement is that the critical methods of twenty years ago are too shop-soiled to be put on sale at all' (1996: 7).

Whatever the reason, the new upsurge of interest in Shakespeare from an historical point of view in the 1980s and 1990s—the newer new historicism—tends to treat historical criticism as though its only representatives in the twentieth century were critics from the era of Tillyard, Stoll, and Lily Campbell whose work once again needs to be traduced and annihilated. And so Mark Breitenberg tells us, as Norman Rabkin told us, that unlike in Tillyard's static world picture, Renaissance life was more like the Witches' cauldron: 'a cauldron of bubbling anxieties, a language of unresolvable contradictions and paradoxes, a world gray and ambivalent rather than clear and categorizable' (1996: 1). And Jonathan Dollimore writes:

> Tillyard's world picture, to the extent that it did still exist, was not shared by all; it was an ideological legitimation of an existing social order, one rendered the more necessary by the apparent instability, actual and imagined, of that order. If this sounds too extreme then we need only recall Bacon's remark to some circuit judges in 1617: 'There will be a perpetual defection, except you keep men in by preaching as well as law doth by punishing' (1992: 48).

The new urgency in the historical criticism of Shakespeare in the 1980s, the new need to resuscitate old scapegoats, was as much in response to the critics' own political situation as was Tillyard's to the political situation of 1943 and 1944 or that of Jan Kott to the political situation in Poland of the late 1950s. The 1980s ushered in a historical criticism that by and large was left-wing (not to say Marxist), radical, and intensely committed—in England anyway—to an instrumental view of literary criticism, particularly Shakespeare criticism, that urged its readers to man the intellectual barricades in the fight against corporate capitalism and Thatcherism generally.

Isobel Armstrong dubs the Shakespeare criticism of these years in England 'Thatcher's Shakespeare' (1989*a*) and reels off the books that began the onslaught: Jonathan Dollimore's *Radical Tragedy: Religion, Ideology and Power in the Drama of Shakespeare and his Contemporaries* (1984), his and Alan Sinfield's *Political Shakespeare: New Essays in Cultural Materialism* (1985), John Drakakis' collection of essays *Alternative Shakespeares* (1985) and Graham Holderness's *The Shakespeare Myth* (1988), Terence Hawkes's *That Shakespeherian Rag* (1986), and Terry Eagleton's *William Shakespeare* (1986). This was oppositional criticism of a particularly tendentious kind in which political history became synonymous with studies in *power* and *ideology*.[17] Don Wayne notes that '[i]n such criticism the figure of *Power* has displaced that of the *Idea* which was the essential constituent of Renaissance scholarship in Tillyard's generation' (1987: 58).

The new Elizabethan World Picture of the second Elizabeth views the world of Shakespeare's plays from the vantage point of the dispossessed and marginalized. Feminism, new historicism (in the United States), Marxism, and cultural materialism (in the United Kingdom) vie with each other in the representation of Shakespeare's history plays in terms not so much of the major royal figures that were the plays' central characters but in terms of the citizenry who opposed them or who suffered under them. Jean Howard and Phyllis Rackin believe that '[t]he predicaments faced by Shakespeare's kings, and the steps they take to confront them, now appear to be shaped as much by the predicaments of the ordinary men in Shakespeare's audience as they were by the historical records that Shakespeare found in his chronicle sources' (1997: 186–7). Walter Cohen writes: 'The vast majority of recent political writing on Shakespeare has sided with the victims of state power, class hierarchy, patriarchy, racism, and imperialism, a partisanship, it is worth asserting, not only compatible with but also necessary to a commitment to objectivity in scholarship' (1987: 20).

Cohen's last phrase illuminates the tendency of these critics to think of their work as redressing a balance that has been badly skewed in favour of an even more tendentious interpretation than theirs of the history plays (and of all the others) that ignored, stifled even, an incipient democratic or proto-democratic opposition. They advocate a kind of aggressive appropriation of the plays in terms of this opposition. In *Reading the Popular* (1989) John Fiske throws light on this process by asking us to consider how Black American urban youth might respond to the stone-throwing Arabs on the news as opposed, say, to the response of members of the National Guard.

In the United Kingdom the target of cultural materialist criticism, however, was not so much new interpretations of Shakespeare— though cultural materialism did and does provide us with many such—but the manner in which Shakespeare's texts have been interpreted in this and other centuries and the political uses to which they have been put. As Richard Wilson says, 'The function of criticism today must be ... to analyze the ways in which meaning has been produced for different social and political purposes in Shakespeare's texts—and ways in which the texts are reproduced today in schools, theatres, newspapers, and Parliament' (Elsom, 1989: 151). Jean Howard and Marion O'Connor concur: 'One end of a political criticism.... Is to explore the ideological functions of texts at various historical junctures and in various cultural practices' (1987: 4). And so they are interested in a criticism that explores how 'Shakespeare' is produced in criticism, and in the classroom, and on the stage. Richard Wilson ends his essay with a provocative call to arms:

Shakespeare is too valuable to British society to be disposed of like the family silver. As an art object, a monument to the old gods, Shakespearean drama must be re-interpreted, re-deployed, re-occupied. In the work of directors such as David Thacker and Michael Bogdanov, Shakespeare may yet prove the Trojan horse to storm the cultural citadel. (1989: 152)

Storming the cultural citadel makes sense only in metaphorical terms. It doesn't seem likely that a socialist literary criticism will bring about or even help to bring about a socialist society. If the world needs to be changed then literary critics who want to change it should seek some other means than literary criticism to make themselves more useful in the coming struggle. None the less when we think of the effectiveness of some dramatic productions in this century in arousing strong emotions and inciting people to man barricades more physical than intellectual, it seems clear that it is in theatrical production (or production in other media) rather than in literary criticism that some kind of direct influence on the larger populace might possibly be achieved. Isobel Armstrong's essay on Thatcher's Shakespeare pleads for the mounting of radical readings and productions like the ones put on by the English Shakespeare Company. Don't abandon Shakespeare, she urges, radicalize him, always bear in mind 'the transgressive pleasure of critique' (1989*a*: 14).

There are numerous examples of the transgressive pleasure that the theatre has given us in this century, as we have seen in Chapter 4, but one of the dangers of political criticism, of whatever stripe, is its tendency to ignore pleasure altogether, whether transgressive or not. Isobel Armstrong seems close to the mark when she argues that '[t]he abandonment of the concept of literature and of the category of the "aesthetic", the philosophical terrain which should support it, is possibly one of the greatest mistakes the left has made this decade' (1989*a*: 13).

In the 1990s as in the 1980s criticism renews its engagement with the ambiguities and multiple voices of Shakespeare's history plays but is frequently more firmly convinced now of the pleasure that Shakespeare took from his exercises in transgression. Thus Paola Pugliatti takes up the notion of perspectivism as described by Michael Hattaway in his editions of the three *Henry VI* plays and gives it more of a cutting edge: 'In my view, however, perspectivism is to be understood as active criticism rather than skepticism or pessimism, and therefore as a sign of involvement rather than of aloofness' (1996: 8). What Shakespeare practised was 'a problem-oriented, multivocal kind of historiography that probed into events in depth rather than in extension' (23). It's a left-wing view: 'But, above all, to have rendered visible and memorable the contradictions and the trivialities of the experience of common people is an instance of historiographical irreverence which can be made to coincide with a political option' (186).

All this constitutes 'a scandal of historiography' (188). As Alvin Kernan remarks: 'Shakespeare's plays were—as generations of readers and audiences since have perceived—deep, searching portrayals of the most serious political and social issues, conservative in their premises but daring in their implications' (1995: 183). And Lynda Boose, taking up once again the notion of Shakespeare the historian, gives it a 1990s spin by arguing that he is a more accurate chronicler of his times in some ways than one of the most distinguished professional Renaissance historians of our own time, Lawrence Stone: 'When we measure Stone's assertions against the Shakespeare canon, the plays must seem startlingly ahistorical in focusing on what would seem to have been the least valued relationship of all: that between father and daughter' (1992: 5). But the fact of the matter is that the plays aren't ahistorical in their portrayal of family life in the sixteenth and seventeenth centuries as intimate and warm-hearted. It's Stone who is ahistorical in this matter, not Shakespeare.

In 1989 the symposium implicitly questioning Kott's position, *Is Shakespeare Still Our Contemporary?*, decided that Shakespeare was more contemporary at some moments of history than at others. And there is no doubt that the historically minded critics of the 1980s and

1990s were (and are) convinced that these two decades comprise such a privileged moment. Jean Howard believes that the 1990s certainly do; she talks of 'the uncanny way in which, at *this* historical moment, an analysis of Renaissance culture can be made to speak to the concerns of late twentieth-century culture' (1992: 15). We too, she argues, are living in a time of transition, a gap in history, where we seem to be moving from established paradigms to future uncertain ones.

The British critic, Lisa Jardine, suggests that '[w]e are beginning to interrogate Shakespeare's texts for clues to our understanding of ethnic conflict in an unstable political world' (1996: 14). But this procedure is reversible as her passion makes clear:

> If we had not watched with horrified fascination on the evening news bulletins as an integrated, multi-racial, multi-faith community in Old Yugoslavia disintegrated into territorial fragments of so-called 'pure' ethnicity and separate religious beliefs, we would not, I contend, be able to recognize as sharply as we currently do the problems lurking within *Henry V*'s depiction of fervour for English nationalism. (7)

This is the dialectic of history working at its most potent.

Then Everything Includes Itself in Power

One of the intriguing differences in the practice of historical criticism of Shakespeare between British and American critics of the late twentieth century may also constitute a minor scandal of historiography. It hinges on the question of potency. American new historicism takes a much more pessimistic view than its British counterpart of the progressiveness of Shakespeare's own politics, of the effectiveness of Elizabethan drama's social role in Shakespeare's time (and in any other), and of the instrumentality of Shakespeare criticism, or any literary criticism, in twentieth-century politics.

A key essay from the most important spokesperson of American new historicism, Stephen Greenblatt, 'Invisible Bullets: Renaissance Authority and its Subversion, *Henry IV* and *Henry V*' (1992), applies Michel Foucault's pessimistic ideas to literary texts, his demolition of the repressive hypothesis or social-control model of authority, and his proposition that power operates through the desires it produces rather than those it forbids. In terms of this thesis, Shakespeare's plays—all of them, not just the histories—'are centrally and repeatedly concerned with the production and containment of subversion and disorder' (1992: 94). In Shakespeare's history plays, '[t]he subversive voices are produced by the affirmation of order, and they are powerfully registered, but they do not undermine that order' (102). Even in *Henry IV, Part 2*,

> where the lies and the self-serving sentiments are utterly inescapable, where the illegitimacy of legitimate authority is repeatedly demonstrated, where the whole state seems—to adapt More's phrase—a conspiracy of the great to enrich and protect their interests under the name of commonwealth, even here the audience does not leave the theatre in a rebellious mood. (105)

It is, of course, impossible to know what kind of mood an Elizabethan and Jacobean audience left the theatre in. Whatever their mood, it is surely unlikely that they would have responded to the play with one mind; like any other audience its members would have been variously affected by the sentiments of the play, as they perceived them, and some of them might very well have left the theatre in a more insurrectionary frame of mind than when they entered it.

Shakespeare's political conservatism, then, as highlighted by Greenblatt, is by and large the burden of American new historicism. But it is a political conservatism whether or not Shakespeare himself was a political conservative. What his political leanings were is not material to the case as far as most new historicists are concerned. As Frank Lentricchia explains, the new historicists are obsessed with the Foucauldian concept of power which is nowhere and everywhere and hence supremely efficacious.[18] It does not therefore matter if the individual writer is a closet radical, or, for that matter, a self-proclaimed public one. He or she has perforce to subscribe to the immutable laws of social containment. Lentricchia points out that in Stephen Greenblatt's famous work, *Renaissance Self-Fashioning: From More to Shakespeare* (1980), state power in Elizabethan England is represented in as totalitarian a manner as in George Orwell's *1984*. And although the new historicists—Greenblatt most notably—proclaim themselves to be anti-determinist, it's determinism that makes them what they are, 'the typically anxious expression of post-Watergate American humanist intellectuals' (Lentricchia 1988: 93). Hence for them 'the Renaissance is *our* culture because it is the origin of our disciplinary society' (97).[19] The most revealing pages in *Renaissance Self-Fashioning*, according to Lentricchia, are those on Marlowe. Here, as with Barabas in *The Jew of Malta*, Greenblatt shows that 'radicalism is a representation of orthodoxy in its most politically cunning form and that all struggle against a dominant ideology is in vain' (98). All we can hope for is radical play: 'we settle for a holiday from reality, a safely sealed space reserved for the expression of aesthetic anarchy, a long weekend that defuses the radical implications of our unhappiness' (101).

Tillyard surely has resurfaced here in this conservative American notion that Shakespeare (and Marlowe) was complicit with the Elizabethan power structure, though Tillyard would never have used the word *complicit*. Just whose side is Shakespeare on? Is it possible to say? We tend, says John Beverley, 'to think of literature as a sanctioned space for the expression of social dissidents' (1993: 25), but the new historicists would stress the fact that the space *is* sanctioned and thus supervised and rendered harmless. All licence is finally contained. Some of them, as Lynda Boose suggests, would argue that Shakespeare was himself 'a co-opted servant of state orthodoxies' (1987: 741) Howard Felperin writes:

A dazzling cast of metadramatic megalomaniacs—Richard III, Falstaff, Volpone, Iago, Vindice, to name but a few—are allowed to turn their worlds into a stage on which they strut and fret their histrionic and directorial fantasies until they are definitively silenced by rigid conventions of closure, which are theatrically, socially and, in the end, theologically sanctioned. (1987: 273)

James Holstun laments that, while the new historicists do not follow Tillyard's model of a 'hierarchical but benevolent collective unconscious unifying women and men, peasants and courtiers, Calvinists and Catholics' (1989: 194), they never consider that there can be a collective movement that is not the 'oppressive construct of a dominant system' (195). What we need is 'the analysis of oppositional collective self-fashioning' (209), the kind that distinguished, so he claims, the birth of the Ranters (and sects like them), and Holstun takes exception to the way the new historicists have ignored groups like these who offer a convincing alternative to the inhibiting status quo that is clearly not the construct of a dominant system.

lament suggests that the new historicists are not
istorical or are too selectively historical. The bits of out-
story they choose to highlight tend to get chosen, con-
t, to illuminate an already firmly held thesis about the
oppressive construct of a dominant system. And according to Pugliatti
(1998) late twentieth-century historical critics are still in some sense in
Tillyard's camp. Although they may emphasize the fact that Shakespeare's plays are resistant to one-sided interpretations, they all more
or less agree that Shakespeare himself was politically conservative. We
still tend to see Shakespeare, she says, as the conservative patriarch and
champion of the status quo, though, as we have seen, she herself thinks
this is not the case.

Let Time Shape, and There an End

Most investigations into Shakespeare's plays these days, whether or
not they are directly concerned with history, are historically inflected.
It is difficult to imagine an approach to Shakespeare, whatever the
critical agenda, that doesn't now take into account the way time shapes
both the play and the criticism of the play. Problems that once might
have been thought to be exclusively aesthetic, for instance, are now
seen to be of a more mongrel kind. So when Leonard Tennenhouse
asks questions in *Power on Display: The Politics of Shakespeare's Genres*
such as—Why is *Henry VIII* so different from *Richard II, Henry IV,
Part 1*, or *Henry V*?, Why did Shakespeare write no romantic comedies
after 1600–2?, Why for that matter are there no romantic comedies by
Shakespeare's contemporaries after this date either?, Why is Jacobean
tragedy so different from Elizabethan tragedy?—his answers to them
are in terms of the politics of the time—the politics, that is, as he puts
it in his title, of Shakespeare's genres. His essential, unimpeachable
claim is that 'during the Renaissance political imperatives were also
aesthetic imperatives' (1986: 6).

This historically inflected approach to Shakespeare's plays, in all its
manifestations, owes a great deal to the seminal work done in this
century in the anthropology of literature. Stephen Greenblatt writes:
'Ever since anthropologists began to speak of the cultures they study as
textual, and literary critics began to speak of the texts they study
as cultural, one of the dreams of cultural poetics has been to link the

text of anthropology and the text of literary criticism' (1994: 97). So when Linda Woodbridge concerns herself with the notion of magical thinking in Shakespeare she acknowledges that the subject does not mean that there is an escape from history: 'What I call magical thinking is a product of this historical collision: inherited medieval magical belief provided the structures, and dawning Renaissance rationalism drove them into the unconscious' (1994: 5).

A sign of the times is the relatively recent concern on the part of feminist criticism with Shakespeare's history plays. Once considered of little interest because they dealt with a politics from which women were patently excluded, the history plays are now seen as central to any feminist investigation of Shakespeare, not only because women *were* excluded in them but because that exclusion turns out to be chimerical. Women are in them as metaphors or as some other linguistic construct or as consciousnesses or consciences. And so Graham Holderness can now write an essay on *Richard II* whose title would at one time itself have seemed chimerical: ' "A Woman's War": A Feminist Reading of *Richard II*'.

What feminist writing there was on the history plays in the early 1980s concentrated on the first tetralogy, which is not surprising considering that there *are* significant female roles in these plays and these roles full of brio. But *King John* has also awakened a new interest. Jean Howard and Phyllis Rackin write:

In *King John* Shakespeare goes as far as he will ever go in making women, women's sceptical voices, and women's truth central to the history he staged, leaving his sources behind and venturing into the realm of the unwritten and the conjectural, and into the inaccessible domain (the no man's land) where the secrets of paternity are kept. (1997: 133)

For them the restriction of women's roles in the second tetralogy represents a move into modernity, while at the same time Mistress Quickly's presence in the plays,

fractures the hermetically sealed world of aristocratic, masculine history to confront London play-goers—both men and women—with a representation of contemporary life in which a woman runs a tavern, both uses and defies the law, exists for a time without a husband, and with her friend Doll Tearsheet probably participates in the sale of sex. (176)

For some feminist critics—Coppelia Kahn is one—the Roman plays 'articulate a critique of the ideology of gender on which the Renaissance understanding of Rome was based' (1997: 1), and even in a play like *Julius Caesar* the feminine is symbolically central.

Recently, a reinvigorated return to the suspect notion of topicality investigates the history plays and others in terms of an intensely focused local history. In *Puzzling Shakespeare: Local Reading and Its Discontents* (1988), Leah Marcus describes this approach as a 'new topicality' but one which reaches its identifications by indirections and assays of bias, responding to what Christopher Highley describes as the manner in which Renaissance drama speaks 'about and to its historical moment in elusive, equivocal, and highly mediated ways' (1997: 6).

This is especially true when the history in question is politically sensitive. Highley argues that 'In *Henry V*, Shakespeare's misgivings about Essex together with an awareness of burgeoning public alarm at the war in Ireland produced a skeptical counter-discourse about English expansionism within the British Isles' (135–6). This is a complicated business, however, where the English in France play the role of the Irish and the French 'are shown in the nervous, defensive posture adopted by the English at the turn-of-the-century' (143). And there are tensions between the representatives in the play of Scotland, Ireland, England, and Wales.

The same elusive topicality, Highley claims, is at work in *Henry IV, Part I* where there is 'a displaced representation of Tyrone's resistance to English authority in Ireland' (87). These strategies in a writer, or a performance, enable some empathy to be shown to the Irish victims of English power. Barbara Hodgdon (1991) proves that the other more narrowly topical historical emphasis continues to flourish as it explores, for instance, the connections between the privately commissioned *Richard II* in February 1601 and Essex's rebellion and the manner in which Richard II reflects Essex himself. And on the larger world stage, Charles Wells (1993) points to a larger topicality at work when he argues that the power struggles between York and Lancaster were seen by the Elizabethans as a parallel to the civil wars of Caesar and Pompey, Octavius and Antony, and the flowering of Elizabeth as the flowering of Rome. The Romans, he says, were routinely compared with Frobisher, Sidney, Grenville, Essex, and Blount.

Untune That String

It may seem to be the case that late twentieth-century Shakespeare criticism has come to be obsessed with history on every level, from the narrowly and indirectly topical to the most far-reaching and wide-ranging political, the politics of our own and everybody else's times. But there have been and continue to be voices of demurral who argue for some kind of history-free investigation of Shakespeare. One such, of course, is from Northrop Frye who finds the application of history to the plays (even to the history plays) a constraint: 'I think Shakespeare uses conceptions taken from the ideology of his time incidentally, and that we always have to look at the structure of the story he's telling us, not what gets said on the way. That is, as a dramatist, he reflects the priority of mythology to ideology...' (1986: 143). Other critics have different reasons and different mythologies for turning their backs on history. Sherman Hawkins, for instance, is more interested in the narrowly psychological. In his view Shakespeare writes histories out of some kind of inner psychic aggression: 'Thus the conflict between aspiration and order in the history plays is deep and real because it is rooted in Shakespeare's personality' (45).

It's *political* history, however, that draws the most fire. Politics may be everything, as Feuerbach claimed, but that does not mean to say that everything is politics. Linda Woodbridge for one is anxious that we should not reduce history to politics.

I strongly resist the tendency of so much new historical writing to value literature only for its public and political moments. *As You Like It's* remarkable conversation about the pitiable death of a deer in the midst of green nature is of value and of interest not only because it talks about usurpation, bankruptcy, and citizens; it is of value and interest because it talks about a deer and green nature. Ecology may be political, but it is not only political. (1994: 191)

The question that Ivo Kamps, echoing Isobel Armstrong, asks about politics will be one, I suspect, that will dog the political criticism of Shakespeare well into the twenty-first century: 'Are recent methods of literary scholarship causing literature and art in general to be displaced by politics?' (1991: 1).

Shakespeare from the Margins

Who's In, Who's Out

Politics in the widest sense of the word has always been a factor in the annals of literary criticism. If literature is what gets taught, as Roland Barthes believed, then what gets taught does not appear on the twentieth-century curriculum by some kind of magical process but as the result of complicated, sometimes obscure, cultural movements. How what gets taught is similarly inflected politically. What was once a dominant method of reading Shakespeare may now be banished to the critical hinterland while something more responsive to the temper of our times takes its place, perhaps rescued from a dusty corner of the past or brought in spanking new from Yale or Paris. Sometimes a dominant method of reading Shakespeare fades into marginality then gets a new lease of life and shifts back to the centre again for a while. This is what has happened to reading Shakespeare as though his characters had inferable identities, though what is now inferred about them at the end of the twentieth century may well be very different from what A. C. Bradley found worthy of inferring about them at the beginning. More often than not, as we have seen in the course of this book, semi-defunct methodologies retain a vestigial flicker of relevance or get transformed into something along similar but more fashionable lines. Hence the diffusion, for instance, of Christian criticism at the end of the century into an undenominational and undoctrinal spirituality. What was once central becomes marginal; what was once on the outside looking in is now the latest orthodoxy.

The Imperial Votaress

It's something of a paradox that the practitioners of feminist criticism, one of the most powerful critical movements over the last thirty years in Shakespeare criticism (and in every other kind), should consider themselves by and large to be on the outside looking in. Yet they feel themselves—no doubt justifiably—to be marginal in the lack of power that they as women (not just as women feminists) have in the academy; and they elect to be marginal in their disinclination to play the game of criticism by the old rules. As far as they are concerned, the critical act has to be a deliberate act of intervention, of renegotiation and rectification, of a setting to rights of what amounts to centuries of distorted interpretation—of Shakespeare's women in particular—by a male-dominated criticism. These acts of critical reparation don't have to be performed by women, of course—though most of them are—and some significant feminist criticism of Shakespeare has come from such male critics as Peter Erickson, Graham Holderness, Mark Breitenberg, and Charles Frey.[1] A parallel criticism of Shakespeare in the late twentieth century, more distinctly marginal, can be found in the recuperative work of critics whose aim is to speak of the love that not long ago dared not speak its name, namely the bonds of homosexual and homosocial affection in Shakespeare's plays and poems (and in Shakespeare's life).

Some sense of the besieged nature of feminist criticism of Shakespeare in the 1990s can be experienced by reading the relevant essays in a couple of anthologies of highly charged ones by critics largely on the political left, *Shakespeare Left and Right* (Kamps 1991) and *Shakespeare and Gender: A History* (Barker and Kamps 1995). In the former collection, for example, Carol Cook writes a piece in angry remonstrance with the work of Richard Levin in particular in whose hands 'feminist criticism becomes the whipping girl on whom a collective aggression is vented' (1991: 68). The moral of her essay is that critical discourse isn't only *about* politics it *is* politics, 'enacting a struggle for power in the academy and in intellectual circles. When this power struggle entails the targeting of feminism, if only "a version of feminism," perhaps it is time to examine criticism's political unconscious' (74). In this climate, it is hardly surprising that Gayle Greene should tell us that feminist criticism of Shakespeare 'is nearly as concerned with the biases of Shakespeare's interpreters—critics, directors, editors—as with Shakespeare himself' (1981: 32), and the title of Linda Fitz's article typifies this concern: 'Egyptian Queens and Male Reviewers: Sexist Attitudes to *Antony and Cleopatra* Criticism' (1977).

It would be a mistake, however, to regard this criticism as monolithic, as a monstrous regiment of feminists marching together in lock step. Marianne Novy reminds us that feminist criticism 'includes accommodation, confrontation and appropriation, opposition to Shakespeare and oppositional use of him' (1993: 7). A properly materialist feminism, Catherine Belsey believes, 'incites heterogeneity' (1991: 264). As with any other ism, and even more so with this one perhaps, there is much variety on offer; as well, the intensity of commitment to its practitioners' revisionist cause guarantees a rapid pace of change. What was the dominant strand of feminist criticism of Shakespeare in the late 1970s and early 1980s had, as far as later feminist critics were/ are concerned, a distinctly old-fashioned air about it. And this is something Carol Cook draws our attention to in the essay mentioned above. Critics of Shakespeare's feminist critics, she says, target feminist criticism written in the early 1980s for its ahistoricism and theoretical weakness, failing to acknowledge (or not knowing) feminism's own increasing sophistication in the late 1980s and 1990s.[2] In 1989 in the opening chapter of the second edition of her book, *Still Harping on Daughters: Women and Drama in the Age of Shakespeare*, Lisa Jardine— feminist, historian, and literary critic—looks back a mere six years to the book's first edition and marvels at the progress that has been made in feminist criticism of Shakespeare. In 1989 what she criticized in 1983 as the prevalent feminist procedure—the mere highlighting of Shakespeare's female characters and the routine condemnation of the sexist views of his male ones—is now no longer the dominant one. Things have moved on apace. Feminist critics of Shakespeare are now much more aware of the necessity to take into account other analytic approaches: Marxist, psychoanalytic, anthropological, and materialist.[3] By 1989 feminist approaches to Shakespeare had matured considerably.

Recuperating Shakespeare's female characters in the face of a grudging, sometimes fearful response to them by mainstream criticism has a lengthy, pre-feminist history. Shakespeare's golden girls, for example, have always had their (often gushing) devotees, as a glance at the work of Mrs M. Leigh Elliott (1885), Helena Faucit Martin (1885), and Agnes Mure MacKenzie (1924) would confirm. As late as 1981, however, a feminist critic, Irene Dash, feels constrained to begin her book on the women in Shakespeare's plays with the supererogatory announcement that '[s]trong, attractive, intelligent, and humane women come to life in Shakespeare's plays' (1981: 1); they're relevant and vital, confident and independent, and through them Shakespeare 'questions the wisdom of a power structure that insists they relinquish personal freedom' (5).

At this stage of the feminist scrutiny of Shakespeare, Shakespeare himself is not seen by most feminist writers to have the biases of his interpreters (or of his male characters). And when we contemplate the sparkling characterizations of women in Shakespeare's plays (especially in the comedies) we don't have to be a Mrs Elliott or a Faucit Martin to respond to the obvious relish he took in giving them wit and intelligence. Indeed, so Juliet Dusinberre argues in the book that some credit with being the first major feminist work on Shakespeare, *Shakespeare and the Nature of Women* (1975), Shakespeare's obvious sympathies with his women characters make him a feminist *avant la lettre*: 'Shakespeare's feminism consists of more than a handful of high-born emancipated heroines: it lies rather in his skepticism about the nature of women' (305). The nature of women, that is, as perceived by the majority of Renaissance thinkers. Shakespeare, Dusinberre insists, rejected the conventional view of women as necessarily inferior to men, siding instead with the Puritan position that 'absorbed both Calvin's idealism about marriage, [and] the concern of Humanists like More for liberal attitudes to women' (4). And would not Shakespeare, she asks, and most of his fellow dramatists, be careful in their work to try to please a major segment of his audiences, the women? A segment of the population, moreover, which, like the members of the dramatic companies, was criticized for play-acting, thus making it the dramatists' natural ally? Dusinberre's claims for a progressive view of women extend beyond Shakespeare's contribution to include most of the drama written between 1590 and 1625. Not just Shakespeare, then, but Marston, Middleton, Dekker, Webster, Heywood, Jonson, and Massinger. And to some extent, Chapman, Beaumont, and Fletcher.

But especially Shakespeare who 'saw men and women as equal in a world which declared them unequal' (308).

Some feminist critics since then have found other ways of exculpating Shakespeare of the charge of sexism. Claire McEachern, for instance, recounts the way Shakespeare differs from his sources in taking the woman's part: 'In revising his sources he recasts and demystifies the role of the father... questions the power of fathers, a power that demands replication for the perpetuation of the patriarchal system' (1988: 272). It's all part of a larger revolt by Shakespeare in reworking his inherited archetypes. Though Shakespeare may not be entirely free of anxiety, McEachern acknowledges, he manages in the end, '[l]ike the daughters in his plays', to defy 'the control of patriarchy, separating and individuating his own identity from that of his literary authority' (289). Shakespeare 'rewrites patriarchy, resists its conclusions, revealing its idealized image of fathers as fictions constructed against the complexity of human desire' (290). The distorted idealized image of the father can be paralleled by the distorted idealized image of the husband, so Gayle Greene believes; the 'accepted ideals of manly and womanly behaviour are distortive and destructive of the human reality'—men's relations must be based, so Shakespeare implies, on 'saner and more certain ground than "this that you call love"' (1995: 61).

As far as Irene Dash and Juliet Dusinberre were concerned it's a question of rescuing Shakespeare's women from a misogynist criticism that sells them and Shakespeare short. Feminist critics need to become the advocates of Shakespeare's women, and their relationship to them should resemble, so Elaine Showalter (1985) argues, that of lawyer to client. Women in Shakespeare's comedies, however, don't usually need feminist lawyers, as Portia in *The Merchant of Venice* makes clear in as literal a sense as possible. In the tragedies it's another matter. Marginalized, often tongue-tied, Shakespeare's tragic women in their limited role as victims of narcissistically articulate men fall far short of the feisty presence of the women in his comedies.

Ophelia and Hamlet's mother are favourite clients for forensically inclined feminists and their team of lawyers stretches back to Carolyn Heilbrun in 1957 with her brief representing Gertrude against a sexist criticism that sees her as 'well-meaning but shallow and feminine, in the pejorative sense of the word: incapable of any sustained rational process, superficial and flighty' (201). Gertrude is, on the contrary, 'intelligent, penetrating, and gifted with a remarkable talent for concise and pithy speech' (206). Nearly thirty years later Jacqueline Rose rewrites the brief for the defence of Gertrude in terms of the delusions of a paranoid male sexuality through which she stands accused 'of too much sexuality, [while] Isabella in *Measure for Measure* of not enough' (1985: 95).

More recent defenders of Shakespeare's tragic women insist that any re-examination of them should not be undertaken in the name of a conventional morality or merely done to list the positive qualities of the women's characters ignored or distorted by traditional criticism. We need, they argue, to recognize that Shakespeare's women are interestingly complex and flawed; like the men they are capable of passion and pain, growth and decay. For Elaine Showalter, for example, Ophelia is the female subtext to the tragedy and 'represents the strong emotions that the Elizabethans as well as the Freudians thought womanish and unmanly' (1985: 79). Showalter's essay epitomizes Carol Neely's third (and in her view most rewarding) feminist mode of Shakespeare criticism, the transformational—the other two she calls the compensatory and justificatory—whereby '[c]ritics in this mode interrogate the relations between male idealization of and degradation of women, between women as heroines and women as victims, between the patriarchal text and the matriarchal subtext' (1981: 9). Hence Catherine Belsey's judgement on *Macbeth*: 'The play magnificently demonstrates the instabilities of a patriarchy which confines woman to motherhood and promises to man everything else that it means to be human' (1991: 261).

Ministers of Chastisement

Earlier feminist critics of Shakespeare, as we have seen, tended to exempt Shakespeare himself from the accusations they brought against his characters and interpreters. In this view, Shakespeare is complicit with the matriarchal subtext of his plays; his not-so secret inclinations are pro-woman and anti-patriarchal. In Coppelia Kahn's words, Shakespeare questions 'the cultural definitions of sexual identity' (1981: 20). But truth to tell it is difficult to decide whether or not Shakespeare criticizes patriarchy, accepts it, or even (in the worst case scenario as far as feminist criticism is concerned) propagandizes on its behalf. More recent feminist critics of Shakespeare tend to identify him with the patriarchal text rather than the matriarchal subtext and view their colleagues' earlier attempts to co-opt Shakespeare to the feminist cause as a species of sentimentality and wishful thinking.

Their revisionist criticism of the revisionist critics can be seen in the larger context of an emerging scepticism about the progress of women in the sixteenth and seventeenth centuries. According to Lisa Jardine the drama does hold a mirror up to society but what we see in it is not progressive:

I maintain the strong interest in women shown by Elizabethan and Jacobean drama does not in fact reflect newly improved social conditions, and greater possibility for women, but rather is related to the patriarchy's unexpressed worry about the great social changes which characterize the period—worries which could be made conveniently concrete in the voluminous and endemic debates about 'the woman question'. (1983: 6)

Thus Shakespeare's tragedies seem, to some feminist critics, a bitter pleasure. For Shirley Nelson Garner, for example, there are so many 'woman-hating voices' (1996: 305) in them. When the tragic heroes go mad they do so misogynistically; indeed it's as though Shakespeare makes them go mad in order to allow them to express their hatred of women. It's wearying, Garner complains, to have to deal with Shakespeare's tragic heroes' relentless fear and hatred of women, and difficult to distinguish between their voices and the voice of Shakespeare himself. (Difficult no doubt, but, some would say, obligatory.)

The later feminist consensus in the twentieth century tends to see Shakespeare's tragedies in terms of an anxious masculinity hostage to a thwart and disnatured view of femininity both in women and in men (and in Shakespeare). Men fear the femininity of women and the female element in themselves. Hence in Jacqueline Rose's commentary on T. S. Eliot's comparison of the *Mona Lisa* and *Hamlet* she asks the question: '[W]hat does it mean to us that one of the most elevated and generally esteemed works of our Western literary tradition should enact such a negative representation of femininity, or even such a violent repudiation of the femininity in man?' (1995: 116–17). What it should mean to us as far as she is concerned is a re-examination of the principles of the Western *critical* tradition that can allow its elevated works of art to speak with such irresponsible partiality without any agitated demurral.

The tragedies—and not just the tragedies—transform the merry war between Signior Benedick and Beatrice into something far more deadly whereby, according to Valerie Traub, the threat posed by female autonomy, maternal power, and sexuality is channelled into a 'strategy of containment' (1995: 121). The three male heroes of *Hamlet*, *Othello*, and *The Winter's Tale*, for instance, long for 'stasis, for a reprieve from the excitations and anxieties of erotic life' (121). Women are imagined in these plays (and in others) as either angels or whores, 'as a psychological defense against the uncomfortable suspicion that underneath, the angel *is* a whore' (123). What these men would like to do is to lock women up, or at least to lock up their sexuality.[4] In her book on Shakespeare Traub notes that the these plays 'seem motivated toward this end: to give women speech only to silence them; to make women move only to still them; to represent their bodies onstage only to enclose them; to infuse their bodies with warmth only to "encorpse" them' (26). According to Paula Berggren the antagonism between the sexes in Shakespeare's plays can be summed up along these polarities: 'Women resent men for oppressing them, while men despise women for reminding them that they are creatures of the flesh' (1980: 26).

Silence, stillness, enclosure, encorpsement: it's a chilling indictment by a feminist of the treatment of women by Shakespeare's tragedies. In their ideal male-dominated world women should be handmaids merely of the masculine ego, so Linda Bamber (1982) concludes, allowing the male characters the freedom of their obsession with themselves, with their frustrations and bewilderment. And if it is the *plays* that treat women in this way (rather than the plays' male characters) then it makes no sense to argue as earlier feminist critics had done that Shakespeare is somehow a proto-feminist, unless we believe that Shakespeare and his plays are separate entities, or that the plays are authorless. As Valerie Traub maintains: 'While dramatically exploring masculine anxieties, and even presenting the crisis of masculinist values, Shakespearean drama nonetheless perpetuates defensive structures of dominance instituted by men' (1992: 48). She does offer, however, less bleak interpretative possibilities, arguing, for example, that the ideological work of the play is not necessarily captured by its formal closure—'it is equally at work in the process of the play' (19)—so that the final containment of women is not necessarily the play's last word, just one of many others that came before it.

Not surprisingly feminist critics tend to concentrate upon Shakespeare's comedies; it is in them, after all, that women have at least as many words as the men, if not the last one (once again). Harriet Hawkins reminds us that 'in giving equal billing to male and female characters as well as their defiantly anti-tribal love, Shakespeare broke new dramatic ground' (1993: 116). Women in the comedies are powerful plot instigators, movers, and developers; they are often more active than the men, reversing the roles of the sexes in the tragedies. The Other has taken over from the Self, to use Linda Bamber's terminology: it 'either rebels against the restraining social order or (more commonly) presides in alliance with forces that challenge its hegemony: romantic love, physical nature, the love of pleasure in all its forms' (1982: 28). In the comedies the women's negotiations with the world come unmediated by father, lover, or husband. The comedies are, to be sure, 'an exercise in sustained poise' (1982: 124). And part of that poise is the women's use of male disguise which is no mere indication, according to Paula Berggren (1980), of women's infirmity, but of their flexibility and astuteness.

In recent years, however, the comedies have come in for a more sceptical scrutiny. Cedric Watts notes that '[t]he most popular and contentious question [for feminism] is whether Shakespeare's women subvert or confirm demeaning stereotypes' (1987: 286), and that question for many feminists remains moot even for the comedies. Jean Howard comes down hard on the sexual politics of *Twelfth Night*, for instance: 'The play disciplines independent women like Olivia and upstart crows such as Malvolio and rewards the self-abnegation of Viola' (1994: 116). So Viola, who has been seen in much of the criticism of the play as the dynamic opposite of her languorous employer, Orsino, here takes on the more familiar role of a version—a more active version to be sure—of the traditional patient Griselda, willing to make the final sacrifice to the wavering fancies of a wealthy Narcissus. Viola, that is, is properly feminine; Olivia, like Portia in *The Merchant of Venice*, is the real threat to the hierarchical gender system and has to be taught the appropriate lesson.[5] For Lisa Jardine Shakespeare's comedies expose 'a serious and deep-rooted ambivalence towards the educated woman' (1996: 64). And Mary Beth Rose considers the significant absence of mothers from the world of romantic comedy arguing that it helps to explain why 'romantic comedy was, and still remains, the most conservative, as well as the most popular, of dramatic genres' (1991: 304). She contrasts the significant presence of the mother in *All's Well that Ends Well* which 'indicates the limitations of male power' (310).

There seem to be no limitations to male power in the romantic comedy that causes feminists most concern, *The Taming of the Shrew*. Most critics in the twentieth century, not all of them feminists by any means, have expressed unease with the sexual politics of this play. Shirley Nelson Garner (1988), for instance, argues that you have to be a man to be able to enjoy the play's humour—it is acted for the benefit of the male characters of the Inductions. Robert Ornstein (1986) says that we have to bite the bullet and face up to the simple fact that Kate *is* a shrew and the only one in Shakespeare.

The more interesting criticism, sometimes feminist, sometimes not, is the one that responds to the play's ambiguous elements, to the teasing quality of the relationship between Petruchio and Katherine, to a deliberately deep-rooted uncertainty about the play's tone. The feminist critic, Coppélia Kahn, responds to these ambiguous elements, and argues that Kate's dependency 'underlies mastery, the strength behind submission' (1981: 118). So too does Marianne Novy (1984) who maintains that the play allows us to see the relationship between Kate and Petruchio as patriarchal or playful or both. The most interesting book along these lines is J. Dennis Huston's *Shakespeare's Comedies of Play* (1981) which concentrates on the fairytale aspect of *The Taming of the Shrew* in which the monstrous is won over by human ingenuity. Kate is like an autistic child, fearing, hating, and yet seeking, isolation. In Petruchio's castle of terrors, so Huston argues, Kate experiences 'a rite of passage which frees her from the tyranny of her infantile self and releases her into the true adulthood of marriage and mutuality' (1981: 88). Lisa Jardine takes as typical of the play's playful instability the difficulty of establishing Kate's tone in her submission to Petruchio at the end of the play: 'Depending on how we take her tone, Kate is seriously tamed, is ironic at Petruchio's expense, has learned comradeship and harmonious coexistence, or will remain a shrew till her death' (1983: 59).

All of these alternatives are plausible, and all have been given expression in various productions of the play in the twentieth-century theatre. (For a discussion of feminist criticism of the history plays see p. 191 in Chapter 5.) Central much more than symbolically—though they are that too—the women in Shakespeare's romances represent an ideal maternity 'that justifies the ways of God to men' (Berggren 1980: 26). Feminist critics have of course responded to the way in which the romances seem to reassert the authority of the women of the comedies (or of some of them anyway) after the nightmare detour through the misogynistic world of the tragedies. The women characters now seem to be the vehicles of the last plays' emphasis on atonement, peace, harmony, renewal; they smile extremity out of act. Even the magician Prospero in *The Tempest*, the play that makes least use of women in anything but the capacity for sweet-natured subservience, credits his angelic daughter for their safe passage through the storm in their journey from Milan to the island. Marianne Novy argues that the conflict between patriarchy and mutuality has been symbolically resolved in the romances (as it had been in the comedies), 'the inadequacy of the traditional masculine stereotype is much more obvious' (1984: 164). Other feminist critics argue that not as much has changed in the romances as has been claimed. Smiling extremity out of act still maintains the traditional lop-sided relationship between the sexes where one has the power to act, the other merely to react (however potently). Charles Frey warns us that the '[romances] may be more patriarchal and patrilineal in perspective than Shakespearean interpreters have yet cared or dared to recognize' (1980a: 213).

Cantons of Contemned Love

Feminists are not the only critics of Shakespeare in the twentieth century to stress the importance of differentiating as is now fashionable between sex and gender, the former biologically constructed, the latter culturally (so the argument runs). Short of an expensive operation, nothing much can be done about changing one's sex; gender, however, can be as malleable as Feste's cheverel glove to a good wit, 'how quickly the wrong side may be turned outward' (*Twelfth Night*, 3.1.12–13).

Turning the wrong side outward, or, more accurately, keeping the wrong side inward, distinguishes for our purposes the most potent form of gender construction in Elizabethan society, that of the boy players playing the roles of girls and women. Feminist critics are divided in their response to this play-acting; some of them see it in the traditional terms of a neutral transparency—the boys are professional actors playing fictional women and there's not much difference between them doing so and women playing fictional women. The majority of feminist critics, however, are alive to the sexual politics and erotics of the indeterminacy of boys playing the woman's part. Lisa Jardine believes that the eroticism of the disguised boys in the comedies (that is, the boys playing girls disguised as boys) depended on their being perceived as boys. Boys will be boys. '"Playing the woman's part"—male effeminacy—is an act for a male audience's appreciation' (1983: 31). It is equally possible to see the boy actor playing the woman's part in terms of his being a boy rather than a woman. In either case, it is a question of male effeminacy designed to titillate a male audience. (How the women in the audience would feel about 'male effeminacy' on the stage is not pursued much in feminist criticism.)[6]

It has been argued by some feminist critics that female roles written by men and acted by boys are caricatures of female roles. Acted by women they may not be that much better off; they are at the mercy— usually—of male intruders, their parts, so Irene Dash tells us, often cut, excised, distorted through 'textual high jinks, directorial liberties, or critical blindness' (1997: 249–50). Even if the woman's part was not cut, however, the actor's vaunted freedom is now considered chimerical by many critics, by no means all of them feminist. Lorraine Helms compares the Shakespearean actress to the prima donna, the ballerina, and the film star all obeying 'rigorous rules for female impersonation . . . within theatrical structures largely controlled by masculinist directors, producers, designers, and promoters; [hence] the energies of the female voice and body are readily channeled into ventriloquism' (1994: 106).

What can be done to counter this inauthenticity is to put on productions of Shakespeare—perhaps by women directors—which would take their cue from a criticism that captures hidden possibilities for the feminist cause. A feminist version of textual high jinks and directorial liberties, perhaps, as when Helms contemplates a production of *Macbeth* geared to Terry Eagleton's *William Shakespeare* which argues for the Witches as the heroes of the piece: 'They are poets, prophetesses and devotees of female cult, radical separatists who scorn male power and lay bare the hollow sound and fury at its heart' (1986: 130–1). In Helms's hypothetical production of Eagleton's reading of the play the Witches would be played by beautiful women actors who would then disguise themselves as witches by putting on masks and behaving theatrically when they meet Macbeth on the heath.

Behind the critical interest in transvestism, gender politics and ideology, cross-dressing, and the like, is the twentieth-century obsession with the body which in some quarters has replaced the traditional and long-standing obsession with the word.[7] Why is this the case? Is it, Dympna Callaghan asks, because the body 'intrinsically constitutes an appropriate and effective site of resistance to the increasingly dense, subtle, and comprehensive conceptual trap of late capitalist patriarchy?' (1993: 431). Lorraine Helms (and Terry Eagleton) might well answer in the affirmative. Actors' bodies, however, according to Keir Elam, have unfortunately been overlooked in most of this criticism: 'Most Shakespearean corporeal criticism is altogether removed from our own theatrical culture, and thus, in a sense, from our own historical moment. The history of Shakespeare's bodies is also and above all the history of their embodiment onstage' (1996: 160).

Embodied on stage—particularly on the English stage—is an often vulgarized homoeroticism that obscures by its adolescent desire to shock genuine moments of tremulous ambiguity in the relationships between some of the male characters in Shakespeare's plays. Antonio and Bassanio in *The Merchant of Venice*, Antonio and Sebastian in *Twelfth Night* (and Orsino and Cesario), Coriolanus and Aufidius, Brutus and Cassius in *Julius Caesar*—these are some of the male bondings in the plays that critics have characterized as homoerotic, less explicit of course than that between the poet and the fair young man of the Sonnets, but just as melancholy. However, in his article 'How to Read *The Merchant of Venice* Without Being Heterosexist' (1996) Alan Sinfield suggests that the Antonios from *The Merchant of Venice* and *Twelfth Night* need not be played on stage at the end of the play as necessarily forlorn and abandoned, which is usually their theatrical fate should the director have decided to dramatize the subterranean erotic feelings they may have towards their friends.

Sinfield's desire to include the Antonios in the final celebrations that Malvolio and Shylock shun reminds us of the recuperative tactics of feminism and also seems to be a positive response in the practical world of mounting a play to the enormous amount of scholarship in the twentieth century on the homosocial ties between the men of Elizabethan and Jacobean England, especially as this scholarship stresses the normalcy in the England of this time for men to have these friendships. Why was Renaissance culture so permissive (for men at least) on this issue?

This is a topic that has fascinated literary critics and social historians alike in this century. Margaret Hunt suggests that passionate male friendships were simply part of 'the complicated system of patronage, faction, protection, and jockeying for status and preferment that largely constituted the "governance" of the Renaissance' (1994: 366). Same-sex relations at this time, Sinfield nonchalantly suggests, were just not terribly important (that is, same-sex relations between men). Bruce Smith agrees with this judgement but notes a subtle distinction: 'In Shakespeare's plays, as presumably in early modern English society, a man can say without shame that he desires to conjoin his body with the body of another male.... What a man cannot say without shame is that he wants to be so desired' (1996: 101).

What cannot be said at all apparently—with or without shame—is an expression of desire for the conjoining of a woman's body with that of another woman. Sinfield believes that men at this time were simply unable to imagine a female sexuality that did not include them. And as the professional playwrights at this time were all men, the lesbian demi-monde remained undramatized. (Although it is not impossible for the boy actors playing girls disguised as boys to convey in their flirtations with the boy actors playing girls a suggestion of a lesbian eroticism.)

The Sweetness of Affiance

Marginalized positions tend to find common ground. Many feminists and critics interested in ethnicity (the ethnicity usually of a subaltern race) see the relationship between the two as homologous and the cause common. Ania Loomba expatiates on the combinatory tendencies of race, sex, and class: 'The processes by which women and black

3. A scene from *Othello* with Paul Robeson and Mary Ure (1959).

people are constructed as the "others" of white patriarchal
similar and connected, and they also reflect upon other sort
sion such as that based on class' (1989: 2). In Shakespeare tl
ture of sex and race is a potent one as *Othello, Titus Andro*
Merchant of Venice, Antony and Cleopatra, and to a lesser ex ... *The*
Tempest illustrate.

Othello is the play that has aroused the greatest passions in its
critics—the greatest passions and the most extreme forms of evasion,
temporizing, revisionism, and rationalization. Even in the twentieth
century—especially in the twentieth century in certain countries at
certain times—there is a strain of criticism unable or unwilling to
accept the play's dramatization of the marriage between Othello and
Desdemona. Karen Newman tells us that the play (and some of the
criticism) is dominated by the fear of miscegenation, particularly of
the black man with the white woman; but femininity in the play is not
opposed to blackness and monstrosity 'but identified with the monstrous . . . [which] makes miscegenation doubly fearful' (1987: 145).
Desdemona's desire is transgressive because Othello is black, Ania
Loomba roundly asserts, and Othello himself as the play wears on
adopts the patriarchal view of women—the Christian patriarchal
view—regarding them as deceivers ever, and he does so—in this
argument—because he is black.

Women and ethnicity become enmeshed at the level of the image.
In an article on Shakespeare and cultural difference, Ania Loomba
asks us to notice the difference in treatment of the body of the woman
in literature about the New World and the Eastern world. 'If the
African or American woman stands in for Woman as Nature, ripe
for ravishing, her Eastern counterpart becomes the embodiment of
Woman as Artifice—ever ready to ensnare' (1996: 177). There are no
African or American women in Shakespeare (except perhaps for
Caliban's mother, Sycorax, in *The Tempest*) but the second part of
Loomba's observation sheds light on Shakespeare's depiction of Cleo-
patra.[8]

And where does Shakespeare stand here? Ethnic criticism of
Shakespeare follows the same trajectory as feminist criticism of
Shakespeare. There is above all an acknowledgement—especially
with regard to *Othello*—of the extraordinary measure of daring and
sophistication on Shakespeare's part to dramatize a love affair between

a black man and a white woman in terms of their mutual admiration, even if Desdemona has to see Othello's visage in his mind in order for the colour of his skin to be acceptable to her. The play's plot, Karen Newman says, 'stands in a contestatory relation to the hegemonic ideologies of race and gender in early modern England' (1987: 157). Though Iago may not be one of the wealthy curled darlings of the Venetian state he has none the less all the advantages of being white in a society—Desdemona's and Shakespeare's—that prizes whiteness. To pit a Christian African against a diabolical white Venetian is, as Ruth Cowhig argues, 'a startling reversal of the norm' (1985: 12). And as though to underscore and at the same time to subvert the vulgar conception of such a union, Shakespeare is more daring still, so Cowhig maintains, in making it clear that Desdemona does not love Othello solely for his mind or for the dangers that he had passed but for the rites 'for why I love him' (*Othello*, 1.3.257). Desdemona is drawn in other words to Othello's sexual potency: 'If [Shakespeare's] purpose was to unsettle or perplex his audience, then he succeeded beyond expectation . . .' (14). And all of this, as many critics point out, takes place against the familiar background of those intolerant sets of beliefs whereby Blacks were thought sinful, bestial, and concupiscent, beyond, as Anthony Barthelemy tells us, 'the realm of grace and civil society' (1987: 6), where if they were Mohammedan, as Jack D'Amico points out, they represented 'a frightening spiritual and political counterforce to European Christianity' (1991: 75) and if they were black they were considered 'sexually unrestrained' (63).

In recent years literary and historical criticism has tended to judge Shakespeare's society as more racist and less homophobic than was formerly thought to be the case. Although the quality and kind of its racism obviously differ from that of the twentieth century in most instances, it's none the less recognizably a prejudiced point of view responding, like ours, more to myth than to reality. But our conception of the reality of the racial situation in Shakespeare's time has also changed. For much of the twentieth century commentators argued that the darker colour of a person's skin in the Renaissance (black, swart, Egyptian, tawny, and so on) fell into the category of exotic strangeness—a category, however, never viewed neutrally or benignly—spiced with traditional theological associations of darkness with things that go bump in the Christian night. G. K. Hunter, for example, in a series of readings,[9] expresses the belief that the Elizabethans had no continuous contact with black people and were not threatened by them economically and could not be said therefore to hold racist views. We have to see their racialism in theological rather than social terms. This one-time popular position is now under siege. Many commentators have pointed out that, *pace* Hunter and others, Blacks were a reasonably familiar sight, at least in London in the late sixteenth century, and were considered by the Elizabethan government late in Elizabeth's reign to be an economic threat. Indeed, as Ania Loomba suggests, '[t]he operations of patriarchalism [sought] to extend the control and authority of man as father over women, and white man as father over black men and women' (1989: 45). In masques and pageants Blacks represented the Other, the always inferior Other, and in stage tradition they were nearly always emblematic of evil (though that theatrical function was no doubt heavily influenced by theology).

Given this revised view of the prejudices of Shakespeare's time, Shakespeare's treatment of the exotic minorities in his plays seems all the more impressive. Anthony Barthelemy considers Shakespeare's presentation, for instance, of Aaron the Moor, the forerunner of Iago, in *Titus Andronicus*, and talks of him in terms of his being a 'chink in the allegory of blackness' (1987: 97), his mite of human kindness undermining the 'univocal symbolism of blackness' (96).

Jack D'Amico thinks Aaron is not only grimly comic but comic 'in a higher sense because through him we glimpse a human capacity for survival and renewal' (1991: 145). The chink widens hugely with Shakespeare's depiction of Othello and we move beyond conventional cultural assumptions 'to confront the question of how we understand and define the relationship between the self and the other' (1991: 3). The representation of the Moor in Shakespeare could, D'Amico asserts, 'lead the dramatist and the audience beyond a comfortable sense of superiority or the superficial titillation provided by a darkly alien villain. The Moor could become a dramatic symbol of the many stereotypes and masks that divide society and alienate the individual' (1991: 212).

Loomba attempts to put the record straight: 'In *Othello* ... commonsense ideas about blacks are evoked but more clearly questioned, disclosed as misrepresentation' (1989: 48). Tawny-fronted Morocco in

The Merchant of Venice and Cleopatra in *Antony and Cleopatra* are given their due as potential or actual partners of Portia and Antony. D'Amico describes the Prince of Morocco as the 'innocent outsider' (1991: 170) and talks of Cleopatra in terms of 'her blessed wantonness' (162), while Ania Loomba argues that in Cleopatra's presentation Shakespeare 'does not simply indicate a stereotype but depicts it as constructed by various male perspectives in the play' (75).

It falls to twentieth-century criticism of Shakespeare to be particularly sensitive to the stereotypes and masks that divide society and alienate the individual, especially the individual as writer and critic. One reason for this is that Shakespeare criticism now is full of strangers in the way Leslie Fiedler claims Shakespeare to be. (The stranger as woman in *Henry VI, Part 1*, the stranger as Jew in *The Merchant of Venice*, the 'savage man called Ind' and the witch 'as they appear in the complex web of the whole Shakespearean corpus' (1973: 16)). Ania Loomba emphasizes the fact that her 1989 book on Shakespeare—her writing generally—is the result of her teaching drama in India; more students, she tells us, read *Othello* in the University of Delhi every year than in all the British universities combined, and the overwhelming majority of these students are women. (And yet the canonical author and the academic hierarchies there as elsewhere are predominantly male.) Jack D'Amico (1991) thinks it important for us to know that he began thinking about the Moor on the English Renaissance stage when he was living and teaching in Beirut, Lebanon, and Rabat, Morocco, and also while teaching in China. Biographies like these are commonplace in the history of twentieth-century criticism. So it is not surprising that there should be much greater urgency in the response of these critics (and of many others for that matter, given the multi-racial constitution of so many modern societies) to questions of race and alienation, of belonging and not belonging. And this identification with questions of ethnicity is equally true of today's historians, the new historicists in particular, who, James Shapiro tells us, 'have re-discovered virtually every marginalized Other that passed through early modern England—including witches, hermaphrodites, Moors, cross-dressers, Turks, sodomites, criminals, prophets, Eskimos, and vagabonds' (1996: 86).

This list doesn't include Caliban from *The Tempest* who seems to combine a number of Shapiro's categories as well as being half-fish.

Whatever shape and colour he may take in any production, the least that can be said for him is that he (along with Ariel) is Shakespeare's major addition to his sources. By making the island inhabited before Prospero's arrival Shakespeare invites the criticism that has dominated twentieth-century discourse about the play, a Conradian obsession with the mutual corruption of colonizer and colonized. 'That single addition', Ania Loomba believes, 'turned the adventure story into an allegory of the colonial encounter' (1989: 2).

In the earlier days of the century's criticism that allegory of the colonial encounter pitted a deformed, bestial, indigenous rapist against a sophisticated bearer of civilized European values. The tendency now is to give Caliban more than his due as the hapless victim of a predatory colonialism. There is enough evidence in the play on both sides, however, to suggest no easy answer to Ania Loomba's question, 'Does *The Tempest* endorse Prospero's view of Caliban as the bestial savage, or does it depict the dehumanisation of colonial rule?' (1989: 74).[10] Perhaps the short answer is that it does both.

James Shapiro's list does not include either the 'Other of Others in the Renaissance, the Jews. And this is all the more strange, perhaps, because so many of these scholars are themselves of Jewish descent' (1996: 86). There was never any need to rediscover the marginalized Jew in *The Merchant of Venice*, however. The history of twentieth-century criticism of the play centres on this marginalized Other in its most basic formulation: is or is not *The Merchant of Venice* anti-semitic? A famous essay of 1911 by E. E. Stoll, reprinted in two important anthologies, one by Harold Bloom (1989) and another by Thomas Wheeler (1991), puts the case starkly when he describes Shylock as 'a sordid miser with a hooked nose' (Wheeler: 262).

Leslie Fiedler is convinced that *The Merchant of Venice* 'in some sense celebrates, certainly releases ritually, the full horror of anti-semitism' (1973: 98). In order to understand what's going on here, Fiedler argues, we don't need to return 'to the historical past in order to reconstruct what men once thought of Jews and witches, but rather... we [need to] descend to the level of what is most archaic in our living selves and there confront the living Shylock and Joan' (99). J. A. Bryant Jr. warns us that the stark truth about *The Merchant of Venice* may be intolerable and would tar everyone in the play except

Portia—even Antonio is 'successively arrogant, servile, and charitable only for purposes of self-interest' (1986: 89).

Critics of this persuasion owe much to A. D. Moody (1964) who declares the play to be egregiously ironic with the Christians and Shylock equally maleficent. Finding all the characters intolerable and equally maleficent is one way, I suppose, of defending the play (and Shakespeare) from the charge of anti-semitism. Another is—*pace* Fiedler—to return to that 'historical past' and urge its distinctness from the twentieth century (a now familiar manoeuvre). A more positive point of view is to emphasize, as many twentieth-century critics have done, the humanity of Shylock (usually at the expense of the Christian merchants). The most extreme form of philosemitism claims Shakespeare to have been a converted Jew, or at least descended from forcibly converted Jews. Shapiro himself isn't interested in whether Shakespeare was anti-or philosemitic. The play is not a diary or a polygraph test, he argues, and it is simply the case that '[i]n seventeenth-century England tolerance and equal, permanent status for Jews were not yet possibilities, not even... for John Locke, the greatest proponent of toleration' (1996: 11).

The Searching Eye of Heaven

It is instructive to look back over the twentieth century and see the extent to which certain ways of perceiving Shakespeare's plays had and lost such a firm hold on the critical imagination. Once taking centre stage, religious, mythic, and archetypal criticism of Shakespeare now languishes on the sidelines. This is especially true of a specifically Christian interpretation of Shakespeare, though Roy Battenhouse's recent anthology of Christian essays, *Shakespeare's Christian Dimension: An Anthology of Commentary* (1994), suggests that the marginality of this critical approach has not yet reached the vanishing point.

Earlier in the century Christian critics were thicker on the ground, and Shakespeare was claimed as one of their own by various denominations and their more radical offshoots. What these claimants had in common was an overwhelmingly positive response to what they perceived as the plays' beneficent providence. Even a tragedy as uncompromising as *King Lear* could be seen *sub specie aeternitatis* as offering some kind of eschatological solace: Lear's 'Look there, look there'(5.3.287),[11] in this view, is joyous, whatever its precise meaning and whether or not it is deluded.

Some plays, of course, are easier to Christianize than others— *Measure for Measure*, for instance, has a tempting narrative for the allegorically minded—but any play by Shakespeare can be moulded to fit the Christian gestalt without overwhelming distortion. (This is hardly surprising given Shakespeare's saturation in a Christian culture.) Hence, S. L. Bethell's account of *The Winter's Tale* in terms of a Christianity 'newly translated into terms of the romance' (1944: 76). In *The Winter's Tale*, he says, 'the religious atmosphere [is] emphatically Christian, while the pagan suggestions give authenticity to the story and serve to "distance" the Christian attitudes' (37); the play 'represents an important moment in the history of Christian civilisation' (118). Secularity, whether or not pagan, is a cover for Christian worship in many, perhaps all, of Shakespeare's plays as he 'does not desert the secular for the sacred but finds the sacred deep down in the secular' (110). As for Shakespeare himself, Bethell (and many others) believes he was undoubtedly a Christian, either a Roman Catholic recusant or an Anglican inclining more to Hooker than to Calvin. Bethell favours the latter: Shakespeare 'wrote consistently from the standpoint of orthodox Christianity' (14).

Bethell's position was (and still is) a common one. For E. M. W. Tillyard Shakespeare was an orthodox Elizabethan at one with Spenser, Sidney, Raleigh, Hooker, and Jonson 'in holding with earnestness, passion and assurance to the major beliefs of his time about God, man and the Universe' (Murray 1969: 88–9). C. J. Sisson thought the tragedies and problem comedies evinced a Christian consciousness; a play like *Measure for Measure* 'is sound to the core, and profoundly Christian in spirit' (1964: 22). And the tragedies are built on a sense of reconciliation and atonement: 'He [Shakespeare] experienced and faced the twin problems of pain and of evil in no spirit of petulance, but with an insight into immanent good of which the tragedy is the clearest proof' (32).

Perhaps, though, Shakespeare was an unorthodox Christian, a Puritan of some persuasion maybe, or, at the other extreme, a Roman Catholic. Throughout the twentieth century (and in all the others) Anglicanism and Roman Catholicism have vied with each other to evangelize Shakespeare. Christopher Devlin, for example, believes that there is evidence from the plays to prove Shakespeare a Roman Catholic and he instances what he regards as corroborating passages from *Hamlet, King John*, and the *Henry IV*s. But it's *Measure for Measure* again that proves conclusive; it is not only the greatest religious play 'that has graced the English stage between the Middle Ages and T. S. Eliot', but 'a great Christian play worked out in terms of explicitly *Roman* Catholic, Papist symbols' (1963: 27). Michael O'Connell argues that, although Shakespeare's plays are formally secular, behind them is an 'incarnational religious aesthetic' (1985: 305) of a late medieval Catholic spirituality.

G. Wilson Knight also conceives of Shakespeare's plays in terms of an incarnational religious aesthetic but it is one, if I understand him correctly, that is more in competition with Christianity as a parallel religious experience in its own right than dependent on Christian doctrine. In *The Christian Renaissance* Knight sees Shakespeare's plays and the New Testament each as sublime poetic experiences that purge the reader of sin: 'The Shakespearian play is ever active, ever in process of new creation and re-creation, and dependent on us to take part in its vital movement and redeeming purpose. It is not a copy of experience, it is itself experience. We burn though it; it is purgatorial' (1962: 40).[12]

1963 saw the publication of a very different kind of book from Devlin's (or from anything from Wilson Knight), R. M. Frye's thoroughgoing investigation, *Shakespeare and Christian Doctrine*. Its attractive thesis argues that it is vainglorious to try to tag Shakespeare with a particular brand of Christianity, though a Christian of some kind he undoubtedly was. Shakespeare's concerns were 'essentially secular, temporal, non-theological' (7), but his work proves him to be 'quite literate in Christian theology' (10); he was 'an intelligent and maturely informed layman' (13) whose view of the secular function of literature differed little from that of Luther, Calvin, and Hooker who 'held to views of art as autonomous, as capable of treating the temporal and secular order independent of theological systems, and as competent to form judgments in that sphere apart from an overall appeal to any particularly or exclusively Christian ethic' (268).

Wilbur Sanders's work in the 1960s is also sensibly undoctrinaire. While it is most certainly true, he argues, that the most outstanding feature of Elizabethan culture is its 'ingrained and ineradicable Christianity' (1968: 329), if 'Shakespeare is Christian at all, he is Christian at a much deeper level than that of theological conformity' (337). This is more or less the position of J. A. Bryant Jr. (1961) whose book follows the principle of poetic interpretation adumbrated by Hippolyta in *A Midsummer Night's Dream:* 'But all the story of the night told over, / And all their minds transfigured so together, / More witnesseth than fancy's images, /And grows to something of great constancy;/But howsoever, strange and admirable' (5.1.23–7). The something of great constancy in Shakespeare is the Christian bedrock on which his plays are built.

The criticism I have been dealing with so far argues for a Shakespeare either explicitly, not to say aggressively, Christian, or passively Christian, unable to avoid the prevailing ideology of the state, or subterraneously Christian in some kind of radical, unorthodox way. While we may not be sure of Shakespeare's precise brand of Christianity, so this argument runs, we can be sure of one thing, namely that he was in some form or other, with whatever degree of attentiveness, a practising Christian.

This is not necessarily a good thing for some critics, and there is a strain of criticism in the twentieth century that takes Shakespeare's Christianity to task as co-extensive with the political ideology of a repressive state. We may sample this left-wing approach to the religious Shakespeare in the work, say, of Richard Wilson. Shakespeare's Christianity, Wilson believes, is a highly inflected one. What is the real function, for instance, of the religious providentialism of the comedies? This aspect of the comic vision, 'so often re-Christianized by critics, is directly pertinent to the accommodation of the English state to contemporary capitalism' (1993: 140). (The same can be said apparently of the way that the comedies emphasize the importance of natural functions: 'Throughout the comedies, childbirth figures to naturalise capitalist relations' (142)). In the same vein, Wilson takes Prospero's religious-sounding abnegation of his doctrinally suspect magic in *The Tempest* and interprets it as anticipatory of the institution of a repressively self-policing society: 'His [Prospero's] would be the system of coercive mercy installed finally at the Restoration, when public relaxation by a "Merry Monarch" would lock into the private self-interrogation of a trembling subject such as Samuel Pepys' (157).

Other critics have argued that the workings of a Christian providence in Shakespeare's plays are purely self-referential, restricted to the world of the theatre, without philosophical, moral, or theological significance. Cynthia Marshall, for instance, explores the disjunctions between the workings of belief in the theatre and in the real world; the image of Hermione's 'resurrection' in *The Winter's Tale*, she says, 'offers a kind of imaginative fulfilment but offers nothing to believe in but the power of the theater' (1991: 59).

Something Rich and Strange

The notion of a religious Shakespeare is not exhausted by examining the variety of doctrinal positions that can be found in his work. Much twentieth-century religious criticism of Shakespeare approaches his plays unfettered by the obligation to find in them evidence of partisanship. Shakespeare as Christian or as anything else organized and doctrinal gives way to Shakespeare as, well, simply religious. The religious element in Shakespeare is seen in other words as something more generalized—as the sacramental, the spiritual, the transcendental, the visionary, the mystical, the ecstatic (these terms are commonplace ones in the criticism).[13]

Expressions of this wider religiosity have been with us for some time. We may look back, for instance, to Swinburne in the late nineteenth century for an ornately Victorian example. He compares Shakespeare to a mystical sea: 'But the limits of that other ocean, the laws of its tides, the motive of its forces, the mystery of its unity and the secret of its change, no seafarer of us all may ever think thoroughly to know. No wind-gauge will help us to the science of its storms, no lead-line sound for us the depth of its divine and terrible serenity' (1965: 2).

A. C. Bradley at his most oracular frequently strikes this note of passionate but vague religiosity: 'What we witness is not the passion and doom of mere individuals [in the tragedies]. The forces that meet in the tragedy stretch far beyond the little group of figures and the tiny tract of space and time in which they appear' (1964: 220).

For Wilson Knight the religious and the mystical comfortably merge. Shakespeare, he says, is clearly religious: 'Once, however, we see that Shakespeare is an artist fit to stand by Dante in point of religious apprehension, then the case for the religious message and purpose of the drama becomes unanswerable' (1930: 296). We are pushed by it (ominously) to a 'thinking beyond thought' (1930: 301), and what differentiates Wilson Knight from other critics, he believes, lies in his willingness, 'or even will, to find in great literature significances that may best, to challenge opposition and avoid all misunderstanding, be called "mystical"' (1931: p. v). Hence 'the Nirvanic mysticism of *Timon of Athens*' (1967: 5), and, more generally, 'the occult and spiritualistic properties of poetry and drama' (8), the 'visionary and imponderable' (10).

This idea of a free-floating spirituality in Shakespeare has proved popular with critics in this century. Wilbur Sanders, for instance, believes Shakespeare's intelligence to be more moral than theological, but we should always be aware of the transcendentalism associated with Elizabethan religion and found throughout his work: 'The indigenous Elizabethan transcendentalism was able to give Shakespeare the kind of support that prevented his realism toppling over into brutality, sentimentality or despair' (1968: 335).

In supporting Bradley's emphasis on an unprogrammatic spirituality in Shakespeare, Barbara Everett describes how the Christianizing of *King Lear* in much criticism makes it sound more like the pious chronicle history *King Leir and his three daughters* than Shakespeare's *King Lear*. She applauds what she describes as Bradley's honest doubt about the redemption of Lear: 'It is perhaps in this way that one could make out a case for a "metaphysical" *King Lear*, that it shows a world of extreme power and vitality embracing its antithesis' (1960: 336–7). This is a far cry from Christ figures, mystical seas, the occult and the visionary.

A favourite target for exercises in spiritualization in this century is *Antony and Cleopatra*. Most critics agree that the central question concerning the play is the degree to which it offers some kind of spiritualized eroticism and/or heroic self-mastery that transcend its presentation of an infinite variety of human deficiencies. John Danby (1952), for one, believes that in *Antony and Cleopatra* the lovers merge finally into an androgynous mysticism as in 'The Phoenix and the Turtle'. Or perhaps the mysticism is not quite so androgynous if we take our cue from Eric Partridge's Lawrentian belief that the pudend, as he calls it, is referred to so frequently in Shakespeare because it has for him 'a mystic as well as a physical goal, something esoteric as well as material, both a haven for the weary mind and harbor for [his] questing sexuality' (1968: 21).

A postwar inclination to see the spiritual and transcendental in the diurnal (and the nightly) round of Shakespeare's characters—for Wilson Knight they embrace the theme of 'a spiritualized nationalism' (1967: 8)—shades into the mid-century's chief mode of secularizing the sacred through an examination of myth and archetype in Shakespeare's plays and in literature generally. (The title of Northrop Frye's book on the romance (including Shakespeare's) speaks to this process: *The Secular Scripture: A Study of the Structure of Romance* (1976)). Richard Halpern writes: 'The New Criticism's main rival after World War II was myth criticism, which evolved directly from modernism's interests in ritual and comparative religion' (1997: 41).

Such an evolution clearly influenced the work of such critics as J. I. M. Stewart. As opposed to E. E. Stoll, say, or to Robert Bridges, Stewart highlights the workings of a poetic drama, which, 'like myth, is part-based on an awareness, largely intuitive, of the recesses of human passion and motive' (1949: 30). In the move away from 'superficial realism' Shakespeare's poetic drama doesn't sacrifice 'nature': 'Rather he is penetrating to nature, and once more giving his fable something of the demonic quality of myth or folk-story, which is commonly nearer to the radical workings of the human mind than are later and rationalised versions of the same material' (36). Stewart talks in terms of 'that deep and sensitive anatomy of the hidden man' (55) or 'the fluid and mysterious personality that lies below' (69), or the 'archaic strata of the mind' (95). Is it possible, he asks, that 'rather queer old stories sometimes afford the poetic dramatist his best field for the scrutiny of the actual hearts and minds of men, rather as the queer world of dreams is the medium of the psychologist's somewhat similar penetrations?' (1949: 6–7).

Perhaps in reaction to modernism's restless experimentation and delight in fragmentation, or even to the generally helter-skelter experience of modern urban living,[14] myth critics sought, as did their religiously minded colleagues, something not just rich and strange in Shakespeare's queer old stories but basic, universal, and invariant. Philip Rahv reminds us that '[t]he mythic is the polar opposite of what we mean by the historical, which stands for process, inexorable change, incessant permutation and innovation' (1966: 7). Myth, however, is based on religious ritual, and ritual, in Naomi Liebler's words, is 'the formal structuring or ordering of the life of any community that seeks to perpetuate itself' (1995: 51). Liebler adds with regard to Shakespeare's tragedies: 'the sacred underpins much of Shakespearean tragedy in the shadows, echoes, and vestiges of ritual that appear, often overtly, in the action of the plays' (53–4). The function of ritual is to preserve spiritual and physical health: 'to prevent the fiend, and to kill vermin' (*King Lear*, 3.4.149). Preservation, perpetuation, universality, and sacred underpinnings: these are the lineaments of ritual as exposed by myth and archetypal criticism.

The most important critic of this school—and of course not just for Shakespeare studies—is Northrop Frye. Like the European structuralists of the 1960s Frye sought to discover the underlying structures of literature that are timeless and self-regulating, uncontaminated by either history or the author's psyche. And although Frye has interesting things to say at times about the nooks and crannies of individual works by Shakespeare, by and large he was less interested in the specifics of any particular play than in its place in the mythic order of world literature.

In a series of books on Shakespeare, Frye assesses Shakespeare's supreme capacity to tap into the rich resources of the mythic narratives that shape all cultures' literatures.[15] The Shakespearean tragic hero, for example, comes from somewhere beyond or above 'the normal limits of experience' (1967: 5); the Shakespearean heroic 'suggests something infinite imprisoned in the finite' (5)—it comes from 'a part of nature that can never be ordered, a colossal exuberance of powers, the tailors of the earth as Enobarbus calls them that weave and unweave the forms of life' (73). When Frye attempts a categorization of Shakespearean tragedy he turns to Blake's prophetic books for an appropriate vocabulary: Shakespeare's social tragedies, with their roots in history, become the tragedies of Urizen; tragedies dramatizing the conflict between duty and passion are the tragedies of Luvah; those of heroic isolation the tragedies of Tharmas. Urizen, Luvah, and Tharmas: mythic or mythic-sounding names that lead us away from the mimetic to a remoter, self-inclosed literary world. In a similar exercise in abstraction, Frye's discussions of Shakespeare's tragic characters concentrate on their functions rather than on their selves; and so, like Wilson Knight, he sees them as hyphenated agents: order-figures, nemesis-figures, counsellor-jester-figures, rebel-figures, Eros-figures; or they are generic types—the traitor, the coward, or the hypocrite; the tragic women are 'white goddesses'; various incidents in the tragedies remind Frye of 'the search of Isis for the body of Osiris' (1967: 51), the tragic themes are those of Tantalus and Sisyphus, or Apollo and Dionysus, and so on, and so on.

In his books on Shakespeare's comedies and romances, Frye argues that, rather than holding the mirror up to nature, they exist for the sake of the story they tell. They retail the 'myth of deliverance' locked in combat with the 'myth of concern' and they obey 'the inner laws of their own structures' (1983: 9). Hence the world of *Measure for Measure* is not significantly realistic and its relation to an actual Vienna is remote. The stories that Shakespeare's comedies and romances tell are popular and conventional and based on the primitive, but Frye insists that the primitive is not being used in its vulgar sense: 'The word primitive . . . suggests, not the old-fashioned, but the archaic, the region of origins and beginnings' (1965: 54). The effect of these archaizing tendencies in Shakespeare is to establish contact with a universal and world-wide dramatic tradition: 'Shakespeare draws away from everything that is local or specialized in the drama of his day, and works toward uncovering a primeval dramatic structure that practically anything in the shape of a human audience can respond to' (1965: 58).

Frye echoes here the sentiments of C. L. Barber who, for instance, believes that the festive comedies 'always produce this effect of a group who are experiencing together a force larger than their individual wills' (1959: 90–1). For Barber '[t]he comedy is a civilized equivalent of the primitive rite' (1959: 209). In the case of Shakespeare's comedy and romance the most important myth is clearly the Christian one as laid out in the greatest of mythic narratives, the Bible. Frye notes: 'The framework of the Christian myth is the comic framework of the Bible, where man loses a peaceful kingdom, staggers through the long nightmare of tyranny and injustice which is human history, and eventually regains his original vision' (1965: 133). On this model are constructed the stories of Prospero in *The Tempest*, Leontes in *The Winter's Tale*, and Pericles, and in more festive terms those of Rosalind and her father in *As You Like It* and Viola and her brother in *Twelfth Night*. In the case of any individual play by Shakespeare, 'the bumps and hollows of the story being told follow the contours of the myth beneath . . . these mythical shapes become the conventions that establish the general framework of narratives' (61). It is these contours, for instance, that give *Macbeth* its 'gigantic and terrifying tragic structure' (62); take them away and there's nothing but chaos left.

Like Wonder-Wounded Hearers

When we deal with Frye we should bear in mind Terry Eagleton's criticism that Frye's work 'emphasises . . . the utopian root of literature because it is marked by a deep fear of the actual social world, a distaste for history itself' (1983: 91).[16] Arthur Eastman points out that in Frye's *A Natural Perspective* (1965) Shakespeare's comedies and romances 'are less mirrorings of life than self-contained conventions that stylize their characters and "may force them to do quite unreasonable things"' (1968: 371). Symptomatic perhaps of his lack of interest in history or the actual social world, Frye never discusses the plays of Shakespeare as theatrical productions or performances; he sees them in terms only of their extracted narratives. Cut off from 'real' history and theatrical performance, Frye's Shakespeare criticism for all its undeniable authority now seems marginal to a criticism so dominated by this-worldly concerns. It's no wonder then that romance plays such a large role in Frye's scheme of things, especially as it can move so easily between what Richard Halpern describes as '[t]he improbabilities of romantic fictions, signs of their frivolous and popular status' and 'high mystery' (1997: 124). At the same time, we can see why new historicists would be so attracted by the Chronicle history plays and the Roman plays. If Frye is indifferent to history, the new historicists seem to be indifferent to literary form.

Frye's response to the sacred underpinnings of mythical structures seems to be a happy convergence of his professions as university lecturer and ordained minister of the United Church of Canada. Certainly, a concern for the sacred, its high mystery, is everywhere in his work, and its ahistorical leanings do not inevitably demand a conservative interpretation. Louis Montrose suggests interesting differences between C. L. Barber and Northrop Frye: 'the former emphasises the cathartic element in festive misrule and the reaffirmation of social norms; the latter emphasises the millenarian element in comic romance and the affirmation of social change. In other words, the differences of perspective between Barber and Fry adumbrates the containment/subversion debate recently raging in Shakespeare studies' (1996: 34). And it is noticeable at the end of the millennium that there are signs of a reawakening in Shakespeare criticism of a positive attitude to Shakespeare's work as secular scripture despite (perhaps because of) our immersion in the postmodern condition which is characterized, in Catherine Belsey's words, 'by a deep distrust of absolutes, a scepticism about truth, and what Lyotard calls "incredulity toward metanarratives"' (1991: 262). Hence the renewed interest in the miraculous last plays in books such as Fawkner's (1992) and Cynthia Marshall's (1991) where in Fawkner's heated language '[t]he hypertranscendental dimensions of William Shakespeare's work cannot be *forbidden*. And partly that is so because those free dimensions simply are there' (1992: 11).

On 16 July 1998 in the *London Review of Books* Michael Dobson reviewed a number of books on Shakespeare dedicated to an exploration of the wonder in Shakespeare's works.[17] He writes, 'historically, Shakespeare criticism begins with wonder, and that it should have returned there in these millennial times should not surprise us' (1998: 24). It might surprise us to realize, however, that this 'new' turn in Shakespeare criticism at the end of the twentieth century harks back to the critic writing at the end of the nineteenth century with whom this book began. It was R. G. Moulton, we remember, who responded most reverentially to Shakespeare's hypertranscendental dimensions. Shakespeare does not only 'compass and comprehend the knowable' but broods 'with a passionate intensity over that which cannot be known' (1893: 34). Like wonder-wounded hearers 'we come anew into the presence of most stupendous mysteries, and, instead of our little piece of comfort, and support, and contentment, we receive the gift with solemn awe, and bow the head in reverential silence' (34). I doubt that the Shakespeare critics of the twenty-first century will be silent or reverential in their reception of the gift of Shakespeare but, if their millennially influenced forebears are anything to go by, they may well continue to respond imaginatively to those free dimensions in his work that simply are there.

Notes

1. G. D. Atkins writes of a later creative phenomenon for criticism in the twentieth century: 'In the hands of writers as different as William H. Gass, Susan Sontag, Roland Barthes, Jacques Derrida, Harold Bloom, Geoffrey Hartman, Barbara Johnson, and Jane Gallop, theory may actually *become* literature, self-consciously displaying its fictive nature and exploiting an impressive arsenal of stylistic devices' (1989: 2).

2. Cf. Richard Wilson: '[I]n the very period when a positivist literary history was amassing data which, when collated by Sir Sidney Lee and E. K. Chambers, would make the Warwickshire writer among the best documented of the Elizabethans, a collective amnesia insisted that none of this counted, because, as James averred, "There should really, to clear the matter up, be no such Person.... There is no such Person"' (1993: 5).

3. What is hugely important to the twentieth-century critical enterprise is the effect the dancing text has on all other hermeneutic activity. As Grace Ioppolo maintains: 'The literary interpretation of a play's imagery, themes, plot, setting, structure, and characters, or any other crucial, interlocking dramatic element, must change when textual scholars demonstrate that any of these aspects was altered by the author in a later version of the text' (1991: 15).

4. To give some idea of the hectic rate of publication in the century, there were—at least—four new *Complete Works* published in the 1990s alone. In 1993 the Yale Shakespeare republished its *Complete Works* under the direction of the Department of English, newly typeset from the text of the original multi-volume set. It seems to have been designed for the poet in all of us: 'By virtue of its size, this spacious one-volume edition presents the reader with an accurate rendering of Shakespeare's poetic rhythms' (7). A three volume set, the *Complete Illustrated Shakespeare*, was put out by Platinum Press in New York in 1995, designed no doubt for the aesthetically motivated as it is a reprint of the 1858–61 original edition 'illuminated with over 800 exquisite engravings and woodcut Illustrations' (4). In the same year an eclectically edited three-volume boxed set appeared from Everyman's Library, with a prestigious general editor, Tony Tanner, aimed at the

student market. The *Norton Shakespeare* was published in 1997 and is based on the 1986 New Oxford edition, with an essay on the Shakespearean stage by Andrew Gurr and edited by Stephen Greenblatt, Jean E. Howard, Katharine Maus. Its *raison d'être* is as a *teaching* version of the Oxford and so it purports to be 'the best student Shakespeare for our times' (p. xii). It, by the way, has *three* versions of *King Lear*, the final one a conflated version of the quarto and Folio editions 'with the reluctant acquiescence of the Oxford editors' (p. xii). For further comment on the *King Lear* phenomenon, see note 6.

5. Lisa Jardine calls Taylor's editorial practice 'buccaneering editing' (1996: 159).

6. There is now a critical consensus on Shakespeare as the revising playwright, *pace* the work of E. K. Chambers who stopped discussion of revision for decades in 1924. The question now being debated is the reasons for Shakespeare's revisions; no doubt they were primarily theatrical, but there must have been some dictated from outside the theatre. The case of *King Lear* is one of the most fascinating and can be explored in Steven Urkowitz's book, *Shakespeare's Revision of King Lear* (1980) and in *The Division of the Kingdoms* (1983) edited by Gary Taylor and Michael Warren. Both these works argue that Shakespeare revised *King Lear*, that he changed the original *King Lear*, printed in the 1608 quarto text, to a new version, printed in the 1623 First Folio. As Jonathan Goldberg notes: 'Shakespeare was a reviser of scripts subject to numerous contingencies; there never was *a King Lear*' (1986: 213). Grace Ioppolo in her influential study *Revising Shakespeare* assesses the importance of Urkowitz's book: 'This book is the first to establish in a materially concrete way that William Shakespeare was a deliberate, consistent, and persistent reviser who worked in an infinite variety of ways, and to recognize his career-long practice of revision as he himself recognized and practiced it' (1991: 5).

7. Cf. Samuel Crowl: 'all great criticism is a form of performance which at the same moment both rivals and reveals the text or texts it seeks to elucidate' (1992: 13).

8. Hawkes's book makes the firm point that 'Shakespeare's texts always yield to, though they can never be reduced to, the readings we give them...' (1992: 67). (There may be much virtue in that 'though' though.)

9. The book of the symposium consists of a collection of eight sessions, the topics of which are all, as is the title of book and symposium, nervously interrogative: Is Shakespeare still our contemporary?; Does Shakespeare translate?; Is Shakespeare sexist?; Is Shakespeare still too English?; Does Shakespeare's verse send you to sleep?; Does Shakespeare write better for

television?; Is Shakespeare a feudal propagandist?; Should Shakespeare be buried or born again?

10. Cf. R. A. Foakes who believes that the future of Shakespeare criticism lies '... towards recuperating a sense of the whole play and of artistic design not in an immutable "formal perfection", but as generated, like meaning, out of a collaboration between viewers or readers and Shakespeare's text in a process that is always subject to change; this requires attending to the cultural transactions and political mood of the age in which the reader or viewer lives as much as to the particular conditions and practices that affected Shakespeare in the writing of his plays' (1993: 223).

11. For more discussion of this phenomenon see Chapter 2.

12. E. K. Chambers wrote in 1924: 'It is perhaps in itself a tribute to the wide appeal of the poet that so much of what is written about him is ill-informed and ill-balanced' (1944*a*: 1).

13. Terry Eagleton eloquently comments on this retreat from the celebration of the well-made: 'Literary theory is in love with failure. It looks with distaste on whatever is integral, self-identical, smugly replete, and is fascinated by lack, belatedness, deadlock, self-undoing. Works of literature catch its attention once they begin to come unstuck or contradict themselves, when they unravel at the edges or betray an eloquent silence at their heart. Like some remorseless therapist, the theorist is bent on exposing just how spiritually troubled such texts really are, despite their pathetic attempt to appear plausible and coherent' (1988: 13).

14. I wouldn't want to paint too rosy a picture. In 1964 Arnold Kettle complained about the lack of 'a living popular dramatic tradition in modern British society' (14) and argued that it 'would be absurd to pretend that in 1964 Shakespeare is a great immediate conscious factor in the lives of the British people as a whole' (14). A remark by Robert Speaight ten years earlier lets us know in unintended comic fashion that the old gung-ho spirit still survived: 'The study and production of Shakespeare, and others of our less familiar classics, is part of our prime business as Englishmen. It is as important, in its way, as the maintenance of the Queen's ships at sea' (1954: 12). The difference between Kettle and Speaight is a nice comment on the divisions in British society in the middle of the century. If you didn't want to join the middle classes, Eric Hobsbawm remarks, you didn't bother about seeing Shakespeare's plays: 'In extreme cases, of which class-divided Britain was a notable example, newspapers addressed respectively to the educated and the uneducated virtually inhabited different universes' (1994: 509).

15. One of those traditions whose heart still infamously beats is bardolatry, the worship of the bard who can do no wrong. Alfred Harbage believes that the

myth of Shakespeare's perfection, 'the critical impulse to treat his work as holy writ' (1964: 9), still flourishes. Terence Hawkes traces it back to Coleridge who leads us to a Romanticism that 'tended to glorify the Shakespearean canon as the benignly rule-flouting, coherence-generating, meaning-conferring work of a genuinely British Bard' (1992: 148).

16. Thus, to take a couple of examples more or less at random, an essay such as Shirley Nelson Garner's on 'Male Bonding and the Myth of Women's Deception in Shakespeare's Plays' (1989) pursues its investigation of the 'problem of trust' in Shakespeare's works through a comparative study of a comedy, a tragedy, a problem comedy, and two romances. Similarly, Emrys Jones's essay 'The Sense of Occasion: Some Shakespearean Night Sequences' (1983) first proclaims Shakespeare's uniqueness in giving us so many scenes set at night and then discusses those found in *Romeo and Juliet*, *Richard III*, *Julius Caesar*, and *Henry V*.

17. Back in 1959 C. L. Barber wrote: 'It is quite possible that *Measure for Measure* and *All's Well That Ends Well* did not seem to Shakespeare and his audiences so different from *Twelfth Night* as they seem to us' (258). On the other hand, a critic like Northrop Frye prefers to deal with *Measure for Measure* in terms of the late romances (1986: 140).

18. The Sonnets are one thing, but it seems almost sacrilegious to claim as Meredith Skura does for *Julius Caesar*—a favourite text for high schools simply because it appears to be sexless—that 'the love between men in this play is based on the erotic tie they deny, and on a vision of devotion as intimate as a Richard II's fantasy about England, nurse of kings' (1993: 191). Sacrilegious though this reading may be, it is more than likely true.

19. Dympna Callaghan tells us that '[r]ouge consisted of red ochre and mercuric sulphide, vermilion or cochineal. Rather less deadly preparations made of powdered brick, cuttle bone, coral and egg shell were available as tooth whiteners' (1996: 198).

20. Barbara Hodgdon in a piece she describes as a 'Barthesian meditation on looking' (1996: 184) writes: 'I view theatrical photography as a practice, a particular mode of textual signification which, when placed within systems of display, distribution, and engagement, helps to constitute or reconstitute a sociocultural imagination' (186).

21. For perhaps the first time, those grotesque experiments in horror and fanaticism, *Titus Andronicus* and *Timon of Athens*, have found a spiritual home, and we can see why when we consider Brian Cox's piece on *Titus*: 'In our century the context for this play has never been more powerful. When Peter Brook produced it in 1951 the shadow of totalitarianism was very much upon us: Stalinism and the purges of the 30s, Hitler's Germany and the subsequent revelations of the Nuremberg trials. And now we have the

rise of Islamic fundamentalism, the breakdown of social units, the mind-less violence of soccer hooliganism, the sectarian violence of Northern Ireland, the disaffection of individuals within society resulting in mass murder, not to mention the ever-increasing rise in rape crimes over the last . forty years. This may seem an over-generalized spectrum of events relating to just one play by Shakespeare, but everyone of those incidents has its parallel in *Titus Andronicus*' (1993: 176). Keir Elam talks again of a Peter Brook production of *Timon* in French in Paris in 1974 in which the play 'finally fulfilled its vocation as a purgative assault on the epidemic of capitalistic "consumption", to abuse its protagonist's medical term' (1996: 162).

That edgy play, *The Life and Death of King John*, also has won converts and adherents in this century. Deborah T. Curren-Aquino emphasizes *King John*'s 'profoundly prophetic affinity with the temper and theater of our time' (1989: 13), and the fact that it speaks to and for 'the flux and aimless drifting of modern man' (14). It smacks, Curren-Aquino goes on to say, of the expressionist, symbolist, and absurdist plays of the twentieth century: 'culturally and theatrically then, *King John* is a kindred spirit' (17). As for the play's notorious ending, we should have a 'sensitivity to the tenuous, contingent, ironic and inconclusive nature of the final moments' (22).

CHAPTER 2

1. Katherine Cooke notes: 'A. C. Bradley lived at the latest time when it was possible to write Shakespeare criticism without a heavy ballast of research material, or at the very least, a reputable record of research behind one' (1972: 77–8).
2. A. D. Nuttall describes Victorian criticism generally as 'a rambling, gen-tlemanly conversation' (1984: 18), before, that is, L. C. Knights's incendiary essay 'How Many Children Had Lady Macbeth?' (1933), written 'in revolt against the over-heated Victorian age' (20).
3. Chris Baldick notes that criticism at this time was an all-male preserve and that the journals that sprung up sounded like ancient and exclusive (all-male) clubs: *The Athenaeum, Belgravia, Pall Mall Magazine, The Savoy*. Baldick goes on to say that the camaraderie of the club was replaced after 1918 with a 'lively ill-will, destructiveness, and contempt in literary criti-cism, by comparison with the clubbish tolerance prevailing in the pre-war years' (1996: 112). Richard Halpern observes that some critics still desire a membership to the club of the civilized like-minded: 'More conservative writers look back wistfully on a time when critics of formidable learning and

readable prose styles illuminated Shakespeare instead of unceremoniously knocking him about' (1997: 1). In a fascinating essay Stephen Foley comments on Virginia Woolf's abhorrence of Bradley's compatriot Walter Raleigh's clubman's style: 'In Raleigh's brusque, manly style, in the jocular style of the boardroom or the club, Woolf found ominous signs of a dark future' (1991: 247). Virginia Woolf links the manly style of Raleigh with the modern rulers of Italy.

4. I don't mean to imply that of the modern critics Bradley is alone in claiming a direct line to the real intentions of character and author. William Empson is one of a number of twentieth-century critics who trade on their powers of persuasion to contradict or countermand what a character appears to be saying. In his essay on *Macbeth*, for instance, Empson argues that when, in Act 2, Scene 4, Ross buttresses the Old Man's alarming descriptions of Nature's waywardness with news that Duncan's horses ate each other, he 'is clearly telling lies to Old Man' (1987: 143). The rhetorical 'clearly' here is followed by an equally specious 'surely': 'Surely even a very superstitious audience would realise that he has waited to see how much Old Man will swallow; he is "spreading alarm and despondency"' (144). Even very sophisticated critics sometimes offer no evidence for an assertion about the credibility of a character's position other than an expression of heartfelt belief. Bert States, for instance, is reduced to a reliance on his intuition, his feelings, when he argues 'that Hamlet's doubts [about the provenance of the Ghost] are decoy doubts at best' (1992: 111). How can he possibly know this?

5. Worshipping, and attempting to understand Shakespeare's living mind, is the characteristic critical pursuit in the late nineteenth and early twentieth centuries. Consider, for instance, Dowden: 'we endeavour to pass through the creation of the artist to the mind of the creator' (1962: 3). However difficult it may be—'we hear only distant ironical laughter' (6)—we must try: 'If we could watch his writings closely, and observe their growth, the laws of that growth would be referable to the nature of the man' (6).

6. There are other forward-sounding judgements. '*No* dramatic language is "natural"; *all* dramatic language is idealized' (1904: 72), Bradley writes, and then issues a prophetic invitation: 'It is very possible to look for subtlety in the wrong places in Shakespeare, but in the right places it is not possible to find too much' (77).

7. Dowden's career is instructive: Professor of English at Trinity College, Dublin from 1867; biographer of Shakespeare, Shelley, and Browning; founder of the Arden editions of Shakespeare. Cf. the career of David Masson, Professor of Rhetoric and English Literature at Edinburgh from 1865.

8. This notorious piece of verse first appeared in *Punch*, 17 February 1926. It was written by Guy Boas (1896–1966), who was, appropriately enough, Vice President of the English Association and the originator and Associate Editor (1935–65) of its journal *English*.

9. Frank Kermode is the most recent critic I've read who wants to save something of this 'fading eminence' (1999: 3) for our time. What Kermode finds particularly praiseworthy in Bradley at the end of a century dominated by Shakespeare idolatry (or so Kermode believes) is Bradley's willingness, like Johnson's, to complain when Shakespeare wanted art. We should, writes Kermode, 'do well to imitate this tone, and perhaps even lower it' (3).

10. She herself, I should point out, happily surrenders to the same urge.

11. We should note that there were other voices—much earlier ones—warning us against the late nineteenth-century obsession with Shakespeare's characters. R. G. Moulton, for instance, writes: 'Character-Interest, which is largely independent of performance, has swallowed up all other interests; and most of the effects which depend upon the connection and relative force of incidents, and on the compression of the details into a given space, have been completely lost' (1966: 322–3). He suggests three more important concerns for the study of Shakespeare's plays—unity, complexity, and movement. Moulton praises the ways in which Shakespeare's plots are interwoven; he admires their economy, their connections, their symmetry, and their balance.

12. See Sigmund Freud (1924: ii. 232).

13. Gary Taylor notes that Freud 'founded the clerisy of psychoanalysis at the very moment when universities were founding the clerisy of academic criticism' (1990: 263).

14. There are, of course, other reasons to focus on the interiority of the male characters in the tragedies. Madelon Gohlke (Sprengnether), while arguing that '[c]omplex language in Shakespeare's plays is an index of complex consciousness' (1982: 157), notes that in the tragedies it's the men who 'develop a sense of interiority' (157) because of 'male sexual anxiety' (158).

15. There is another kind of interiority entirely that has recently become fashionable in criticism—a literal, corporeal one, alimentary and gustatory—endoscopic even—rather than cerebral. See Elam (1996).

16. It's an exuberance that responds to the energy of Shakespeare's art that Stoll describes as 'positive, opulent, redundant, not negative or corrective, frugal or austere' (1933: 50).

17. The line from Stoll stretches to the crack of doom and includes such luminaries as M. C. Bradbrook, Bernard Spivack, Alfred Harbage, and

even Northrop Frye. Eastman notes that in *A Natural Perspective* (1965) Frye argues that Shakespeare's comedies and romances 'are less mirrorings of life than self-contained conventions that stylize their characters and "may force them to do quite unreasonable things"' (Eastman 1968: 371). Frye is 'an anthropologically sophisticated E. E. Stoll' (381). An astute observer in this tradition is James Calderwood who throws light on the curious shadowy conduct of Horatio in *Hamlet* by seeing him in terms of his theatrical function as 'Hamlet's messenger in residence at Elsinore' (1983: 120). He is, in other words, 'less a realistic personage in Denmark than a function of Shakespearean dramaturgy' (121).

18. Compare a later remark of his about *King Lear*: 'A stage-play is not a riddle, and Shakespeare's least of all' (1933: 139).

19. Gabriele Bernhard Jackson writes about *Othello*. 'I would argue that in Act 1 Othello had not given Desdemona a magic handkerchief as his first gift, but in Act 3 he had. It is a matter of the character's consonance with the key into which the movement of the play has modulated' (1988: 43).

20. Edward Pechter begins his essay on *Othello* with the sentence, 'We discovered Bianca this century' (1998: 364).

21. An exemplary instance of this kind of attention can be found in Peter Holland's essay (1989) on the role and function of the First Senator in *Othello*.

22. I should perhaps say that both books—Bishop's and Gillies's—are fascinating contributions in many ways to the cultural significance of Shakespeare's work. M. M. Mahood writes sensibly about this subject: 'Criticism which probes the unconscious mind of Lear or of Leontes is only a modern refinement of the fallacy which led earlier critics to speculate about Lear's wife, Lady Macbeth's children and Hamlet's studies at Wittenberg' (1957: 41).

23. Philip Bock—in a rather pedestrian book—attempts to give silence an anthropological context in a chapter called ' "I think but dare not speak": silence in Elizabethan culture' (1984).

24. That doesn't of course stop the critics speculating. One of the more interesting trains of thought is Lachlan Mackinnon's: 'Her silence at the end of the play is awesome because we are suddenly aware that she has a core of being beyond what we have yet seen, a core which continues to live and is capable of surprising us' (1988: 156). For a critic like H. W. Fawkner silence, or 'muteness' as he calls it, takes on an extraordinary potency both for Shakespeare's characters (in the last plays especially) and for Shakespeare himself. 'This is the secret of the mute person, of a protest whose passivity is completely pure: that power grows spontaneously out of impotency' (1992: 28).

25. See especially Bakhtin's *Rabelais and His World* (1968) translated by Helene Iswolsky.
26. See, for example, Michael Taylor's reconstruction of them (1983–84).
27. This argument crops up frequently in Levin's writings, most notably in 'Feminist Thematics and Shakespearean Tragedy' (1988: 125–38).
28. Pavis explores the usefulness of the term *actant* rather than *actor* or *character.* 'The advantage of such a notion is that it does not artificially separate *character* from *action* but reveals the dialectics between them and gradual transition from one to the other' (1998: 4).
29. Interesting (and amusing) pieces on John Dover Wilson and Walter Raleigh (the twentieth-century critic) can be found in Hawkes (1986), and on Joseph Wright, the editor of the *English Dialect Dictionary*, and E. K. Chambers in Foley (1991). Contrasting Chambers with Raleigh, Foley writes: '[T]hese essays never rise to the imperialist jingoism and phallic, bardolatrous rhetoric Raleigh exhibits' (249). James Shapiro pursues the career of Israel Gollancz, the first Jewish professor in English literature in England and a Shakespearean. Shapiro talks about the large problem 'of how Shakespeare scholarship has been shaped in this century by the social and religious identifications of those whose profession it is to interpret and teach his works' (1996: 87–8). Peter Donaldson pursues this approach in his study of some Shakespearean films and their directors; he talks of the way in which psychological issues in the director's childhood 'even at times specific images associated with early fears or traumas, are revived in the work of adaptation and contribute to its interest' (1990: p. xii).
30. Even as late as 1988 we are still invited by Peter Levi to endorse the claim that 'history and family connection do as much to throw light on Shakespeare as a poet as academic criticism has done, and maybe more' (p. xvii).
31. T. J. B. Spencer's British Academy lecture, 'The Tyranny of Shakespeare', however, alerts us to the misanthropic strain running throughout the criticism of Shakespeare. There always has been, Spencer points out, considerable resistance to Shakespeare and he instances Arnold in the nineteenth century who was especially anxious about Shakespeare's pernicious effect on the language, and Arnold's strictures echo ones by Dryden, Pope, Dr Johnson, Shelley, and Leigh Hunt, to name just a few. This sort of thing can be found in the nineteenth century: 'The Victorian books about Shakespeare have to be read to be believed' (1964: 167). All this leads Spencer to conclude that '[n]one of the great poets of the world has suffered such persistent disparagement nor from so many of the greatest minds of Europe' (169).

32. I am referring here to Strachey's hard-nosed biographical studies *Eminent Victorians* (1918) and *Queen Victoria* (1921).

33. There have been a number of sarcastic responses to this kind of investigation. One of the most memorable is C. J. Sisson's 1934 British Academy lecture 'The Mythical Sorrows of Shakespeare'. He describes how Shakespeare has been seen as 'the outcome of twentieth-century blues, which lay hold of Shakespeare as a fellow-sufferer from pessimism and disillusionment, the victim of seventeenth-century blues' (1964: 10). He is particularly amused by the manifest incongruities in this approach: 'It appears that in 1607 Shakespeare's brother Edmund died, an event which helped to infuriate him. Fortunately, in 1608 his mother died, an event which restored him into a kindlier mood' (15). A more considered scepticism perhaps can be found in Richard Strier who addresses the problem of knowing what Shakespeare's views were. He suggests the following procedure: 'We must see whether certain views are expressed by characters of whom, it seems clear, we are meant to approve or with whom we are meant to sympathize; we must see if there is a *pattern* of such views being expressed, so that they seem to be something that the playwright was truly interested in; and, finally, we must see whether such views are expressed in a number of plays, whenever contexts arise when they might be appropriate' (1995: 166–7).

34. Richard Levin has coined the term 'bardicide' to describe the death (or murder) of Shakespeare: what replaces the author after the death of the author is the 'text' which has a mind, a will (but not a Will) of its own, it has a project, and it has tendencies, contradictions that it is (desperately) trying to conceal from its lynx-eyed critics: '. . . the text is personified, reified, mystified, hypostatized, alterized, and demonized and so is constructed as the enemy, bent on defeating us; but it is a very vulnerable enemy that can easily be defeated. Its project is to lie, yet even as it lies it reveals the truth—to the right critics' (1990: 498).

35. The 'death' of Shakespeare is given rich theoretical rites. Roland Barthes's 'The Death of the Author' is perhaps the most famous of triumphant twentieth-century announcements of the passing of authorial agencies: 'writing is the destruction of every voice, of every point of origin' (1977: 142). Paola Pugliatti notes: 'The politics of refutation by quotation marks and its assumptions has been energetically challenged by Richard Levin' (1996: 25).

36. 'Editing exercises power, and it can only be understood by an analysis of power' (1988: 19).

CHAPTER 3

1. Isocolon is the name for the structural phenomenon v
   clauses or sentences are of equal length; anaphora is the
   word beginning successive clauses or sentences (or in p
   cessive lines). The world of rhetoric is full of corrugated t
   some ways it's unfortunate that the terminology is not more reader-friendly
   as any structural analysis of verse or prose cannot do without some version of
   it. M. M. Mahood notes: 'The nomenclature of the rhetoricians is not a
   helpful language for the twentieth-century reader who is trying to make
   explicit his pleasure in Shakespeare' (1957: 19). And Helen Vendler declines
   to use the terminology: 'I use ordinary language to describe Shakespeare's
   rhetorical figuration' (1997: 24).

2. In his study on metaphor in Shakespeare Ralph Berry warns against confining any investigation to figurative language. 'One has to be on one's
   guard against assuming an absolute divergence between literal and figurative in Shakespeare' (1978: 3), for '[t]he essence of the matter is repetition
   and recall: a word retained in a new context receives new meanings, and
   retroactively affects the old' (6). R. B. Heilman notes: 'A recurrent word is
   found to exist in a dual relationship: one of its links is to the thing to be
   noted, the other is to the sum total of the word.... Repetition itself is a
   mode of meaning' (1963: 9). Maurice Charney (1961) says that the iteration
   of a word can have the force of an image in a play, and he instances serpents
   in *Antony and Cleopatra*, blood in *Julius Caesar* or in *Macbeth*; food and
   eating in *Coriolanus*.

3. Foakes maintains that Shakespeare is full of passages of 'magic incantation,
   not reducible to "sense"' (1993: 140). Of 'Come seeling night' (*Macbeth*,
   3.2.46–51) Foakes says there are a 'mind-boggling variety of glosses' (139).

4. The opening metaphorical clause—'that knits up the ravelled sleeve of
   care'—kicks off the sequence, and is clearly not a cliché. Caroline Spurgeon
   describes it as 'a wonderful picture of knitting up the loose fluffy all-
   pervading substance of frayed-out floss silk' (1935: 125). Sister Miriam
   Joseph notes that the ravelled sleeve begins a sequence of heaped-up
   definitions of one thing that is called systrophe (1947: 109).

5. James Calderwood, however, cheerfully admits to being guilty of over-
   ingenuity: 'The rich voluptuousness of Shakespearean meaning—which is
   rather like the multi-flected female in Roethke's "Light Listened" who had
   "more sides than the seal"—will seduce any critic into taking interpretive
   liberties now and then, and no doubt I have committed my fair share of
   indiscretions' (1971: 17). R. A. Foakes takes a more censorious view of the
   hypertrophic critical imagination, lamenting the small returns of much

scholarly investigation: 'It would not be difficult to compile an anthology of entertaining notes in which editors and others have chased elusive meanings through thickets of curious possibilities, without finally telling us a great deal about a troublesome passage in Shakespeare' (1980: 79).

6. One pair among the innumerable belongs to Jan Kott. Consider his misleadingly superfluous comment on Orsino's 'But when in other habits you are seen, / Orsino's mistress, and his fancy's queen' in *Twelfth Night* (5.1.383–4): 'in England from the Elizabethan period until the present day and in America, a "queen" is a man in drag' (1992: 16). On the other hand, for a level-headed analysis of Shakespeare's immersion in sex and bawdy and the history of the critical reception to it the reader should consult Gordon Williams (1996).

7. See Michael Taylor (1974).

8. We should remember, though, that many New Critics commented on social, historical, and political issues of the time. Consider, for instance, the case of William Empson.

9. The same charge could be brought, with greater justice, I think, against the twentieth-century's inattention to Shakespeare's metrics. It was not until 1988 that a major work appeared—George Wright's *Shakespeare's Metrical Art*—that incisively pursues throughout Shakespeare's career his verse's 'constant obligation to maintain a creative equilibrium between two poles of linguistic force: the continually recurring metrical pattern and the rhythmic phrase' (1988: 281).

10. I should mention two of the other important contributions that this essay makes to Shakespeare criticism: it shows the relevance of scenes that hitherto had been thought irrelevant or digressive in the structure of their plays, and it usefully discusses the choral, impersonal use at times of some of the play's characters.

11. Besides works on Chaucer, Dante, and T. S. Eliot this influential writer has other books on Shakespeare: one on the last plays (1950), the second tetralogy (1957), the Roman plays (1963), and the early comedies (1964).

12. An essay almost as famous as Brooks's 'The Naked Babe' by the dean of the Chicago critics, R. S. Crane (1952), casts doubt in a more general way on Brooks's critical position in *The Well-Wrought Urn*.

13. S. L. Bethell speaks of the dangers of 'subjective' imagery: 'To talk of Othello's poetic nature because he speaks of Anthropophagi, Arabian trees and turbaned Turks is to fall victim to a crude aesthetic' (1952: 64). In any case, as he then adds, '[f]requently imagery used in characterization refers not to the character of the speaker but to the person spoken about' (65).

14. The soliloquy is a notable case in point, and W. H. Clemen has written an interesting book (1972) on it. No work to my knowledge has been devoted

to the aside perhaps because it was never marked off as such in the original texts, so that anyone dealing with it would first have to prove that it was one, and there are quite a number of them that are debatable. The oration and the monologue are two other abstractions that have been treated by this century's criticism. A whole book indeed, by Milton Kennedy (1942) was devoted to the former. Plot, too, in Shakespeare's plays, though not extractable in the same way, has received a fair amount of attention in this century from Bradley to the present day. A common theme stresses Shakespeare's expertise in arousing and sustaining interest in the forward movement of the plot. Bradley notes in Shakespeare's tragedies how there is 'a constant alternation of rises and falls in . . . tension or in the emotional pitch of the work, a regular sequence of more exciting and less exciting sections' (1904: 48). Shakespeare is very good at the creation of dramatic tension, suspense, expectation, and dramatic contrast. W. H. Clemen describes this technique as a kind of flirtation with the reader and play-goer: 'The dramatist must alternately unveil and veil, promise and again withdraw his promise, he must proceed rather by "hints and guesses" than by obvious and obtrusive indications' (1972: 6). It is the art of progressive revelation.

15. This is not always true of course. Nobody could accuse the Second Witch's sublime piece of doggerel in *Macbeth*—'By the pricking of my thumbs, / Something wicked this way comes' (4.1.61–2)—of being old-fashioned or homespun. Or if it is old-fashioned it is so in a knowing, sophisticated, up-to-date way.

16. Barbara Everett's criticism of L. C. Knights can be applied more generally: 'It is a pity, when poetry and morality are two of the great gifts of civilisation, that they should ever be so confused that each loses its character' (1960: 176).

17. See especially his articles in 1975, 1977, 1980, and 1988, and his book in 1979.

CHAPTER 4

1. A major difference from conventional thinking that the Rose discovery suggested has to do with the shape of the stage in the Elizabethan theatre. Instead of the familiar rectangle shape, the Rose foundations suggest that the stage was wedge-shaped with its sides tapered towards the front.

2. As I write this chapter I read in the last issue of *The Economist* for 1999, in a piece entitled 'This Wooden O', that London is abuzz with the dispute over the replica of the 1599 Globe Theatre, built largely at the instigation of the late Sam Wanamaker, the American actor and director. 'This being Shakespeare', the anonymous essayist writes, 'don't expect the Globe's

reopening to signal a happy ending or final curtain' (70). The piece goes on to explore the 'bitter dispute' among scholars about the accuracy of the replica and, despite its phenomenal success with the play-going public, about the validity of the entire enterprise. The article concludes with the prediction that the Globe will quite likely have to be pulled (or burned) down in ten or so years' time to be rebuilt to more authentic specifications. (Though it is unclear where these will come from.)

3. Compare Robert Hapgood's 'Shakespeare's Choreography: Pace and Rhythm' (1980): 'It is time for concern with "spatial values" in Shakespeare to be balanced by an awareness of sequential ones' (141). Other works that deal with Shakespeare in charge of the performance are Honigmann's (1976) and Howard's (1984) as well as Hapgood's (1988).

4. Stanley Cavell has a just remark on the illogicality of Stoll's thought-processes here: 'the idea that these conventions supply [Shakespeare] with solutions to his artistic purposes, rather than problems or media within which those purposes are worked out, is as sensible as supposing that one has explained why a particular couple have decided to divorce by saying that divorce is a social form' (1987: 48).

5. Harley Granville Barker notes that in the nineteenth century 'the theater began to think of its Shakespeare from the point of view of the pictur-esque, and, later, in terms of upholstery' (1957: 1).

6. The use of this term is not as widespread as Kennedy implicitly suggests. It cannot be found, for instance, in Pavis (1998). 'Scenology' is there but this word is not restricted to the purely visual: it comprises 'all the constituent elements of stage production' (323).

7. They began as seven volumes called the *Players' Shakespeare*, appearing in 1923, 1925, and 1927. In 1927 Barker signed an agreement which saw a revision of these early volumes called *Prefaces to Shakespeare*. The first series appeared in 1927, others in 1930, 1937, 1945, and 1947.

8. It will never be the same because of the sweeping reforms Barker made in simplifying the play's presentation. In this production only two full stage sets were used; drops were used instead and the play proceeded without interruption at a speed, Kennedy says, 'unthought of in the carpenter-dominated theatres of Irving and Tree' (1985: 125). The location of the scenes was established primarily by the actors themselves.

9. Peter Thomson notes that at least one of the innovative touring compa-nies he discusses, Footsbarn, dispensed with a director, and its actors are 'musicians, mimes, and acrobats, and the cultural world they inhabit is closer to circus than to theatre' (1996: 171).

10. In the 1950s and 1960s the Royal Shakespeare Company was under the artistic and administrative control of Cambridge men. Peter Hall, John

Barton, Trevor Nunn had all read English literature at Cambridge under F. R. Leavis who therefore became a kind of director *ex machina* in the wings. This academic, literary affiliation, as Dennis Kennedy points out, meant that '[t]he director had become, in one sense at least, a literary critic, whose job was to explain the meaning of the play, first to actors and then to audiences' (1993: 182).

11. Robert Hapgood writes: 'It is sometimes said backstage that a play belongs at first to the playwright. During rehearsals, it belongs to the director. After opening night, it belongs to the actors. And after it has run for a few weeks, it belongs to the audience, to whose responses the actors cater' (1988: 49).

12. Amy Green (1994) calls these productions 'simile' productions: those in which directors re-deposit plays wholesale into different historical or geographical contexts.

13. Russell Jackson describes Marowitz as 'a leading worrier at the heels of conventional or comfortable Shakespeare' (1996a: 224). He later talks of Marowitz's impatience with 'what he sees as the pallid liberal co-opting of potentially revolutionary forces which are present in the plays' subtext' (228). Marowitz's egregiously solipsistic book, *Recycling Shakespeare* (1991), dedicated to Peter Brook and Jan Kott, is, he says, 'directed at two enemies—the academics and the traditionalists' (p. ix).

14. James Calderwood writes eloquently: 'But the life of theatrical speech rides on breath itself, exhalations of eloquence that cannot survive their own saying; and the grand spectacles of the stage are transient as a gesture—as Prospero's gesture dismissing the revels' (1983: 142).

15. Cf Bert States: 'There are as many things about *Hamlet* that one cannot possibly appreciate in a performance as there are things in a performance that elude the most sensitive reading' (1985: 130).

16. These generalizations need considerable refinement. Things were never as clear-cut as this argument suggests, though I think the broad outline is a reasonable one. Where do we put Stratford-upon-Avon for instance? In the provinces but not of them, we might say. Neither regional nor metropolitan, but more metropolitan than regional, especially since the purchase of the Aldwych Theatre in London. The Stratford phenomenon has attracted a number of critics in its capacity as the first theatre in history specifically dedicated to the work of a single playwright. Built in 1879 and rebuilt in 1932, the Shakespeare Memorial Theatre didn't attain intellectual prominence until 1960 when Peter Hall reorganized the company as the Royal Shakespeare Company, renaming the building the Royal Shakespeare Theatre. He began to establish a permanent core of actors, directors, and designers to produce Shakespeare for the contemporary stage.

17. Mutual animation tends to become more and more comprehensive. W. B. Worthen makes an interesting connection between textual editing and the situation of contemporary performance. Editors and directors have similar problems: 'how to ground the authority of texts in a notion of the work, how the figure of the author does or does not provide an instrument for producing texts' (1997: 16). In this account of editing the production of a text sounds like the production of a performance. Barbara Hodgdon argues for similar processes at work in study and theatre: 'both practices share similar methodologies and processes of selection' (1985: 58). What is called cutting in the theatre, in the study is called 'making an argument' (58).

18. Maurice Charney writes: '. . . suspicion of the theater is a part of our literary tradition, if not of our moral tradition as well' (1961: 2).

19. Booth writes about Antony: 'The chances to shine that Shakespeare gives an actor who goes out on stage with Cleopatra in the first scene of *Antony and Cleopatra* are comparable to those of an actor who had to play a scene with a two-year-old and a puppy' (558). As for Cleopatra, she is a wonder, and she is so because the actor fails to deliver her: 'The actor is blamed for Shakespeare's success in creating an unbelievable character we believe in' (563). Brutus has 'the built-in inability of the actor to make us glory in him' (566) which makes the play better even though it defeats the actor. As for Hal: 'We do not get the play we expect. Shakespeare makes that play impossible by making it nearly impossible for its central figure to be central in our affections or the center of our attention; he thus makes it nearly impossible for an actor to please us with his performance' (568).

20. Two of the most interesting are by the Russian director, Grigorii Kozint-sev (1966) and (1977).

21. Salter's argument need not be confined to postcolonial settings. Everything he says about actors in Canada would apply, it seems to me, to actors working virtually anywhere outside of London and Stratford-upon-Avon.

22. Consider the frequent invocation in Jonathan Bate's *Shakespeare and Ovid* of the 'mythologically literate Elizabethan' (1993: 194).

23. For a corrective to both Cook and Harbage see Martin Butler's fourteen-page appendix (1984).

24. The notion of the bifurcated audience, however, one part in the know and one not, continues to find adherents for the cinema, and other newer art forms, as much as for the theatre. In the cinema, Eric Hobsbawm writes, the sophisticated directors 'advertised their cinematic erudition to the elite which understood their allusions while keeping the masses (and hopefully the box office) happy with blood and sperm' (1994: 510).

25. Even the bad productions in the BBC series can be pedagogically bene-ficial, according to James Bulman: 'Students who have read the text

responsively will pick up on those unaddressed potentials and ask questions: Is pastoral love the same as love in a "real" wood? Did Shakespeare mean Romeo to be as raw as a spaghetti western? Is Cleopatra's allure really more cerebral than physical? Isn't Othello's color important? Such questions lead students to a fuller appreciation of the play and of the power of performance to manipulate their responses.' (Bulman and Coursen 1988: 59).

26. *To Be and Not To Be: Negation and Metadrama in Hamlet* (1983), *Shakespearean Metadrama* (1971), *If It Were Done: 'Macbeth' and Tragic Action* (1986), *Metadrama in Shakespeare's Henriad: 'Richard II' to 'Henry V'* (1979). In *Shakespearean Metadrama* he notes that there are various kinds of metadramatic subjects in the plays: *Romeo and Juliet*, for instance, focuses on literary style and form; *Love's Labour's Lost* on language and the durability of art; *Richard II* on poetic versus dramatic language; *A Midsummer Night's Dream* on the theatrical interaction of playwright, play, and audience.

CHAPTER 5

1. We should note that Heather Dubrow suggests that Tillyard in his own time was thought rather unsophisticated and that Hardin Craig's *The Enchanted Glass* (1936) or Theodore Spencer's *Shakespeare and the Nature of Man* (1943) were thought the more profound.

2. I assume that Tillyard knew that a section of any Elizabethan audience would be intelligent women. If he did he presumably didn't think that their views would differ from the men's.

3. Theodore Spencer, Tillyard's contemporary, was also fascinated by the contrast between theoretical good and evil fact in Shakespeare's time, a time which, as in Spencer's (1943), demonstrated a particular urgency in confronting essential problems of human nature: 'Shakespeare's age was breaking into chaos, while our age is trying to turn chaos into order' (1943: p. ix). On the one hand, an optimistic theory of human nature depended upon certain commonplaces of neo-Platonism that every 'thoughtful Elizabethan took for granted' (5). On the other hand, there was a growing pessimism, for, after all, 'in the inherited, the universally accepted, Christian view of man and his universe there was a basic conflict between man's dignity and his wretchedness' (28).

4. Compare John Palmer's still popular book, *Shakespeare's Political Characters* (1945).

5. Cf. Moody Prior: 'When we attempt to reconstruct the age by means of scholarship, what emerges for the most part is the common denominator, a

synthesis deeply colored by the contributions of those less creative minds, the official ideologists, the popularizers, the shapers of common opinion, the propagandists, the second-rate poets, the slogan-makers, and all the other useful drudges who try to create a common intellectual environment for their age, formalize its sensibilities, and guide its conduct' (1973: p. xii).

6. Howard Horwitz dubs the historical criticism in the 1960s an earlier new historicism. He argues that in, say, R. B. Heilman and Roy Harvey Pearce in *Historicism Once More* (1969) and Wesley Morris *Toward a New Historicism* (1972) there was a revival of historicism, but 'the humanist premises and goals of this generally existential historicism ... differ greatly from those of the current, post-structuralist and neo-Marxist New Historicism' (1988: 814).

7. In a latter-day attempt to turn back the historical tide A. D. Nuttall in *A New Mimesis: Shakespeare and the Representation of Reality* returns to a version of the old pieties. Despite his impressive scholarship I don't find the argument especially convincing. But we can certainly agree with him that Shakespeare was 'the poet of reverent and attentive perception' (1983: 100), astute and knowledgeable enough in his Roman plays, for example, not merely to 'distinguish Romans from English, [but to distinguish] early Romans from later Romans' (102).

8. Rossiter's iconoclasm makes enjoyable reading. He describes Pistol memorably as 'mouthfuls of Theatre masquerading as a man' (57).

9. Don Wayne describes Kettle's *Shakespeare in a Changing World* as calling for a new kind of historical criticism that 'would measure the distance between the social conditions that produced the Shakespeare plays and the conditions in which those plays are performed and studied today' (1987: 63).

10. In 1990 G. K. Hunter refines this: 'a providential pattern emerges, but not as an overall explanation, only as a justification for the humanly inexplicable' (18).

11. As late as 1992 Jan Kott praises a production in Dubrovnik of *Hamlet* that had the Ghost wearing a striped concentration camp uniform. In a Jonathan Miller production commended by Kott the same actor played the Ghost and Fortinbras—they thus 'appear as signs of history' (85), but the history is clearly that of the twentieth century not Shakespeare's.

12. *A Midsummer Night's Dream* is a popular play for revisionist treatments. In the theatre sado-masochistic interpretations of it have become fashionable. Cf. Michael Taylor (1969).

13. In the symposium, *Is Shakespeare Our Contemporary?*, Richard Wilson considers the case of Kott. In his view, Kott's version of human behaviour as animal-like belongs to the last days of modernism and the postwar recoil

from politics. Kott's point of view, as Wilson understands it, is essentially conservative.

14. There are voices raised in protest in the 1990s. Margreta de Grazia, for instance, is disturbed by the tendency to read the Renaissance as the Early-Now: 'as if *the* relevant history were a prior version of what we already are and live' (1996: 21). In this essay she shows us how *King Lear* 'blocks the mobility identified since the nineteenth century with the Modern . . . in an attempt to withstand flux or fluidity, superflux or superfluity' (21).

15. We should note, however, that in a 1988 essay Heather Dubrow and Richard Strier point out that it is often difficult to sort out the new from the old historicism (clearly, by old historicism they don't mean the old old historicism of the 1940s).

16. We should remember, though, that many New Critics commented on social, historical, and political issues of the time.

17. They were not the first on the scene as Moody Prior's title witnesses (1973).

18. David Cressy writes that '[i]t's arguable that Shakespeare . . . has become a testing ground for Foucault, an arena of validation for cultural theory rather than a social and cultural problem in his own right' (1991: 124).

19. Stephen Bretzius believes the modern-day university is similar to Shakespearean drama in that it encourages 'an institutionalized subversion that actually strengthens the very centralizing authority it ostensibly opposes' (1997: 39).

CHAPTER 6

1. Consider, for example, Erickson (1985), Holderness (1991), Breitenberg (1996), Frey (1980*a* and *b*).

2. The books that get singled out, according to her, are Dusinberre (1975), Lenz *et al.* (1980), Dash (1981), French (1982), Kahn (1984), Bamber (1982).

3. The history of feminism's various alliances and divorces with other movements can be sampled in Logan and Rudnytsky (1991: history, psychology, and feminism); McEachern (1988: source study and feminism); Sargent (1981: Marxism and feminism); Wayne (1991: materialism and feminism). A major alliance is that between feminist critics and psychoanalysis (in a Freudian direction with US critics, and a Lacanian one with French). What Lenz *et al.* point out as a persistent theme in Shakespeare is 'men's inability to reconcile tender affection with sexual desire and their consequent vacillation between idealization and degradation of women' (1980: 9). The troubled alliance between Marxism and feminism is examined by a number of feminists (and Marxists). Like Marxism, as Gayle Greene explains, feminism involves 'an understanding of the social dimensions of

244 *Notes to Pages 201–05*

consciousness' (1981: 29). But feminism is also concerned as Marxism *per se* is not with 'the liberation of women from oppressive social structures and stereotypes' (30). The focus of Wayne's collection of feminist materialist essays is as various as materialism itself. The contributors write 'on money and women's work, rape in English law and drama, prosecutions for sexual crimes and slander, on the circulation of homoerotic desire, the disarticulation between oppressions of class and gender, changes brought about by the material conventions of theatre attendance, and rhetorical practices in this profession' (12).

4. The most extreme form of masculine anxiety in the plays is sexual jealousy. Breitenberg argues that it's 'an anxiety and a potential source of violence engendered in men by an economy that constructs masculine identity as dependent on the coercive and symbolic regulation of women's sexuality' (1996: 175). So Iago isn't 'motiveless malignity' but someone 'articulating and activating the cultural anxieties that produce jealousy as a condition of romantic love, indeed, of male subjectivity itself' (176). Garner goes further in arguing that at some level in *Othello, The Winter's Tale, Cymbeline,* and *Troilus and Cressida,* 'all four figures *need* the women who love them to betray them' (1989: 136).

5. According to Dympna Callaghan that lesson involves the 'degradation'—at one or two removes—of Olivia's body. In the scene (2.5) where Malvolio reads aloud the letter from Olivia, forged by Maria, he comments on the way Olivia forms certain letters: 'These be her very c's, her u's, and her t's, and thus makes she her great P's' (2.5.85–6). Sir Andrew draws our attention to the fleeting obscenity, 'Her c's, her u's, and her t's? Why that?' (2.5.88). Why that indeed unless as an allusion to 'cut', bawdy slang for the female genitals. Callaghan, however, focuses on Olivia's great P's: 'The allusion to Olivia's copious urination further deforms veiled, cloistered, aristocratic femininity into the grotesque and, paradoxically, more suitable object of Malvolio's sexual and social ambitions' (1993: 437). The reference to Olivia's copious urination becomes part of the scene's 'social enactment of women's oppression' (449). It hardly seems likely. The target here—if there is one—is veiled and cloistered male incomprehension, Malvolio's and Sir Andrew's. The cleverness is Maria's and the audience's, Olivia's great P's the mere mechanism of the joke. Earlier in her article Callaghan had argued that by materialism she did not mean raw physicality nor the materiality of signs but 'the way the social and cultural always *exceed* the discursive' (430). Her analysis of these lines from *Twelfth Night* might be considered the perfect example of the way the social and cultural have exceeded the discursive.

6. A subtly argued piece by Catherine Belsey considers the famous speech by Enobarbus in *Antony and Cleopatra* where the description of Cleopatra

climaxes with lines about 'pretty dimpled boys, like smiling cupids' rather than the expected lines about Cleopatra herself. Belsey then pursues these dimpled cupids in European paintings after Shakespeare. 'If this argument proves in anyway persuasive, it implies that for more than a century, all over Europe, boys were involved, implicated, somehow incorporated into female seductiveness' (1996: 60). This tradition disappears in the nineteenth century.

7. Keir Elam (1996) provides us with an itemization of our fascination with bodies in various states: bodies tremulous; bodies single-sexed; bodies double-natured; bodies enclosed; bodies intestinal; bodies consumed; bodies carnivalized; bodies feminized; bodies embarrassed; bodies sodomized; bodies emblazoned or dissected; bodies castrated; bodies disease-ridden.

8. Lynda Boose agrees with Loomba that the black male consorting with the white female is 'the ultimate romantic-transgressive model of erotic love' (1994: 41) in drama, epic, and pastoral. But, she asks, where's the black woman/white man union? The answer is nowhere (though Lorenzo in *The Merchant of Venice* accuses Lancelot of 'the getting up of the Negro's belly' (3.5.36–7)): 'in the untold story about the son produced by a "faire English man" and an "Ethiopian woman black as a cole" lurks the impetus for a patriarchal culture's profound anxieties about gender to spill over into a virulent system of racial anathema' (46). We might consider here the case of the converging prejudices. James Shapiro notes in his book on Shakespeare and the Jews that '[t]o early modern Englishman, the fantasy of Christian men marrying converting Jewesses was far more appealing than the idea of Jewish men, even converted ones, marrying Christian women' (1996: 132).

9. See Hunter's articles of 1964 (two) and 1967 and his book *Dramatic Identities and Cultural Traditions: Studies in Shakespeare and his Contemporaries* (1978). A recent reworking of Hunter's position can be found in John Gillies's book *Shakespeare and the Geography of Difference* (1994). Shakespeare's 'geographic imagination' (4), Gillies claims, comes from a rich tradition—moralized and 'poetic'. In this tradition Shakespeare's 'moorish' other 'is completely independent of the anachronistic terminology of "race", "colour" and "prejudice"' (25). The 'moorish' other has to be seen in structural rather than moral terms as a polluting sexual partner: Aaron in *Titus Andronicus*, Morocco in *The Merchant of Venice*, Othello, Cleopatra, and Claribel's 'Ethiope' in *The Tempest*.

10. Consider Loomba's parallel question about *Othello*: 'Does *Othello* serve as a warning against inter-racial love, or an indictment of the society which does not allow it?' (1989: 74).

11. 'Look there, look there' only occurs in the Folio text of *King Lear*. The 1608 quarto does not offer this cryptic invitation to witness a possible change of mood. If the Folio text is Shakespeare's revision, as is now thought to be the case, then this addition (and some others only to be found in the 1623 Folio) lessens the bleakness of the original ending. (Though there is the argument that Lear's dying in deluded joy intensifies the anguish at the end for the audience.)

12. In *Shakespeare and Religion* Wilson Knight argues that there is in Shakespeare more of Christ than the Christian. He talks of the 'clear divergence, even a challenge, in respect to Church doctrine' (1967: 14) in Shakespeare's plays; and, again, '[i]t will be clear that Shakespeare's tragedies do not submit to a simple interpretation in terms of Christian orthodoxy' (20). Shakespeare, indeed, trumps Christianity; he 'differs from orthodox Christianity not by being less, nor alien, but by a greater inclusiveness' (24–5).

13. Some aren't quite so commonplace. Consider, for example, H. W. Fawkner's use of the term 'hyperontological' in his own hyperontological works, *Deconstructing 'Macbeth' the Hyperontological View* (1990), *Shakespeare's Hyperontology: 'Antony and Cleopatra'* (1990) and *Shakespeare's Miracle Plays* (1992).

14. Richard Halpern argues that it is possible to see Frye's work as an attempt to capture criticism for the universities from influential poet-critics like Eliot, Allen Tate, and John Crowe Ransom. 'Myth is modernism's primary resource for imposing imaginative unity on a shattered and fragmented experience of modern life; indeed, it posits modernity as the broken remnants of a lost totality which it attempts to reconstruct' (1997: 120).

15. Giles Gunn writes that for Frye '[l]iterary works participate in the "order of words" because their embedded narratives or plots resonate with, and find a place in the overarching narrative or mythic cycle which Frye maps in the *Anatomy*' (1987: 118).

16. Richard Halpern (1997) notes that Frye's relationship with the products of mass culture was an uneasy one. Frye compared the student movement of the 1960s with the Nazis.

17. The three books on Shakespeare he is considering here are *Reason Diminished: Shakespeare and the Marvellous* (1998) by Peter Platt, *Shakespeare and the Theatre of Wonder* (1996) by T. G. Bishop, and *The Genius of Shakespeare* (1997) by Jonathan Bate.

List of Works Cited

Abbott, E. A. (1869). *Shakespearian Grammar: An Attempt to Illustrate some of the Differences between Elizabethan and Modern English*. London

Abrams, M. H. (1997). 'The Transformation of English Studies: 1930–1995', *Daedalus* 126: 105–31

Adams, Joseph Quincy (1917). *Shakespeare's Playhouse: A History of English Theatres from the Beginnings to the Restoration*. Gloucester, Mass

Adelman, Janet (1996). '"Born of Woman": Fantasies of Maternal Power in *Macbeth*', in *Shakespearean Tragedy and Gender*, eds. Shirley Nelson Garner and Madelon Sprengnether. Bloomington, Ind., 105–34

Arber, Edward, ed. (1875–94). *Transcript of the Registers of the Company of Stationers, 1554–1640*. 5 vols. London

Armstrong, Edward A. (1946). *Shakespeare's Imagination: A Study of the Psychology of Association and Inspiration*. London

Armstrong, Isobel. (1989a). 'Thatcher's Shakespeare?' *Textual Practice* 3: 1–14

—— (1989b). 'English in Higher Education: "Justifying" the Subject', *Essays and Studies* 42: 9–24

Astington, John H., ed. (1992). *The Development of Shakespeare's Theatre*. New York

Atkins, G. Douglas. (1989). 'Introduction: Literary Theory, Critical Practice, and the Classroom', in *Contemporary Literary Theory*, eds. G. Douglas Atkins and Laura Morrow. Amherst, Mass. 1–23

Auden, W. H. (1968). 'The Joker in the Pack', in *The Dyer's Hand and Other Essays*. New York, 246–72

Babcock, R. W. (1948). 'Mr. Stoll Revisited 20 Years After', *Philological Quarterly* 27: 289–313

—— (1952). 'Historical Criticism of Shakespeare', *Modern Language Quarterly* 13: 6–20

Bakhtin, Mikhail (1968). *Rabelais and His World*, trans. Helene Iswolsky. Cambridge, Mass

Baldick, Chris (1983). *The Social Mission of English Criticism*. Oxford

—— (1996). *Criticism and Literary Theory 1890 to the Present*. London and New York

Baldwin, T. W. (1947). *Shakspere's Five Act Structure*. Urbana, Ill.

Ball, Robert Hamilton (1968). *Shakespeare on Silent Film: A Strange Eventful History*. London

Bamber, Linda (1982). *Comic Women, Tragic Men: A Study of Gender and Genre in Shakespeare*. Stanford, Calif

Barber, C. L. (1959). *Shakespeare's Festive Comedy: A Study of Dramatic Form and its Relation to Social Custom*. Princeton

—— (1959–60). 'Shakespeare in His Sonnets', *Massachusetts Review* 1: 648–72

—— and Wheeler, Richard P. (1986). *The Whole Journey: Shakespeare's Power of Development*. Berkeley and Los Angeles

—— (1989). 'Shakespeare in the Rising Middle Class', in *Shakespeare's Personality*, eds. Norman N. Holland, Sidney Homan, and Bernard J. Paris. Berkeley, 17–40

Barish, Jonas (1981). *The Antitheatrical Prejudice*. Berkeley

Barker, Deborah, and Kamps, Ivo, eds. (1995). *Shakespeare and Gender: A History*. London

Barker, Harley Granville (1957). *Preface to Hamlet*. 1927. New York

Barrell, John (1988). *Poetry, Language and Politics*. Manchester

Barroll, J. Leeds (1974). *Artificial Persons: The Formation of Character in the Tragedies of Shakespeare*. New York

Barthelemy, Anthony (1987). *Black Face, Maligned Race: The Representation of Blacks in English Drama from Shakespeare to Southerne*. Baton Rouge, La

Barthes, Roland (1977). 'The Death of the Author', in *Image Music Text*, trans. Stephen Heath. New York

Bartlett, John (1953). *New and Complete Concordance of the Dramatic Works and Poems of Shakespeare*. 1894. London

Bate, Jonathan (1993). *Shakespeare and Ovid*. Oxford

—— (1997). *The Genius of Shakespeare*. London

Battenhouse, Roy, ed. (1994). *Shakespeare's Christian Dimension: An Anthology of Commentary* Bloomington, Ind

Belsey, Catherine (1991). 'Afterward: A Future for Materialist Feminist Criticism?' in *The Matter of Difference: Materialist Feminist Criticism of Shakespeare*, ed. Valerie Wayne. Hemel Hempstead, 257–70

—— (1996). 'Cleopatra's Seduction', in *Alternative Shakespeares Volume 2*, ed. Terence Hawkes. London and New York, 38–62

Bennett, Susan (1996). *Performing Nostalgia: Shifting Shakespeare and the Contemporary Past*. London

Bentley, G. E. (1941–68). *The Jacobean and Caroline Stage*. 7 vols. Oxford

Berger, Harry, Jr. (1987). 'Bodies and Texts', *Representations* 17: 144–66

—— (1997). *Making Trifles of Terrors: Redistributing Complicities in Shakespeare*. New York

Berger, Peter L. (1986). *The Capitalist Revolution: Fifty Propositions About Prosperity, Equality & Liberty*. New York

Berggren, Paula S. (1980). 'The Woman's Part: Female Sexuality as Power in Shakespeare's Plays', in *The Woman's Part: Feminist Criticism of Shakespeare*, eds. C. R. Lenz, Gayle Green, and C. T. Nealy. Chicago, 17–34

Berry, Cicely (1973). *Voice and the Actor.* London

Berry, Ralph (1978). *The Shakespearean Metaphor: Studies in Language and Form.* London

Bethell, S. L. (1944). *Shakespeare and the Popular Dramatic Tradition.* London

—— (1952). 'Shakespeare's Imagery: The Diabolic Images in *Othello*', *Shakespeare Survey* 5: 62–80

Beverley, John (1993). *Against Literature.* Minneapolis

Bishop, T. G. (1996). *Shakespeare and the Theatre of Wonder.* Cambridge

Bloom, Harold (1989). *Shylock: Major Literary Characters.* New York

Bock, Philip K. (1984). *Shakespeare & Elizabethan Culture: An Anthropological View.* New York

Boose, Lynda E. (1987). 'The Family in Shakespeare Studies: or—Studies in the Family of Shakespeareans; or—the Politics of Politics', *Renaissance Quarterly* 40: 707–42

—— (1992). 'The Father and the Bride in Shakespeare', in *Ideological Approaches to Shakespeare: The Practice of Theory*, eds. Robert P. Merrix and Nicholas Ranson. Lewiston, NY, 3–38

—— (1994). '"The Getting of a Lawful Race": Racial Discourse in Early Modern England and the Unrepresentable Black Woman', in *Women, "Race," and Writing in the Early Modern Period*, eds. Margo Hendricks and Patricia Parker. London and New York, 35–54

—— and Richard Burt, eds. (1997). *Shakespeare the Movie: Popularizing the Plays on Film, TV, and Video.* London

Booth, Stephen (1985). 'The Shakespearean Actor as Kamikaze Pilot', *Shakespeare Quarterly* 36: 553–70

—— (1990). 'The Function of Criticism at the Present Time and All Others', *Shakespeare Quarterly* 41: 262–8

Bove, Paul (1986). *Intellectuals in Power: A Genealogy of Critical Humanism.* New York

Bradbrook, M. C. (1935). *Themes and Conventions of Elizabethan Tragedy.* Cambridge

—— (1954). 'Fifty Years of the Criticism of Shakespeare's Style: A Retrospect', *Shakespeare Survey* 7: 1–11

—— (1964). *The Rise of the Common Player: A Study of Actor and Society in Shakespeare's England.* 1962. Cambridge, Mass

—— (1976). *The Living Monument: Shakespeare and the Theatre of His Time.* Cambridge

Bradley, A. C. (1904). *Shakespearean Tragedy.* London and New York

—— (1964). 'Coriolanus', British Academy Lecture. 1912. Repr. in *Studies in Shakespeare*, ed. Peter Alexander. London

—— (1965). *Oxford Lectures on Poetry*. 1909. London and New York

Bradshaw, Graham (1993). *Misrepresentations: Shakespeare and the Materialists*. Ithaca, NY and London

Brandes, Georg (1905). *William Shakespeare*. 1898. London

Braunmuller, A. R. (1983). 'Characterization through Language in the Early Plays of Shakespeare and his Contemporaries', in *Shakespeare, Man of the Theater*, eds. Kenneth Muir, Jay Halio, and D. J Palmer. Newark, NJ, 128–47

—— (1990). 'The Arts of the Dramatist', in *The Cambridge Companion to English Renaissance Drama*, eds. A. R. Braunmuller and Michael Hattaway. Cambridge, 53–90

Breitenberg, Mark (1996). *Anxious Masculinity in Early Modern England*. Cambridge Studies in Renaissance Literature and Culture 10. Cambridge

Bretzius, Stephen (1997). *Shakespeare in Theory: The Postmodern Academy and the Early Modern Theater*. Ann Arbor

Bridges, Robert (1927). 'On the Influence of the Audience', *Collected Essays*. 1904. Oxford

Bristol, Michael D. (1985). *Carnival and Theater: Plebeian Culture and the Structure of Authority in Renaissance England*. New York and London

—— (1996). *Big-Time Shakespeare*. New York

Bromley, John C. (1971). *The Shakespearean Kings*. Boulder, Colo

Brook, Peter (1968). *The Empty Space*. New York

Brooks, Cleanth (1947). 'The Naked Babe and the Cloak of Manliness', in *The Well-Wrought Urn: Studies in the Structure of Poetry*. New York 22–49

Brown, Ivor, and Fearon George (1939). *The Shakespeare Industry: Amazing Monument*. London

Brown, John Russell (1974). *Free Shakespeare*. London

—— (1996). *William Shakespeare: Writing for Performance*. New York

Bruster, Douglas (1992). *Drama and the Market in the Age of Shakespeare*. Cambridge Studies in Renaissance Literature and Culture 1. Cambridge

Bryant, J. A., Jr. (1961). *Hippolyta's View: Some Christian Aspects of Shakespeare's Plays*. Lexington, Ky

—— (1986). *Shakespeare and the Uses of Comedy*. Lexington, Ky

Bulman, James C., ed. (1996). *Shakespeare, Theory, and Performance*. London and New York

—— and Coursen, Herbert R., eds. (1988). *Shakespeare on Television: An Anthology of Essays and Reviews*. Hanover, NH

Butler, Martin (1984). *Theatre and Crisis*. Cambridge

Buzacott, Martin (1991). *The Death of the Actor: Shakespeare on Page and Stage*. London and New York

Calderwood, James L. (1971). *Shakespearean Metadrama*. Minneapolis
—— (1979). *Metadrama in Shakespeare's Henriad: 'Richard II' to 'Henry V'*. Berkeley
—— (1983). *To Be and Not To Be: Negation and Metadrama in Hamlet*. New York
—— (1986). *If It Were Done: 'Macbeth' and Tragic Action*. Amherst, Mass
Callaghan, Dympna (1993). '"And All is Semblative a Woman's Part": Body Politics and *Twelfth Night*', *Textual Practice* 7: 428–52
—— (1996). '"Othello Was a White Man": Properties of Race on Shakespeare's Stage', in *Alternative Shakespeares Vol. 2*, ed. Terence Hawkes. London and New York, 192–215
Campbell, Lily B. (1930). *Shakespeare's Tragic Heroes*. Cambridge
—— (1965). *Shakespeare's 'Histories': Mirrors of Elizabethan Policy*. 1947. San Marino, Calif
Cavell, Stanley (1987). *Disowning Knowledge in Six Plays of Shakespeare*. Cambridge
Chambers, E. K. (1923). *The Elizabethan Stage*. 4 vols. Oxford
—— (1944a). 'The Disintegration of Shakespeare', British Academy Annual Shakespeare Lecture. 1924. Repr. in *Shakespearean Gleanings*. Oxford, 1–21
—— (1944b). 'The Unrest in Shakespeare Studies', in *Shakespearean Gleanings*. 1927. Oxford, 22–34
Charlton, H. B. (1938). *Shakespearian Comedy*. London
—— (1948). *Shakespearian Tragedy*. Cambridge
Charney, Maurice (1961). *Shakespeare's Roman Plays: The Function of Imagery in the Drama*. Cambridge, Mass
—— (1971). *How To Read Shakespeare*. New York
Clemen, W. H. (1951). *The Development of Shakespeare's Imagery*. London
—— (1972). *Shakespeare's Dramatic Art: Collected Essays*. London and New York
—— (1987). *Shakespeare's Soliloquies*. 1972. London and New York
Cohen, Derek (1988). *Shakespearean Motives*. New York
Cohen, Walter (1987). 'Political Criticism of Shakespeare', in *Shakespeare Reproduced: The Text in History and Ideology*, eds. Jean E. Howard and Marion F. O'Connor. New York and London 18–46
Collick, John (1989). *Shakespeare, Cinema, and Society*. Manchester
Colman, E. A. M. (1974). *The Dramatic Use of Bawdy in Shakespeare*. London
Cook, Ann Jennalie (1981). *The Privileged Playgoers of Shakespeare's London, 1576–1642*. Princeton
Cook, Carol (1991). 'Straw Women and Whipping Girls: The (Sexual) Politics of Critical Self-fashioning', in *Shakespeare Left and Right*, ed. Ivo Kamps. New York and London, 61–78

Cooke, Katherine (1972). *A. C. Bradley and his Influence on Twentieth Century Shakespeare Criticism*. Oxford

Coursen, H. R. (1993). *Watching Shakespeare on Television*. London and Toronto

Cowhig, Ruth (1985). 'Blacks in English Renaissance Drama and the Role of Shakespeare's Othello', in *The Black Presence in English Literature*, ed. David Dabydeen. Manchester, 1–20

Cox, Brian (1993). 'Titus Andronicus', in *Players of Shakespeare 3: Further Essays in Shakespearian Performance by Players with the Royal Shakespeare Company*, eds. Russell Jackson and Robert Smallwood. Cambridge and New York, 174–88

Craig, Hardin (1936). *The Enchanted Glass: The Elizabethan Mind in Literature*. New York

—— (1949). 'Trends of Shakespeare Scholarship', *Shakespeare Survey* 2: 107–14

Crane, R. S. (1952). 'The Critical Monism of Cleanth Brooks', in *Critics and Criticism Ancient and Modern*. Chicago and London, 83–107

Cressy, David (1991). 'Foucault, Stone, Shakespeare and Social History', *English Literary Renaissance* 21: 121–33

Crowl, Samuel (1992). *Shakespeare Observed: Studies in Performance on Stage and Screen*. Athens, Oh

Culler, Jonathan (1988). *Framing the Sign: Criticism and its Institutions*. Oxford

—— (1997). *Literary Theory: A Very Short Introduction*. Oxford

Curren-Aquino, Deborah (1989). *King John: New Perspectives*. Newark, NJ

D'Amico, Jack (1991). *The Moor in English Renaissance Drama*. Tampa, Fla

Danby, J. F. (1952). *Poets on Fortune's Hill*. London

Danson, Lawrence (1986). 'Continuity and Character in Shakespeare and Marlowe', *Studies in English Literature* 26: 217–34

Dash, Irene G. (1981). *Wooing, Wedding and Power: Women in Shakespeare's Plays*. New York

—— (1997). *Women's Worlds in Shakespeare's Plays*. London

Davies, Anthony (1987). 'Shakespeare and the Media of Film, Radio and Television: A Retrospect', *Shakespeare Survey* 39: 1–11

—— (1988). *Filming Shakespeare's Plays*. Cambridge

Dawson, Anthony B. (1991). 'The Impasse over the Stage', *English Literary Renaissance* 21: 309–27

de Grazia, Margreta (1996). 'The Ideology of Superfluous Things: *King Lear* as Period Piece', in *Subject and Object in Renaissance Culture*, eds. Margreta de Grazia, Maureen Quilligan and Peter Stallybrass. Cambridge, 17–42

—— (1997). 'Love among the Ruins: Response to Pechter', *Textual Practice* 11: 67–72

Delany, Paul (1995). '*King Lear* and the Decline of Feudalism', in *Materialist Shakespeare: A History*, ed. Ivo Kamps. London, 20–38

Dessen, Alan, C. (1980). 'Shakespeare's Patterns for the Viewer's Eye: Dramaturgy for the Open Stage', in *Shakespeare's More than Words Can Witness: Essays on Visual and Nonverbal Enactment in the Plays*, ed. Sidney Homan. Lewisburg Pa., 92–107

—— (1995). *Recovering Shakespeare's Theatrical Vocabulary.* Cambridge

Devlin, Christopher (1963). *Hamlet's Divinity and Other Essays.* London

Dobson, Michael (1998). 'Gobsmacked', *London Review of Books* 20 14 (16 July), 24–6

Dollimore, Jonathan (1984). *Radical Tragedy: Religion, Ideology and Power in the Drama of Shakespeare and his Contemporaries.* Brighton

—— (1989–90). 'Shakespeare, Cultural Materialism, and Marxist Humanism', *New Literary History* 21: 471–93

—— (1990). 'Critical Developments: Cultural Materialism, Feminism and Gender Critique, and New Historicism', in *Shakespeare A Bibliographical Guide*, ed. Stanley Wells. Oxford, 405–28

—— (1992). 'Shakespeare, Cultural Materialism and the New Historicism', in *Political Shakespeare: New Essays in Cultural Materialism*, eds. Jonathan Dollimore and Alan Sinfield. Ithaca, NY, 1985, 2–18. Repr. *New Historicism and Renaissance Drama*, eds. Richard Wilson and Richard Dutton. London and New York, 45–56

—— and Sinfield, Alan, eds. (1985). *Political Shakespeare: New Essays in Cultural Materialism.* Ithaca, NY

Donaldson, Peter S. (1990). *Shakespearean Films/Shakespearean Directors.* Boston

Dowden, Edward (1962). *Shakspere: A Critical Study of his Mind and Art.* 1875. New York

Drakakis, John, ed. (1985). *Alternative Shakespeares.* London and New York

Dubrow, Heather (1987). *Captive Victors: Shakespeare's Narrative Poems and Sonnets.* Ithaca, NY

—— (1997). 'Twentieth-Century Shakespeare Criticism', in *The Riverside Shakespeare*, 2nd. edn., vol. i. Boston, 27–54

—— and Strier, Richard (1988). 'Introduction: The Historical Renaissance', in *The Historical Renaissance: New Essays on Tudor and Stuart Literature and Culture*, eds. Heather Dubrow and Richard Strier. Chicago, 1–14

Dusinberre, Juliet (1975). *Shakespeare and the Nature of Women.* New York

Eagleton, Terry (1983). *Literary Theory: An Introduction.* Oxford

—— (1986). *William Shakespeare.* Rereading Literature Series. Oxford

—— (1988). 'Afterword', in *The Shakespeare Myth.* Cultural Politics Series. Ed. Graham Holderness. Manchester, 203–8

—— (1992). 'The Ideology of the Aesthetic', in *The Politics of Pleasure: Aesthetics and Cultural Theory*, ed. S. Regan. Buckingham, Pa., 25–37

254 List of Works Cited

—— (1998). 'Good Dinners Pass Away, So do Tyrants and Toothache', *London Review of Books* 208 (16 Apr.), 13–14

Eastman, Arthur M. (1968). *A Short History of Shakespearean Criticism*. New York

Edgar, David (1999). 'Be Flippant', *London Review of Books* 21 24 (9 Dec), 27–9

Edwards, Philip (1968). *Shakespeare and the Confines of Art*. London

Elam, Keir (1996). ' "In what chapter of his bosom?": Reading Shakespeare's Bodies', in *Alternative Shakespeares Volume 2*, ed. Terence Hawkes. London and New York, 140–63

Eliot, T. S. (1950). *Selected Essays*. 1932. New York

Elliott, M. Leigh (1885). *Shakespeare's Garden of Girls*. London

Ellis-Fermor, Una (1964). *The Frontiers of Drama*. 1945. London

Elsom, John, ed. (1989). *Is Shakespeare Still Our Contemporary?* London and New York

Elton, W. R. (1966). *King Lear and the Gods*. San Marino, Calif

Empson, William (1951). *The Structure of Complex Words*. London

—— (1987). *Essays on Shakespeare*. Cambridge

Engle, Lars (1993). *Shakespearean Pragmatism: Market of His Time*. Chicago and London

Erickson, Peter (1985). 'Shakespeare and the "Author-Function" ', in *Shakespeare's 'Rough Magic': Renaissance Essays in Honor of C. L. Barber*, eds. Peter Erickson and Coppelia Kahn. London and Toronto, 231–55

Everett, Barbara (1960). 'The Figure in Professor Knights's Carpet', *Critical Quarterly* 2: 171–6

—— (1998). 'Shakespeare in the Twentieth Century', in *Shakespeare and the Twentieth Century*, eds. Jonathan Bate, Jill Levenson, and Dieter Mehl. Newark, NJ and London, 215–30

Farmer, J. S., and Henley, W. E., eds. (1965). *Slang and its Analogues Past and Present*. 7 vols. 1890. New York

Farnham, Willard (1956). *The Medieval Heritage of Elizabethan Tragedy*. Oxford

Fawkner, H. W. (1990a). *Shakespeare's Hyperontology: 'Antony and Cleopatra'*. Rutherford, NJ

—— (1990b). *Deconstructing 'Macbeth': The Hyperontological View*. Rutherford, NJ

—— (1992). *Shakespeare's Miracle Plays*. London and Toronto

Felperin, Howard (1987). 'Making it "Neo": The New Historicism and Renaissance Literature', *Textual Practice* 1: 262–77

Ferry, Anne (1983). *The 'Inward' Language: Sonnets of Wyatt, Sidney, Shakespeare, and Donne*. Chicago

Fiedler, Leslie (1973). *The Stranger in Shakespeare*. London

Fineman, Joel (1986). *Shakespeare's Perjured Eye: The Invention of Poetic Subjectivity in the Sonnets.* Berkeley

Fish, Stanley (1995). *Professional Correctness: Literary Studies and Political Change.* New York

Fiske, John (1989). *Reading the Popular.* London and New York

Fitz, Linda (1977). 'Egyptian Queens and Male Reviewers: Sexist Attitudes to *Antony and Cleopatra* Criticism', *Shakespeare Quarterly* 28: 297–316

Foakes, R. A. (1952). 'Suggestions for a New Approach to Shakespeare's Imagery', *Shakespeare Survey* 5: 81–92

—— (1980). 'Poetic Language and Dramatic Significance in Shakespeare', in *Shakespeare's Styles: Essays in Honour of Kenneth Muir*, eds. Philip Edwards, Inga-Stina Ewbank, and G. K. Hunter. Cambridge, 79–93

—— (1993). *Hamlet Versus Lear: Cultural Politics and Shakespeare's Art.* Cambridge

—— (1996). 'Shakespeare's Elizabethan Stages', in *Shakespeare: An Illustrated Stage History*, eds. Jonathan Bate and Russell Jackson. Oxford, 10–22

Foley, Stephen (1991). 'Nostalgia and the "Rise of English": Rhetorical Questions', in *The Matter of Difference: Materialist Feminist Criticism of Shakespeare*, ed. Valerie Wayne. Hemel Hempstead, 237–55

Freedman, Barbara (1989). 'Misrecognizing Shakespeare', in *Shakespeare's Personality*, eds. Norman N. Holland, Sidney Homan, and Bernard J. Paris. Berkeley, 244–60

French, Marilyn (1982). *Shakespeare's Division of Experience.* London

Freud, Sigmund (1924). *Collected Papers.* 5 vols. London

Frey, Charles (1980a) *Shakespeare's Vast Romance: A Study of 'The Winter's Tale'.* New York

—— (1980b). '"O Sacred, Shadowy, Cold, and Constant Queen": Shakespeare's Imperiled and Chastening Daughters of Romance', in *The Woman's Part: Feminist Criticism of Shakespeare*, eds. Carolyn Lenz *et al.* Chicago, 295–313

Frye, Northrop (1965). *A Natural Perspective: The Development of Shakespearean Comedy and Romance.* New York

—— (1967). *Fools of Time: Studies in Shakespearean Tragedy.* Toronto and Buffalo

—— (1976). *The Secular Scripture: A Study of the Structure of Romance.* Cambridge, Mass. and London

—— (1983). *The Myth of Deliverance: Reflections on Shakespeare's Problem Comedies.* Toronto

—— (1986). *Northrop Frye on Shakespeare*, ed. Robert Sandler. Markham, Ont

Frye, R. M. (1963). *Shakespeare and Christian Doctrine.* London

Garner, Shirley Nelson (1988). '*The Taming of the Shrew*: Inside or Outside the Joke?' in *'Bad' Shakespeare: Revaluations of the Shakespeare Canon*, ed. Maurice Charney. Rutherford, NJ., 105–19

—— (1989). 'Male Bonding and the Myth of Women's Deception in Shakespeare's Plays', in *Shakespeare's Personality*, eds. Norman N. Holland, Sidney Homan, and Bernard J. Paris. Berkeley, 135–50

—— (1996). 'Shakespeare in My Time and Place', in *Shakespearean Tragedy and Gender*, eds. Shirley Nelson Garner and Madelon Sprengnether. Bloomington, Ind., 287–306

Gillies, John (1994). *Shakespeare and the Geography of Difference*. Cambridge Studies in Renaissance Literature and Culture 4. Cambridge

Girard, René (1991). *A Theater of Envy: William Shakespeare*. New York

Gitlin, Todd (1988). 'Hip-Deep in Post-modernism', *New York Times Book Review*. 6 Nov., 3 and 35

Gohlke (Sprengnether), Madelon (1982). ' "All that is Spoke is Marred": Language and Consciousness in *Othello*', *Women's Studies* 9: 157–76

Goldberg, Jonathan (1986). *Voice Terminal Echo: Postmodernism and English Renaissance Texts*. New York

Goldman, Michael (1981). 'Characterizing Coriolanus', *Shakespeare Survey* 34: 73–84

Gottschalk, Paul (1972). *The Meanings of 'Hamlet': Modes of Literary Interpretation since Bradley*. Albuquerque, N. Mex

Grady, Hugh (1991*a*). *The Modernist Shakespeare: Critical Texts in a Material World*. Oxford

—— (1991*b*). 'Disintegration and its Reverberations', in *The Appropriation of Shakespeare: Post-Renaissance Reconstructions of the Works and the Myth*, ed. Jean I. Marsden. London, 111–28

Graff, Gerald (1987). *Professing Literature: An Institutional History*. Chicago

Green, Amy S. (1994). *The Revisionist Stage: American Directors Reinvent the Classics*. Cambridge

Green, Martin (1974). *The Labyrinth of Shakespeare's Sonnets: An Examination of the Sexual Elements of Shakespeare's Language*. London

Greenblatt, Stephen (1980). *Renaissance Self-Fashioning: From More to Shakespeare*. Chicago and London

—— (1992). 'Invisible Bullets: Renaissance Authority and its Subversion, *Henry IV* and *Henry V*', in *Political Shakespeare: New Essays in Cultural Materialism*, eds. Jonathan Dollimore and Alan Sinfield. Manchester, 1985. Repr. *New Historicism and Renaissance Drama*, eds. Richard Wilson and Richard Dutton. London and New York

—— (1994). 'The Eating of the Soul', *Representations* 48: 97–116

Greene, Gayle (1981). 'Feminist and Marxist Criticism: An Argument for Alliances', *Women's Studies* 9: 29–45

——— (1995). '"This that You Call Love": Sexual and Social Tragedy in *Othello*', in *Shakespeare and Gender: A History*, eds. Deborah Barker and Ivo Kamps. London, 47–62

Greg, W. W. (1955). *The Shakespeare First Folio*. Oxford

Grivelet, Michel (1963). 'Shakespeare as "Corrupter of Words"', *Shakespeare Survey* 16: 70–6

Gunn, Giles (1987). *The Culture of Criticism and the Criticism of Culture*. New York and Oxford

Gurr, Andrew (1987). *Playgoing in Shakespeare's London*. Cambridge

——— (1992). *The Shakespearean Stage, 1574–1642*. 3rd edn. Cambridge

Halio, Jay L. (1977). '"This Wide and Universal Stage": Shakespeare's Plays as Plays', in *Teaching Shakespeare*, ed. Walter Edens. Princeton, 273–89

Hallett, Charles A., and Hallett, Elaine S. (1991). *Analyzing Shakespeare's Action: Scene Versus Sequence*. Cambridge

Halpern, Richard (1991). *Poetics of Primitive Accumulation: English Renaissance Culture and the Genealogy of Capital*. Ithaca, NY

——— (1997). *Shakespeare among the Moderns*. Ithaca, NY and London

Hammond, Antony (1994). 'The Noisy Comma: Searching for the Signal in Renaissance Dramatic Texts', in *Crisis in Editing: Texts of the English Renaissance*, ed. Randall McLeod. New York, 203–49

Hapgood, Robert (1962). 'Shakespeare and the Ritualists', *Shakespeare Survey* 15: 111–24

——— (1980). 'Shakespeare's Choreography: Pace and Rhythm', in *Shakespeare's more than Words can Witness: Essays on Visual and Nonverbal Enactment in the Plays*. Lewisburg, Pa., 130–41

——— (1988). *Shakespeare the Theatre-Poet*. Oxford

Harbage, Alfred (1950). *Shakespeare and the Rival Traditions*. New York

——— (1964). 'Shakespeare and the "Myth of Perfection"', *Shakespeare Quarterly* 15: 1–10

——— (1966). *Conceptions of Shakespeare*. Cambridge, Mass

——— (1969). *Shakespeare's Audience 1941*. New York and London

Harris, Frank (1969). *The Man Shakespeare and His Tragic Life-Story. 1909*. New York

Hart, Jonathan (1992). *Theater and World: The Problematics of Shakespeare's History*. Boston

Hartwig, Joan (1983). *Shakespeare's Analogical Scene*. Lincoln, Nebr. and London

Hattaway, Michael (1990). *The First Part of King Henry VI*, New Cambridge Shakespeare. Cambridge

Hawkes, Terence (1981). 'Opening Closure', *Modern Drama* 24: 353–6

—— (1986). *That Shakespeherian Rag: Essays on a Critical Process*. London and New York

—— (1992). *Meaning by Shakespeare*. London

Hawkins, Harriett (1987). *Measure for Measure*. Harvester Introductions. Brighton

—— (1993). 'Disrupting Tribal Difference: Critical and Artistic Responses to Shakespeare's Radical Romanticism', *Studies in the Literary Imagination* 26: 115–26

Hawkins, Sherman (1991). 'Structural Pattern in Shakespeare's Histories', *Studies in Philology* 88: 16–45

Heilbrun, Carolyn (1957). 'The Character of Hamlet's Mother', *Shakespeare Quarterly* 8: 201–6

Heilman, Robert (1963). *This Great Stage: Image and Structure in 'King Lear'*. 1948. Washington

—— and Pearce, Roy Harvey (1969). *Historicism Once More*. Princeton

Hellenga, Robert R. (1981). 'Elizabethan Dramatic Conventions and Elizabethan Reality', *Renaissance Drama* 12: 27–49

Helms, Lorraine (1994). 'Acts of Resistance: The Feminist Player', in *The Weyward Sisters: Shakespeare and Feminist Politics*, eds. Dympna Callaghan, Lorraine Helms, and Jyotsna Singh. Cambridge, Mass., 102–56

Herford, C. H. (1923). *A Sketch of Recent Shakespearean Investigation*. London

Highley, Christopher (1997). *Shakespeare, Spenser, and the Crisis in Ireland*. Cambridge

Hildy, Franklin J., ed. (1990). *New Issues in the Reconstruction of Shakespeare's Theatre*. New York

Hobsbawm, Eric (1994). *Age of Extremes: The Short Twentieth Century 1914–1991*. London

Hodgdon, Barbara (1985). 'Parallel Practices, or the Un-Necessary Difference', *Kenyon Review*, n.s. 7: 57–65

—— (1991). *The End Crowns All: Closure and Contradiction in Shakespeare's History*. Princeton

—— (1996). ' "Here Apparent": Photography, History, and the Theatrical Unconscious', in *Textual and Theatrical Shakespeare: Questions of Evidence*, ed. Edward Pechter. Iowa City, 181–209

Hodges, C. Walter (1939). *The Globe Restored*. London

—— (1999). *Enter the Whole Army: A Pictorial Study of Shakespearean Staging 1576–1616*. Cambridge

Holderness, Graham (1984). 'Agincourt 1944: Readings in the Shakespeare Myth', *Literature and History* 10: 24–45

—— ed. (1988). *The Shakespeare Myth*. Manchester

—— (1991). ' "A Woman's War": A Feminist Reading of *Richard II* ', in *Shakespeare Left and Right*, ed. Ivo Kamps. New York and London, 167–83

—— Potter, Nick, and Turner, John (1988). *Shakespeare: The Play of History*. London

Holland, Norman, N. (1989). 'Introduction', in *Shakespeare's Personality*, eds. Norman N. Holland, Sidney Homan, and Bernard J. Paris. Berkeley

Holland, Peter (1989). 'The Resources of Characterization in *Othello* ', *Shakespeare Survey* 41: 119–32

—— (1997a). *English Shakespeares: Shakespeare on the English Stage in the 1990s*. Cambridge

—— (1997b). 'Reade him Therefore—and Againe and Againe', *Times Literary Supplement*, No. 4936 (7 Nov.), 24–5

Holstun, James (1989). 'Ranting at the New Historicism', *English Literary Renaissance* 19: 189–225

Honigmann, E. A. J. (1976). *Shakespeare: Seven Tragedies: The Dramatist's Manipulation of Response*. New York

—— (1982). *Shakespeare's Impact on his Contemporaries*. London

—— (1985). *Shakespeare: The 'Lost Years'*. Manchester

—— (1989). *Myriad-Minded Shakespeare: Essays, Chiefly on the Tragedies and Problem Comedies*. London

Horwitz, Howard (1988). ' "I Can't Remember": Skepticism, Synthetic Histories, Critical Action', *South Atlantic Quarterly* 87: 787–819

Hotson, J. L. (1934). *The Companion to Shakespeare Studies*. New York

Howard, Jean E. (1984). *Shakespeare's Art of Orchestration: Stage Technique and Audience Response* Urbana, Ill. and Chicago

—— (1986). 'Scholarship, Theory, and More New Readings: Shakespeare for the 1990s', in *Shakespeare Study Today*, ed. Georgianna Ziegler. New York, 127–51

—— (1992). 'The New Historicism in Renaissance Studies', in *New Historicism and Renaissance Drama*, eds. Richard Wilson and Richard Dutton. London and New York

—— (1994). *Stage and Social Struggle in Early Modern England*. London

—— and O'Connor, Marion F., eds. (1987). *Shakespeare Reproduced: The Text in History and Ideology*. New York and London

—— and Rackin, Phyllis, (1997). *Engendering a Nation: A Feminist Account of Shakespeare's English Histories*. Feminist Readings of Shakespeare. London and New York

Howarth, Herbert (1961). 'Shakespeare's Gentleness', *Shakespeare Survey* 14: 90–7

Hughes, Robert (1981). *The Shock of the New*. New York

Hulme, H. N. (1962). *Explorations in Shakespeare's Language: Some Problems of Lexical Word Meaning in the Dramatic Text*. London

Hunt, Margaret (1994). 'Afterword', in *Queering the Renaissance*, ed. Jonathan Goldberg. Durham and London, 359–77

Hunter, G. K. (1964*a*). 'Elizabethans and Foreigners', *Shakespeare Survey* 17: 37–52

—— (1964*b*). 'The Theology of Marlowe's *Jew of Malta*', *The Journal of the Warburg and Cortauld Institutes* 27: 211–40

—— (1967). 'Othello and Colour Prejudice', *Proceedings of the British Academy* 53: 139–63

—— (1968). 'A. C. Bradley's *Shakespearean Tragedy*', *Essays and Studies* 21: 101–17

—— (1978). *Dramatic Identities and Cultural Traditions: Studies in Shakespeare and his Contemporaries*. Liverpool

—— (1990). 'Truth and Art in History Plays', *Shakespeare Survey* 42: 15–24

Huston, J. Dennis (1981). *Shakespeare's Comedies of Play*. New York

Ingram, William (1992). *The Business of Playing: The Beginnings of the Adult Professional Theater in Elizabethan London*. Ithaca, NY and London

Ioppolo, Grace (1991). *Revising Shakespeare*. Cambridge, Mass

Jackson, Gabriele Bernhard (1988). 'Topical Ideology: Witches, Amazons, and Shakespeare's Joan of Arc', *English Literary Renaissance* 18: 40–65

Jackson, Russell (1996*a*). 'Shakespeare in Opposition: From the 1950s to the 1990s', in *Shakespeare: An Illustrated Stage History*, eds. Jonathan Bate and Russell Jackson. Oxford, 211–30

—— (1996*b*). 'Actor-Managers and the Spectacular', in *Shakespeare: An Illustrated Stage History*, eds. Jonathan Bate and Russell Jackson. Oxford, 112–27

James, Henry (1964). 'Introduction to *The Tempest*', in *Selected Literary Criticism*, ed. M. Shapira. New York, 297–310

Jardine, Lisa (1983). *Still Harping on Daughters: Women and Drama in the Age of Shakespeare*. Brighton

—— (1996). *Reading Shakespeare Historically*. London and New York

Jones, Emrys (1971). *Scenic Form in Shakespeare*. Oxford

—— (1983). 'The Sense of Occasion: Some Shakespearean Night Sequences', in *Shakespeare, Man of the Theater*, eds. Kenneth Muir, Jay Halio, and D. J Palmer. Newark, NJ, 98–104

Jones, Ernest (1949). *Hamlet and Oedipus*. New York

Jorgens, Jack (1977). *Shakespeare on Film*. London

Jorgensen, Paul A. (1962). *Redeeming Shakespeare's Words*. Berkeley and Los Angeles

Joseph, Sister Miriam (1947). *Shakespeare's Use of the Arts of Language*. London

Joyce, James (1966). *Ulysses*. 1922. New York

Kahn, Coppélia (1984). *Man's Estate: Masculine identity in Shakespeare*. Berkeley and Los Angeles

—— (1997). *Roman Shakespeare: Warriors, Wounds and Women*. London and New York

Kamps, Ivo, ed. (1991). *Shakespeare Left and Right*. New York and London

Keats, John (1942). *The Letters of John Keats*, ed. M. B. Forman. London

Kelly, H. A. (1970). *Providence in the England of Shakespeare's Histories*. Cambridge, Mass

Kennedy, Dennis (1985). *Granville Barker and the Dream of Theatre*. Cambridge

—— (1993). *Looking at Shakespeare: A Visual History of Twentieth Century Performance*. Cambridge

—— (1996). 'Shakespeare without his Language', in *Shakespeare, Theory, and Performance*, ed. James C. Bulman. London and New York, 133–48

Kennedy, Milton B. (1942). *The Oration in Shakespeare*. Chapel Hill, NC

Kermode, Frank (1999). 'Writing About Shakespeare', *London Review of Books*, 21 24 (9 Dec.), 3–8

Kernan, Alvin (1986). 'The New Historicism in Renaissance Studies', *English Literary Renaissance* 16: 13–43

—— (1987). 'Criticism as Theodicy: The Institutional Role of Literary Criticism', *Yale Review* 77: 86–102

—— (1995). *Shakespeare, the King's Playwright: Theater in the Stuart Court 1603–1613*. New Haven and London

Kerrigan, William (1989). 'The Personal Shakespeare: Three Clues', in *Shakespeare's Personality*, eds. Norman N. Holland, Sidney Homan and Bernard J. Paris. Berkeley, 175–90

—— (1994). *Hamlet's Perfection*. Baltimore

Kettle, Arnold, ed. (1964). *Shakespeare in a Changing World*. London

Knight, G. Wilson (1930). *The Wheel of Fire*. Oxford

—— (1931). *The Imperial Theme*. Oxford

—— (1962). *The Christian Renaissance*. New York

—— (1967). *Shakespeare and Religion: Essays of Forty Years*. London

Knights, L. C. (1963a). 'How Many Children Had Lady Macbeth?' 1933. Repr. in *Explorations: Essays in Criticism Mainly on the Literature of the Seventeenth Century*. London, 1–39

—— (1963b). 'Shakespeare's Sonnets' 1934. Repr. in *Explorations: Essays in Criticism Mainly on the Literature of the Seventeenth Century*. London, 40–65

—— (1965). *Further Explorations*. London

Knowles, Richard Paul (1996). 'Shakespeare, Voice, and Ideology: Interrogating the Natural Voice', in *Shakespeare, Theory, and Performance*, ed. James C. Bulman. London and New York, 92–112

Kolbe, F. C. (1930). *Shakespeare's Way: A Psychological Study*. London

Kott, Jan (1964). *Shakespeare Our Contemporary*. New York

—— (1992). *The Gender of Rosalind*. Evanston, Ill

Kozintsev, Grigorii (1966). *Shakespeare: Time and Conscience*, trans. Joyce Vining. New York

—— (1977). *King Lear: The Space of Tragedy*, trans. Mary Mackintosh. Berkeley

Kroeber, Karl (1984). 'The Evolution of Literary Study 1883–1983', *PMLA* 99: 326–9

Krupnick, Mark (1986). *Lionel Trilling and the Fate of Cultural Criticism*. Evanston, Ill

Laroque, Francois (1991). *Shakespeare's Festive World: Elizabethan Seasonal Entertainment and the Professional Stage*, trans. Janet Lloyd. Cambridge

Lawrence, W. J. (1913). *Elizabethan Playhouses and Other Studies*. Stratford-upon-Avon

Lawrence, W. W. (1931). *Shakespeare's Problem Comedies*. New York

Leavis, F. R. (1952). 'Diabolic Intellect and the Noble Hero: or the Sentimentalist's Othello', *Scrutiny* 6 (1937), 259–83. Repr. in *The Common Pursuit*. London

—— (1942). 'The Greatness of *Measure for Measure*', *Scrutiny* 10: 234–47

Lee, Sir S. (1898). *A Life of William Shakespeare*. London

—— (1906). *Shakespeare and the Modern Stage*. New York

Leggatt, Alexander (1988). *Shakespeare's Political Drama: The History Plays and the Roman Plays*. London and New York

Leinwand, Theodore, B. (1993). 'Shakespeare and the Middling Sort', *Shakespeare Quarterly* 44: 284–303

Lentricchia, Frank (1983). *Criticism and Social Change*. Chicago and London

—— (1988). *Ariel and the Police: Michael Foucault, William James, Wallace Stevens*. Madison

Lenz, C. R., Green, Gayle, and Nealy, C. T., eds. (1980). *The Woman's Part: Feminist Criticism of Shakespeare*. Chicago

Lever, J. W. (1976). 'Shakespeare and the Ideas of His Time', *Shakespeare Survey* 29: 79–91

—— (1987). *The Tragedy of State: A Study of Jacobean Drama*. 1971. London

Levi, Peter (1988). *The Life and Times of William Shakespeare*. London

Levin, Richard (1975). 'Refuting Shakespeare's Endings—Part I', *Modern Philology* 72: 337–49

—— (1977). 'Refuting Shakespeare's Endings—Part II', *Modern Philology* 75: 132–58

—— (1978). 'The Delapsing of Shakespeare', in *Shakespeare, Pattern of Excelling Nature*, eds. David Bevington and Jay L. Halio. Newark, NJ 174–82

—— (1979). *New Readings vs Old Plays: Recent Trends in the Reinterpretation of English Renaissance Drama*. Chicago

—— (1980). 'The Relation of External Evidence to the Allegorical and Thematic Interpretation of Shakespeare', *Shakespeare Studies* 13: 1–29

—— (1986). 'Performance Critics *vs.* Close Readers in the Study of English Renaissance Drama', *Modern Language Review* 81: 545–59

—— (1988). 'Feminist Thematics and Shakespearean Tragedy', *PMLA* 103: 125–38

—— (1990). 'The Poetics and Politics of Bardicide', *PMLA* 105: 491–504

Levine, Lawrence W. (1988). 'William Shakespeare in America', in *Highbrow/ Lowbrow: The Emergence of Cultural Hierarchy in America*. Cambridge, Mass., 11–82

Lewis, C. S. (1964). 'Hamlet: The Prince or the Poem' 1942. Repr. in *Studies in Shakespeare: British Academy Lectures*, ed. Peter Alexander. Oxford, 201–18

Lewis, Wyndham (1966). *The Lion and the Fox: The Role of the Hero in the Plays of Shakespeare*. 1927. New York

Liebler, Naomi Conn (1995). *Shakespeare's Festive Tragedy: The Ritual Foundations of Genre*. London and New York

Logan, Marie-Rose, and Rudnytsky, Peter L., eds. (1991). *Contending Kingdoms: Historical, Psychological and Feminist Approaches to the Literature of Sixteenth Century England*. Detroit

Loomba, Ania (1989). *Gender, Race, Renaissance Drama*. Cultural Politics Series. Manchester

—— (1996). 'Shakespeare and Cultural Difference', in *Alternative Shakespeares Volume 2*, ed. Terence Hawkes. London and New York 164–91

Lupton, Julia, and Reinhard, Kenneth (1993). *After Oedipus: Shakespeare in Psychoanalysis*. Ithaca, NY and London

McEachern, Claire (1988). 'Fathering Herself: A Source Study of Shakespeare's Feminism', *Shakespeare Quarterly* 39: 269–90

McGann, Jerome J. (1991). *The Textual Condition*. Princeton

Mackenzie, Agnes Mure (1924). *The Women in Shakespeare's Plays*. London

McKerrow, R. B. (1951). *An Introduction to Bibliography for Literary Students*. Oxford

Mackinnon, Lachlan (1988). *Shakespeare the Aesthete: An Exploration of Literary Theory*. London

Mahood, M. M. (1957). *Shakespeare's Wordplay*. London

—— (1993). *Bit Parts in Shakespeare*. Cambridge

Manvell, Roger (1979). *Shakespeare and the Film*. New York

Marcus, Leah S. (1988). *Puzzling Shakespeare: Local Reading and its Discontents*. Berkeley

Marder, Louis (1963). *His Exits and His Entrances: The Story of Shakespeare's Reputation*. London

Margolies, David (1988). 'Teaching the Handsaw to Fly: Shakespeare as a Hegemonic Instrument', *The Shakespeare Myth*, ed. Graham Holderness. Manchester, 42–53

Marowitz, Charles (1991). *Recycling Shakespeare*. London

Marshall, Cynthia (1991). *Last Things and Last Plays: Shakespearean Eschatology*. Carbondale, Ill

Martin, Helena Faucit (1885). *On Some of Shakespeare's Female Characters*. London

Mazer, Cary M. (1981). *Shakespeare Refashioned: Elizabethan Plays on Edwardian Stages*. Ann Arbor

Meagher, John C. (1997). *Shakespeare's Shakespeare: How the Plays Were Made*. New York

Melchiori, Giorgio (1981). 'The Rhetoric of Character Construction: *Othello*', *Shakespeare Survey* 34: 61–72

—— (1994). *Shakespeare's Garter Plays: 'Edward III' to 'The Merry Wives of Windsor'*. London

Miles, Rosalind (1976). *The Problem of Measure for Measure: A Historical Investigation*. London

Miller, Jonathan (1986). *Subsequent Performances*. New York

Mills, Howard (1993). *Working With Shakespeare*. Hemel Hempstead

Montrose, Louis (1983). '"Shaping Fantasies": Figurations of Gender and Power in Elizabethan Culture', *Representations* 1: 61–94

—— (1996). *The Purpose of Playing: Shakespeare and the Cultural Politics of the Elizabethan Theatre*. Chicago and London

Moody, A. D. (1964). *Shakespeare: The Merchant of Venice*. London

Morgann, Maurice (1777). *Essay on the Dramatic Character of Falstaff*. London

Morris, Wesley (1972). *Toward a New Historicism*. Princeton

Moulton, R. G. (1903). *The Moral System of Shakespeare: A Popular Illustration of Fiction as the Experimental Side of Philosophy*. London

—— (1966). *Shakespeare as a Dramatic Artist: A Popular Illustration of the Principles of Scientific Criticism*. 1885 With a New Introduction by Eric Bentley. New York

Muir, Kenneth (1965). 'Shakespeare's Imagery—Then and Now', *Shakespeare Survey* 18: 46–57

—— (1981). 'Shakespeare's Open Secret', *Shakespeare Survey* 34: 1–9

Mullaney, Steven (1988). *The Place of the Stage: License, Play, and Power in Renaissance England*. Chicago

Murray, Patrick (1969). *The Shakespearian Scene*. London

Neely, C. T. (1981). 'Feminist Modes of Shakespearean Criticism: Compensatory, Justificatory, Transformational', *Women's Studies* 9: 3–15

—— (1985). *Broken Nuptials in Shakespeare's Plays*. New Haven

—— (1988). 'Constructing the Subject: Feminist Practice and the New Renaissance Discourses', *English Literary Renaissance* 18: 5–18

—— (1995). 'Circumscriptions and Unhousedness: *Othello* in the Borderlands', in *Shakespeare and Gender: A History*, eds. Deborah Barker and Ivo Kamps. London, 302–15

Nelson, Robert J. (1958). *Play within a Play: The Dramatist's Conception of His Art*. New Haven

Ness, Frederic W. (1969). *The Use of Rhyme in Shakespeare's Plays*. 1941. New Haven

A New English Dictionary on Historical Principles. (1888–1928) 10 vols. Oxford

Newman, Karen (1985). *Shakespeare's Rhetoric of Comic Character: Dramatic Convention in Classical and Renaissance Comedy*. New York and London

—— (1987). '"And Wash the Ethiop White": Femininity and the Monstrous in *Othello*', in *Shakespeare Reproduced: Text in History and Ideology*, eds. Jean E. Howard and Marion F. O'Connor. New York, 143–62

Nietzsche, F. (1909–11). *Complete Works*, ed. Oscar Levy, vol. vi. New York

Novy, Marianne (1984). *Love's Argument: Gender Relations in Shakespeare*. Chapel Hill and London

—— ed. (1993). *Cross-Cultural Performance: Differences in Women's Re-visions of Shakespeare*. Urbana, Ill

Nuttall, A. D. (1983). *A New Mimesis: Shakespeare and the Representation of Reality*. London

—— (1984). 'The Argument about Shakespeare's Characters', *Critical Quarterly* 7 (1965), 107–19. Repr. in *Shakespeare's Wide and Universal Stage*, eds. C. B. Cox and D. J. Palmer. Manchester, 18–31

—— (1989). *Timon of Athens*. New York

O'Connell, Michael (1985). 'The Idolatrous Eye: Iconoclasm, Anti-Theatricalism, and the Image of the Elizabethan Theater', *English Literary History* 52: 279–310

Orgel, Stephen (1986). 'Prospero's Wife', in *Rewriting the Renaissance: The Discourses of Sexual Difference in Early Modern Europe*, eds. Margaret Ferguson, Maureen Quilligan and Nancy J. Vickers. Chicago and London, 50–64

—— (1988). 'The Authentic Shakespeare', *Representations* 21: 1–26

—— (1991). 'The Poetics of Incomprehensibility', *Shakespeare Quarterly* 42: 431–8

Ornstein, Robert (1959). 'Historical Criticism and the Interpretation of Shakespeare', *Shakespeare Quarterly* 10: 3–9

—— (1986). *Shakespeare's Comedies: From Roman Farce to Romantic Mystery.* Newark, NJ

Palmer, D. J. (1965). *The Rise of English Studies.* London

Palmer, John (1945). *Shakespeare's Political Characters.* New York

Partridge, Eric (1968). *Shakespeare's Bawdy.* 1947. London

Pasternak Slater, Anne (1982). *Shakespeare the Director.* Brighton

Pavis, Patrice (1998). *Dictionary of the Theatre: Terms, Concepts, and Analysis,* trans. Christine Shantz. Toronto

Pechter, Edward (1998). 'Why Should We Call Her Whore? Bianca in *Othello*', in *Shakespeare and the Twentieth Century,* eds. Jonathan Bate, Jill Levenson, and Dieter Mehl. Newark, NJ and London, 364–77

Pilkington, Ace G. (1991). *Screening Shakespeare from 'Richard II' to 'Henry V'.* London and Toronto

Platt, Peter (1998). *Reason Diminished: Shakespeare and the Marvellous.* Lincoln, Nebr.

Poel, William (1913). *Shakespeare in the Theatre.* London

—— (1929). *Monthly Letters.* London

Pollard, A. W. (1909). *Shakespeare's Folios and Quartos: A Study in the Bibliography of Shakespeare's Plays, 1594–1685.* London

Porter, Carolyn (1988). 'Are We Being Historical Yet?' *South Atlantic Quarterly,* 87: 743–86

Porter, Joseph A. (1991). 'Character and Ideology in Shakespeare', in *Shakespeare Left and Right,* ed. Ivo Kamps. New York and London, 131–46

Prior, Moody E. (1973). *The Drama of Power: Studies in Shakespeare's History Plays.* Evanston, Ill

Pugliatti, Paola (1996). *Shakespeare the Historian.* New York

—— (1998). 'Shakespeare's Historicism: Visions and Revisions', in *Shakespeare and the Twentieth Century,* eds. Jonathan Bate, Jill Levenson, and Dieter Mehl. Newark, NJ and London, 336–49

Pye, Christopher (1990). *The Regal Phantasm: Shakespeare and the Politics of Spectacle.* New York

Rabkin, Norman (1967). *Shakespeare and the Common Understanding.* New York

—— (1981). *Shakespeare and the Problem of Meaning.* Chicago

Racevskis, Karlis (1989). 'Genealogical Critique: Michel Foucault and the Systems of Thought', in *Contemporary Literary Theory,* eds. G. Douglas Atkins and Laura Morrow. Amherst, Mass., 229–45

Rackin, Phyllis (1990). *Stages of History: Shakespeare's English Chronicles.* Ithaca, NY

Rahv, Philip (1966). *The Myth and the Powerhouse.* New York

Raleigh, Walter (1907). *Shakespeare*. London

Reynolds, Peter (1988). *'As You Like It': A Dramatic Commentary*. The Penguin Critical Studies Series. Harmondsworth

Righter, Anne (1962). *Shakespeare and the Idea of the Play*. London

Rose, Jacqueline (1985). 'Sexuality in the Reading of Shakespeare: *Hamlet* and *Measure for Measure*', in *Alternative Shakespeares*, ed. John Drakakis. London and New York 95–118

—— (1995). 'Hamlet—The *Mona Lisa* of Literature', in *Shakespeare and Gender: A History*, eds. Deborah Barker and Ivo Kamps. London, 104–19

Rose, Mark (1972). *Shakespearean Design*. Cambridge, Mass

Rose, Mary Beth (1991). 'Where are the Mothers in Shakespeare? Options for Gender Representation in the English Renaissance', *Shakespeare Quarterly* 42: 291–314

Rossiter, A. P. (1961). 'Ambivalence: The Dialectic of the Histories', in *Angel with Horns*. London, 40–64

Rubinstein, Frankie (1989). *A Dictionary of Shakespeare's Sexual Puns and their Significance*. 1984. London

Saccio, Peter (1977). *Shakespeare's English Kings: History, Chronicle, and Drama*. New York

Salingar, Leo (1974). *Shakespeare and the Traditions of Comedy*. Cambridge

Salter, Dennis (1996). 'Acting Shakespeare in Postcolonial Space', in *Shakespeare, Theory, and Performance*, ed. James C. Bulman. London and New York, 113–32

Sanders, Wilbur (1968). *The Dramatist and the Received Idea*. Cambridge

Sargent, Lydia, ed. (1981). *Women and Revolution: A Discussion of the Unhappy Marriage of Marxism and Feminism*. Boston

Schmidt, Alexander (1874–75). *Shakespeare-Lexicon*. 2 vols. Berlin

Schücking, Levin L. (1922). *Character Problems in Shakespeare's Plays*. London

Shakespeare, William (1981). *Much Ado About Nothing*, ed. A. R. Humphreys. London

—— (1986). *The Oxford Shakespeare: The Complete Works*, eds. Stanley Wells, Gary Taylor, John Jowett, and William Montgomery. Oxford

—— (1988). *Much Ado About Nothing*, ed. F. H. Mares. Cambridge

—— (1993). *Much Ado About Nothing*, ed. Sheldon Zitner. Oxford

—— (1995a). *The Complete Illustrated Shakespeare*. 3 vols. Ed. Howard Staunton. New York

—— (1995b). *William Shakespeare: Comedies, Tragedies, Histories*. 3 vols. Ed. Tony Tanner. New York and Toronto

—— (1997). *The Norton Shakespeare*. Based on the New Oxford edn. With an essay on the Shakespearean stage by Andrew Gurr. Eds. Stephen Greenblatt, Jean E. Howard, and Katharine Maus. New York

Shapiro, James (1996). *Shakespeare and the Jews*. New York

Showalter, Elaine (1985). 'Representing Ophelia: Women, Madness, and the Responsibilities of Feminist Criticism', in *Shakespeare and the Question of Theory*, eds. Patricia Parker and Geoffrey Hartman. New York and London, 77–94

Simpson, Richard (1874). 'The Politics of Shakspere's Historical Plays', *Transactions of the New Shakspere Society* 1: 396–441

—— (1874) 'The Political Use of the Stage in Shakespeare's Time', *Transactions of the New Shakspere Society* 1: 371–95

Sinfield, Alan (1992). *Faultlines: Cultural Materialism and the Politics of Dissident Reading*. Oxford

—— (1996). 'How to Read *The Merchant of Venice* Without Being Heterosexist', in *Alternative Shakespeares Volume 2*, ed. Terence Hawkes. London and New York, 122–39

Sisson, C. J. (1964). 'The Mythical Sorrows of Shakespeare', British Academy Lecture (1934). Repr. in *Studies in Shakespeare: British Academy Lectures*, ed. Peter Alexander. Oxford, 9–32

Skura, Meredith Anne (1993). *Shakespeare the Actor and the Purposes of Playing*. Chicago and London

Smallwood, Robert (1996). 'Directors' Shakespeare', in *Shakespeare: An Illustrated Stage History*, eds. Jonathan Bate and Russell Jackson. Oxford, 176–96

Smith, Bruce R. (1991). *Homosexual Desire in Shakespeare's England: A Cultural Poetics*. Chicago and London

—— (1996). 'L[o]cating the Sexual Subject', in *Alternative Shakespeare* vol. ii, ed. Terence Hawkes. London and New York, 95–121

Snyder, Susan (1979). *The Comic Matrix of Shakespeare's Tragedies*. Princeton.

Speaight, R. (1954). *William Poel and the Elizabethan Revival*. London

Spencer, T. J. B. (1964). 'The Tyranny of Shakespeare'. 1959. Repr. in *Studies in Shakespeare: British Academy Lectures*, ed. Peter Alexander. Oxford, 149–70

—— (1973). 'Shakespeare's Careless Art', in *Shakespeare's Art: Seven Essays*, ed. Milton Crane. Chicago and London, 115–36

Spencer, Theodore (1943). *Shakespeare and the Nature of Man*. New York

Spurgeon, Caroline F. E. (1935). *Shakespeare's Imagery and What it Tells Us*. London

—— (1964). 'Shakespeare's Iterative Imagery'. 1931. Repr. in *Studies in Shakespeare: British Academy Lectures*, ed. Peter Alexander. Oxford, 171–200

States, Bert, O. (1985). *Great Reckonings in Little Rooms: On the Phenomenology of Theater*. Berkeley

—— (1992). *'Hamlet' and the Concept of Character*. Baltimore and London

Steiner, George. (1970). 'Shakespeare—Four Hundredth', in *Language and Silence: Essays on Language, Literature, and the Inhuman*. New York

Stevenson, D. L. (1966). *The Achievement of Measure for Measure*. Ithaca, NY

Stewart, J. I. M. (1949). *Character and Motive in Shakespeare*. London

Stoll, E. E. (1927). *Shakespearian Studies: Historical and Comparative in Method*. New York

—— (1933). *Art and Artifice in Shakespeare: A Study in Dramatic Contrast and Illusion*. Cambridge

—— (1944). *From Shakespeare to Joyce*. New York

—— (1991). 'Shylock', in *'The Merchant of Venice': Critical Essays*, ed. Thomas Wheeler. New York and London, 247–62

Strachey, Lytton (1918). *Eminent Victorians*. London

—— (1921). *Queen Victoria*. London

—— (1948). 'Shakespeare's Final Period', *Independent Review* 3 (Aug. 1904), 405–18. Repr. in *Books and Characters* (London, 1922) and in *Literary Essays*. London

Strier, Richard (1988). 'Faithful Servants: Shakespeare's Praise of Disobedience', in *The Historical Renaissance: New Essays on Tudor and Stuart Literature and Culture*, eds. Heather Dubrow and Richard Strier. Chicago, 104–33

—— (1995). *Resistant Structures: Particularity, Radicalism, and Renaissance Texts*. Berkeley

Styan, J. L. (1977). *The Shakespeare Revolution: Criticism and Performance in the Twentieth Century*. Cambridge

Sundelson, David (1983). *Shakespeare's Restorations of the Father*. New Brunswick, NJ

Swinburne, A. C. (1965). *A Study of Shakespeare*. 1880. New York

Taylor, Gary (1985). *To Analyze Delight: A Hedonist Criticism of Shakespeare*. Newark, NJ

—— (1988). 'The Rhetorics of Reaction', in *Crisis in Editing: Texts of the English Renaissance*, ed. Randall McLeod. New York, 19–60

—— (1990). *Reinventing Shakespeare: A Cultural History from the Restoration to the Present*. London

—— ed. (1998). ed. *Henry V*. The Oxford Shakespeare. 1982. Oxford

—— (1983). and Michael Warren, eds. *The Division of the Kingdoms: Shakespeare's Two Versions of 'King Lear'*. Oxford

Taylor, Michael (1969). 'The Darker Purpose of *A Midsummer Night's Dream*', *Studies in English Literature* 9: 259–73

—— (1974). '*Twelfth Night* and *What You Will*', *Critical Quarterly* 16: 71–80

—— (1983–4). 'The Case of Rosencrantz and Guildenstern', *Dalhousie Review* 63: 645–53

Tennenhouse, Leonard (1986). *Power on Display: The Politics of Shakespeare's Genres*. New York and London

Thomson, Peter (1992). *Shakespeare's Professional Career*. Cambridge

—— (1996). 'Shakespeare and the Public Purse', in *Shakespeare: An Illustrated Stage History*, eds. Jonathan Bate and Russell Jackson. Oxford, 160–75

Thorndike, A. H. (1916). *Shakespeare's Theater*. New York

Tillyard, E. M. W. (1938). *Shakespeare's Last Plays*. New York

—— (1943). *The Elizabethan World Picture: A Study of the Idea of Order in the Age of Shakespeare, Donne and Milton*. London

—— (1965). *Shakespeare's Early Comedies*. London

—— (1986). *Shakespeare's Problem Plays*. Toronto

—— (1986). *Shakespeare's History Plays*. 1944. Harmondsworth

Traub, Valerie (1992). *Desire and Anxiety: Circulations of Sexuality in Shakespearean Drama*. London and New York

—— (1995). 'Jewels, Statues, and Corpses: Containment of Female Erotic Power in Shakespeare's Plays', in *Shakespeare and Gender: A History*, eds. Deborah Barker and Ivo Kamps. London, 120–41

Traversi, Derek (1938). *Approach to Shakespeare*. London

—— (1950). *Shakespeare: the Last Phase*. New York

—— (1957). *Shakespeare from 'Richard II' to 'Henry V'*. Stanford, Calif

—— (1963). *Shakespeare: The Roman Plays*. London

—— (1964). *William Shakespeare: The Early Comedies*. London

Trousdale, Marion (1982). *Shakespeare and the Rhetoricians*. London

Urkowitz, Stephen (1980). *Shakespeare's Revision of 'King Lear'*. Princeton

Vendler, Helen (1997). *The Art of Shakespeare's Sonnets*. Cambridge, Mass

Vickers, Brian (1968). *The Artistry of Shakespeare's Prose*. London

Viswanathan, S. (1980). *The Shakespearean Play as Poem: A Critical Tradition in Perspective*. Cambridge

Watts, Cedric (1986). 'Recent Developments in Shakespeare Studies', in *New History of Literature III: English Drama to 1710*, ed. Christopher Ricks. New York, 276–88

Wayne, Don E. (1987). 'Power, Politics, and the Shakespearean Text: Recent Criticism in England and the United States', in *Shakespeare Reproduced: The Text in History and Ideology*, eds. Jean E. Howard and Marion F. O'Connor. New York and London, 47–67

Wayne, Valerie, ed. (1991). *The Matter of Difference: Materialist Feminist Criticism of Shakespeare*. Hemel Hempstead

Weimann, Robert (1974). 'Shakespeare and the Study of Metaphor', *New Literary History* 6: 149–67

Weitz, M. (1964). *Hamlet and the Philosophy of Literary Criticism*. Chicago and London

Wells, Charles (1993). *The Wide Arch: Roman Values in Shakespeare*. New York

Wells, Stanley (1994). *Shakespeare: A Dramatic Life*. London

—— and Taylor, Gary, eds. (1987). *William Shakespeare: A Textual Companion*. Oxford

Wharton, T. F. (1989). *Measure for Measure*. The Critics Debate. Houndmills, Basingstoke

Wheeler, Thomas, ed. (1991). *The Merchant of Venice: Critical Essays*. New York

Willbern, David (1989). 'What Is Shakespeare?', in *Shakespeare's Personality*, eds. Norman N. Holland, Sidney Homan, and Bernard J. Paris Berkeley, 226–43

Williams, Gordon (1996). *Shakespeare, Sex and the Print Revolution*. London

Williams, Raymond (1952). *Drama from Ibsen to Eliot*. London

Wilson, John Dover (1932). *The Essential Shakespeare: A Biographical Adventure*. Cambridge

—— (1944). *The Fortunes of Falstaff*. London

Wilson, Richard (1993). *Will Power: Essays on Shakespearean Authority*. Detroit

—— and Dutton, Richard, eds. (1992). *New Historicism and Renaissance Drama*. London and New York

—— (1989). 'Session 7: Is Shakespeare a Feudal Propagandist?' in *Is Shakespeare Still Our Contemporary?* ed. Elsom, John. London and New York, 140–68

Wilson, Scott (1995). *Cultural Materialism: Theory and Practice*. Oxford

Woodbridge, L. (1994). *The Scythe of Saturn: Magical Thinking in Shakespeare*. Urbana, Ill

—— and Berry, E. eds. (1992). *True Rites and Maimed Rites: Ritual and Anti-Ritual in Shakespeare and His Age*. Urbana, Ill

Worthen, W. B. (1989). 'Deeper Meanings and Theatrical Technique: The Rhetoric of Performance Criticism', *Shakespeare Quarterly* 40: 441–55

—— (1996a). 'Invisible Bullets, Violet Beards: Reading Actors Reading', in *Textual and Theatrical Shakespeare: Questions of Evidence*, ed. Edward Pechter. Iowa City, 210–29

—— (1996b). 'Staging "Shakespeare": Acting, Authority, and the Rhetoric of Performance', in *Shakespeare, Theory, and Performance*, ed. James C. Bulman. London and New York, 12–28

—— (1997). *Shakespeare and the Authority of Performance*. Cambridge

Wright, George T. (1988). *Shakespeare's Metrical Art*. Berkeley

—— (1998). 'The Silent Speech of Shakespeare's *Sonnets*', in *Shakespeare and the Twentieth Century*, eds. Jonathan Bate, Jill Levenson, and Dieter Mehl. Newark NJ and London, 314–35

Wright, Joseph (1890–1904). *English Dialect Dictionary*. 6 vols. London

Young, David (1990). *The Action to the Word: Structure and Style in Shakespearean Tragedy*. New Haven and London